THE CHURCH IN THE MAKING

REDISCOVERING VATICAN II

Series Editor: Christopher M. Bellitto, Ph.D.

Rediscovering Vatican II is an eight-book series in commemoration of the fortieth anniversary of Vatican II. These books place the council in dialogue with today's church and are not just historical expositions. They answer the question: What do today's Catholics need to know?

This series will appeal to readers who have heard much about Vatican II, but who have never sat down to understand certain aspects of the council. Its main objectives are to educate people as to the origins and developments of Vatican II's key documents as well as to introduce them to the documents' major points; to review how the church (at large and in its many parts) since the council's conclusion has accepted and/or rejected and/or revised the documents' points in practical terms; and to take stock of the council's reforms and paradigm shifts, as well as of the directions that the church appears to be heading.

The completed series will comprise these titles:

Ecumenism and Interreligious Dialogue: Unitatis Redintegratio, Nostra Aetate by Cardinal Edward Cassidy

The Church and the World: Gaudium et Spes, Inter Mirifica by Norman Tanner, SJ

The Laity and Christian Education: Apostolicam Actuositatem, Gravissimum Educationis by Dolores Leckey

Liturgy: Sacrosanctum Concilium by Rita Ferrone

Scripture: Dei Verbum by Ronald Witherup, SS

The Church in the Making: Lumen Gentium, Christus Dominus, Orientalium Ecclesiarum by Richard Gaillardetz

Evangelization and Religious Freedom: Ad Gentes, Dignitatis Humanae by Jeffrey Gros and Stephen Bevans

Religious Life and Priesthood: Perfectae Caritatis, Optatam Totius, Presbyterorum Ordinis by Maryanne Confoy, RSC

The Church in the Making

Lumen Gentium, Christus Dominus, Orientalium Ecclesiarum

Richard R. Gaillardetz

Paulist Press
New York/Mahwah, NJ

Cover design by Amy King

Book design by Celine M. Allen

Library of Congress Cataloging-in-Publication Data

Gaillardetz, Richard R., 1958–
    The church in the making : Lumen gentium, Christus Dominus, Orientalium Ecclesiarum / Richard. R. Gaillardetz.
        p. cm. — (Rediscovering Vatican II)
    Includes bibliographical references and index.
    ISBN 0-8091-4276-7 (alk. paper)
    1. Church. 2. Catholic Church—Doctrines—History—20th century. 3. Vatican Council (2nd : 1962–1965) I. Title. II. Series.
    BX1753.G255 2006
    262'.02—dc22

                                                              2006008248

Published by Paulist Press
997 Macarthur Boulevard
Mahwah, New Jersey 07430

www.paulistpress.com

Printed and bound in the
United States of America

Dedicated to my son, David,
in gratitude for his gentle and playful spirit

CONTENTS

Acknowledgments

I would like to acknowledge the colleagues who have assisted me in this project. Ormond Rush, Robert Rivers, Edward Hahnenberg, and James Bacik all read versions of the manuscript and offered valuable suggestions. Chris Bellitto at Paulist Press has been a wonderfully congenial editor who provided not only expert editorial assistance but the insights of a fine church historian. I wish to extend my thanks to the Jesuit community at Weston Jesuit School of Theology for offering such warm hospitality during a research trip I made to Boston in February of 2005 and the University of Toledo for granting me a sabbatical during which time I was able to bring this project to a conclusion.

As always, a much more personal expression of gratitude must be extended to my sons, David, Andrew, Brian, and Gregory and to my wife Diana for offering their customary patience and support for my work.

Unless otherwise indicated, English translations of both Vatican II and post-conciliar documents are from the the Vatican website, http://www.vatican.va/archive/hist_councils/ii_vatican_council/index.htm. Limited emendations to render the texts more gender inclusive have been inserted in brackets.

At certain points in this volume I have reworked short sections of material that I have published elsewhere. That material is taken from the following: "Ecclesiological Perspectives on Church Reform," forthcoming in *Church Ethics and its Organizational Context: Learning from the Sex Abuse Scandal in the Catholic Church*, edited by Jean Bartunek, Mary Ann Hinsdale, and James F. Keenan (Kansas City: Rowman and Littlefield); "Catholic Teaching on Membership in the Body of Christ," forthcoming in *Through Divine Love: The Church in Each Place and All Places*, edited by Jeffrey Gros and Walter Klaiber (Sherborne, England: Kingswood Books); "The Selection of Bishops: Recovering the Enduring Values of Our Tradition," (co-authored with John Huels) *The Jurist* 59 (1999): 348–76; "Reflections on the Future of Papal Primacy," *New*

Theology Review 13 (November, 2000): 52–66; "Toward a Contemporary Theology of the Diaconate," *Worship* 79 (September, 2005): 419–38; "The Ecclesial Foundations of Ministry within an Ordered Communion," in *Ordering the Baptismal Priesthood,* edited by Susan K. Wood (Collegeville: Liturgical Press, 2003), 26–51; "Shifting Meanings in the Lay-Clergy Distinction," *Irish Theological Quarterly* 64 (1999): 115–39.

ABBREVIATIONS

Documents of Vatican II

AA	*Apostolicam Actuositatem* (Apostolate of the Laity)
AG	*Ad Gentes* (Missionary Activity)
CD	*Christus Dominus* (Bishops)
DH	*Dignitatis Humanae* (Religious Freedom)
DV	*Dei Verbum* (Revelation)
GE	*Gravissimum Educationis* (Christian Education)
GS	*Gaudium et Spes* (The Church in the World of Today)
IM	*Inter Mirifica* (Means of Social Communication/Mass Media)
LG	*Lumen Gentium* (The Church)
NA	*Nostra Aetate* (Non-Christian Religions)
OE	*Orientalium Ecclesiarum* (Eastern Catholic Churches)
OT	*Optatam Totius* (Priestly Formation)
PC	*Perfectae Caritatis* (Religious Life)
PO	*Presbyterorum Ordinis* (Ministry and Life of Priests)
SC	*Sacrosanctum Concilium* (Liturgy)
UR	*Unitatis Redintegratio* (Ecumenism)

Books

Alberigo, *Vatican II*	G. Alberigo and J. Komonchak, eds., *History of Vatican II* (Maryknoll, NY: Orbis 1995–)
Acta Synodalia	*Acta Synodalia Sacrosancti Concilii Oecumenici Vaticani II*, 4 vols. (Vatican City: Typis Polyglottis Vaticanis, 1970–80)
Latourelle, *Vatican II*	René Latourelle, *Vatican II: Assessment and Perspectives Twenty-Five Years After (1962–1987)*, 3 vols. (New York/Mahwah, NJ: Paulist Press, 1988–89)
Vorgrimler, *Commentary*	Herbert Vorgrimler, ed. *Commentary on the Documents of Vatican II*. 5 vols. (New York: Crossroad, 1989)

Other Abbreviations

AAS   *Acta Apostolicae Sedis*

ARCIC   Anglican–Roman Catholic International Commission

CCEO   *Codex Canonum Ecclesiarum Orientalium* (Code of Canons of the Eastern Churches)

CCC   *Catechism of the Catholic Church*

CDF   Congregation for the Doctrine of the Faith

CELAM   Spanish acronym for the Episcopal Conference of Latin America

CL   *Christifideles Laici* (Pope Paul VI's apostolic exhortation on The Laity)

CN   *Communionis notio* (Congregation for the Doctrine of the Faith's instruction on Some Aspects of the Church Understood as Communion)

DS   Denzinger-Schönmetzer, *Enchiridion Symbolorum*

EN   *Evangelii Nuntiandi* (Pope Paul VI's apostolic exhortation on Evangelization in the Modern World)

MC   *Marialis Cultis* (Pope Paul VI's apostolic exhortation on the Right Ordering and Development of Devotion to the Blessed Virgin)

NMI   *Novo Millennio Ineunte* (Pope John Paul II's apostolic letter at the close of the Great Jubilee of the Year 2000)

OL   *Orientale Lumen* (Pope John Paul II's apostolic letter to mark the centenary of Pope Leo XIII's *Orientalium Dignitas)*

PB   *Pastor Bonus* (Pope John Paul II's apostolic constitution on The Roman Curia)

PDV   *Pastores Dabo Vobis* (Pope John Paul II's post-synodal apostolic exhortation on the Formation of Priests in the Circumstances of the Present Day)

PG   *Pastores Gregis* (Pope John Paul II's apostolic exhortation on The Bishop, Servant of the Gospel of Jesus Christ for the Hope of the World)

RM   *Redemptoris Missio* (Pope John Paul II's encyclical on Mission)

SCU   Secretariat for Christian Unity

UUS   *Ut Unum Sint* (Pope John Paul II's encyclical on Ecumenism)

PREFACE

"We are a 'Vatican II' parish." "What can we do about our pastor, who is 'pre–Vatican II'?" "Many of the problems facing the church today are because of Vatican II." "Vatican II clearly taught…"

We hear statements like these regularly if we are active in the Catholic Church today. "Vatican II" has become a place marker in the ecclesiastical and ideological geography of contemporary Catholicism. Yet forty years after the council, few who refer to the council and its teachings, whether with approval or in criticism, demonstrate a solid grasp of the council's teaching. Even fewer are aware of the important debates that have taken place in the past four decades regarding the council's authentic reception and implementation.

Paulist Press has responded to this pastoral reality by sponsoring a series of eight volumes dedicated, first, to making more accessible the conciliar teaching found in the sixteen documents of the Second Vatican Council and, second, to helping Catholics and those interested in contemporary Catholicism to better grasp the issues still alive in the Catholic Church as it continues the work of implementing conciliar teaching. As part of this series, this volume will consider three of those sixteen documents: (1) the Dogmatic Constitution on the Church (*Lumen Gentium*), (2) the Decree on the Pastoral Office of Bishops in the Church (*Christus Dominus*), and (3) the Decree on the Catholic Churches of the Eastern Rite (*Orientalium Ecclesiarum*).

The true import of the Second Vatican Council, however, goes far beyond any of its documents. As with every ecumenical council, Vatican II was an ecclesial event. By this I do not mean merely that it was the twenty-first in a series of ecclesiastical meetings of bishops and other church leaders. Vatican II was an ecclesial event in the sense that in the planning and conduct of the council we see the nature of the church itself in microcosm.

Ecumenical councils put the church "on display." What happens at
ecumenical councils is more than the writing, debate, revision, and
approval of documents. What happens at an ecumenical council is an
expression, in a more dramatic and concentrated form, of what the
church always is. Saints and sinners, the learned and the ignorant, gather
together. So gathered, they share their faith, voice their concerns, pray
together, argue, gossip, forge alliances and compromises, enter into
political intrigue, rise above that intrigue to discern the movements of
the Spirit, worry about preserving the great tradition in which their identity is rooted, seek to understand the demands of the present moment,
and hope for a better future. That those who gather at a council carry
lofty titles (pope, patriarch, archbishop, bishop, religious superior, theologian) and wear somewhat unusual garb should not distract us from
the fact that, at heart, they are brothers and sisters (for women did play
their part, however circumscribed it may have been) in the faith to all
Catholic Christians and their actions and deliberations represent in concentrated form who we all are as members of this pilgrim church.

In the first centuries of the church, bishops would gather in regional
synods (the term is a compound of two Greek words, *syn*, meaning
"together," and *hodos*, meaning "way" or "road"—hence a "synod"
involves the church in walking or meeting together) to address matters of
common concern. For example, in the early church several regional synods were devoted to the pastoral issue concerning how to handle the
return of apostates (those who had rejected the faith under persecution)
to the church. By the fourth century some of these synods would turn to
more formal questions of the faith. These synods or councils played a
decisive role in the development of Christian doctrine concerning the
mystery of the triune God encountered in Jesus Christ by the power of
the Spirit. In like manner, the Second Vatican Council, although rightly
characterized as "pastoral," attended to foundational theological and
doctrinal questions as well. Virtually every one of the sixteen council
documents addressed some aspect of the church's nature and mission in
the world. Cumulatively, these documents effected a profound shift in
Catholicism's contemporary self-understanding.

The nature and extent of this shift has been much debated in the
decades since the council. Recently, Pope Benedict XVI has identified
a conflict between two different manners of interpreting the teaching
of the council.[1] He characterizes the first approach as presupposing a

"hermeneutics of discontinuity and rupture." In his view, this inter-pretive stance highlights a marked discontinuity between earlier Cath-olic tradition and what was effected at Vatican II. Advocates of this hermeneutical perspective, it is held, presume a radical break and even repudiation of much of the earlier tradition. In the view of some fig-ures in the Vatican, this hermeneutics of discontinuity and rupture has achieved dominance in contemporary Catholic thought. It is, they contend, embodied in the major five-volume study of the council undertaken by the "Bologna School" under the leadership of Giuseppe Alberigo.[2]

The pope rejects this hermeneutical perspective and advocates instead a "hermeneutics of reform." This approach focuses less on Vat-ican II as an ecclesial event and more on the authoritative status of the final form of the council documents themselves. It is these documents, in their final form, and not a larger textual history or a vague appeal to "the spirit of the council" that should command the assent of Cath-olics. Such an approach would privilege the broader continuity of the council's teaching with earlier Catholic tradition. This hermeneutics of reform is proposed in the major new study on the council offered by noted church historian Bishop Agostino Marchetto, who now serves as secretary for the Pontifical Council for the Pastoral Care of Migrants and Itinerant People.[3]

The pope is certainly right to be concerned that studies of the council not exaggerate the elements of discontinuity found in council teaching. Yet one might wonder whether these two hermeneutical approaches can be so easily opposed to one another. Would not an adequate hermeneutics of the council need to attend to both continu-ity and discontinuity? Moreover, it seems to me that it would run counter to the great Catholic tradition to reduce the impact of an ecu-menical council to its formal documents. Ecclesiologically, councils derive their authority not from the juridical force of their documents but from their status as ecclesial events manifesting, in concentrated form, the reality and faith witness of the church as communion.

That great Catholic insight which governs the interpretation of scripture holds true for council documents as well. Catholics (and many mainline Protestants!) reject a fundamentalist absolutizing of the written biblical text. They recall that Jesus did not come to leave a written text, but to create a community of disciples. The scriptural texts emerged out of the lived faith witness of the people of Israel and the apostolic community. Catholics believe that scripture cannot be adequately interpreted apart from an awareness of both the faith experience that gave rise to the biblical testimony (sometimes called by biblical scholars "the meaning behind the text") and the ways in which the biblical texts have been received, interpreted, and implemented in the life of the church (biblical scholars refer to this as "the meaning in front of the text").

Just as scripture and tradition cannot be opposed to one another but are inextricably linked, so too one cannot oppose to one another (1) the dynamic ecclesial event which is a council itself conjoined with the dynamic process by which that council is received in the life of the church and (2) the official promulgation of the council's teaching in its final documents.

Australian theologian Ormond Rush has provided the most balanced hermeneutical framework to date for interpreting council documents, one which avoids a false absolutizing of either continuity or discontinuity, Rush distinguishes between a "macro-rupture," a fundamental severance with the great tradition of the church, and a "micro-rupture," which reflects a genuine innovation or shift that must be considered discontinuous with some aspect of the previous tradition but which can also be read as "rejuvenating that broader tradition."[4] I agree with Rush that we need to affirm the genuine micro-ruptures evident in the conciliar documents that constituted a break, particularly with the baroque or post-Tridentine Catholicism of the previous four centuries, while remaining in continuity with a more ancient tradition.

As we study the documents of the council, it would be a mistake to try and lift out of those documents a systematic and internally coherent ecclesiology. Attempts at developing a nascent conciliar ecclesiology around a particular biblical image, like the people of God, or one theological concept, like that of communion, risk imposing on the texts a theological unity that simply is not there. It is unrealistic to expect that a council in which between two and three thousand bishops and numerous other theologians played some part would be able to construct a rigorously systematic theology of the church.

The work of the council was grounded less in a common theology of the church than in a shared commitment to two impulses that impelled the bishops to seek ecclesial reform and renewal. One is captured by the French term *ressourcement*, a "return to the sources." This term referred to a commitment to recover the theological vision of the early church that had been eclipsed by the static neo-scholastic view dominant on the eve of the council. This *ressourcement* led to a recovery of a more theological understanding of the church grounded in baptism and Eucharist rather than in law and jurisdiction. It meant a return to the liturgical spirituality of the first millennium in preference to the arid mechanistic view of the liturgy and sacraments that dominated in neo-scholasticism.

The second impulse for renewal is captured in the Italian word *aggiornamento*, which can be translated as "bringing up to date." Advocates of this view feared that the church had become largely irrelevant to the concerns of the modern world. The work of *aggiornamento* demanded a policy of active and respectful engagement with the world out of a confident expectation that the hand of God was at work in the world. It called for a new ecumenical impulse. This theological perspective, with its relatively greater confidence in God's action in the world, reflected not so much the patristic theological vision of the first millennium as the theological vision associated with the thirteenth-century Dominican, St. Thomas Aquinas.

Pope Paul VI, early in his pontificate, expressed a concern that the documents of the council might engender harmful church divisions. Consequently, though the rules of the council allowed a document to be approved with a two-thirds majority, Pope Paul made it known that he wished the documents to be approved by a moral (rather than absolute) unanimity among the bishops. A cursory review of the final voting suggests that the pope got what he desired, as no document was opposed in the final vote by more than a handful of bishops. But there was a price to be paid for this high level of unanimity. Significant compromises were made. When achieving full consensus was unlikely, one way of obtaining approval of a document was to juxtapose, sometimes in the same paragraph, alternative formulations.[5] Sometimes this juxtaposition occurred merely at the level of formulation, with diverse formulae employed to express a deeper consensus. At other times the compromise required was much more profound, occurring at the level of content, where two or more fundamental views which could not be reconciled were placed side by side.[6] Some of the tensions in post-conciliar interpretation were a direct consequence of this latter form of juxtaposition or compromise.

To some extent this form of compromise is evident at every council. It is why conciliar documents should never be considered to be systematic treatises. Indeed, anyone who has ever served on a committee to draft a common document is aware of this fact. However, because of the uniquely transitional character of Vatican II, juxtaposition appears particularly striking in its documents. At the council, the advantage of this method of juxtaposition was that it ultimately enabled passage of sixteen conciliar documents. The disadvantage was that it would become possible for various ideological camps to appeal to certain passages that appeared to support their particular ecclesiastical agenda.

In an influential study, Antonio Acerbi maintained that in *Lumen Gentium* two fundamentally different ecclesiologies were being juxtaposed, one more juridical in character and the other oriented toward the priority of baptism and the church as communion.[7] The result has been the creation of a "canon within the canon," in which each group cites texts in justification of its agenda without any consideration of the whole corpus of documents.

The only way out of this impasse is to adopt an explicit, interpretive methodology, a conciliar hermeneutic that goes beyond the juxtaposition of discrete passages in an effort to discern the emerging theological vision that is evident in the conciliar documents. Rush contends that an adequate conciliar hermeneutic requires a threefold reading of the council documents.[8] First, a diachronic reading of the council documents presumes that one must study the historical development of the documents from the pre-conciliar, preparatory period through the four sessions and three intersessions of the council itself.[9] This reading requires a careful consideration of the sources from which a text draws, the history of its development, and a consideration of the questions it was intended and not intended to address. Such a reading will also identify an emerging trajectory of development that may in fact point beyond the council. A diachronic interpretation of conciliar documents must respond to the following kinds of questions:

1. How does the history of a text as it moved from preparatory schema to its final promulgation affect our understanding of it?

2. Did a particular teaching grow or lessen in importance over the course of the council?

3. Did the council anticipate and provide for further development of a given topic after the close of the council?

4. How did the council critically "receive" earlier insights and theological perspectives?

5. Did the council intentionally leave some theological/doctrinal questions open?

6. What significance do we attach to the council's decision to avoid certain theological formulations in its teaching?

This diachronic approach will be employed in Part One as we consider the history of *Lumen Gentium, Christus Dominus,* and *Orientalium Ecclesiarum.*

Second, alongside this diachronic reading, the texts must also be read synchronically, that is, each text must be read in relation to other companion texts among the council documents.[10] Questions that must be considered in a synchronic reading include:

1. When considering a particular text, how does a sense of the whole corpus of conciliar documents shape the way that a particular text is read?

2. Are there texts that ought to provide a hermeneutical key for interpreting other texts?

3. What weight should be given to any particular document with respect to the others?

This more synchronic reading will be used in Part Two to identify common themes in the documents.

Finally, diachronic and synchronic interpretations have to be accompanied by a third reading, one that considers the conciliar texts in the light of their subsequent reception in the life of the church.[11] Such a reading must consider:

1. What themes have been emphasized and/or neglected in post-conciliar church teaching?

2. What themes have been emphasized or neglected in post-conciliar theological literature?

3. What conciliar teachings have or have not given rise to concrete changes in church law, structures, and pastoral practice?

This third mode of interpretation will be undertaken in Part Three. In conclusion, Part Four will look to the future with some constructive proposals for continued church reform and renewal.

There will be an inevitable overlap between themes addressed in the three conciliar documents considered in this volume and the thirteen documents treated in the other volumes of this series. In certain instances, where themes found in these three documents received much more substantial development in other documents, as in the case of ecumenism or the ministerial priesthood, I have been content to make only summary observations. What I hope will emerge is a dynamic and vital image of the church, faithful to its great tradition, yet attentive to the distinctive challenges of the present and open to a graced future.

PART I

THE DOCUMENTS

LOCATING THE "BEGINNING" OF THE STORY: CATHOLIC ECCLESIOLOGY FROM THE COUNCIL OF TRENT TO VATICAN II

In one sense, the story of Vatican II began on January 25, 1959, at the Basilica of St. Paul Outside-the-Walls when newly elected Pope John XXIII announced to a gathering of his advisors his plans to convene a new ecumenical council. In another sense, the story of Vatican II reaches back to the mid-sixteenth century. Many of the issues and questions that dominated discussion at Vatican II emerged from the significant developments in the Catholic Church that had transpired in the previous four centuries.

The Council of Trent met between 1545 and 1563 to respond to attacks leveled against the Roman Catholic Church by the reformers. That council marked the beginning of a period in Roman Catholic history characterized by significant reform but also by a pattern of ecclesiastical defensiveness. Protestant attacks—on the efficacy of the sacraments, the ministerial priesthood, the authority of the pope and bishops—all led to a defense of these institutional features within Roman Catholicism. Since it was the integrity of the visible and institutional church that was under attack, it was the visible, institutional integrity of the church that would receive a most spirited defense. For example, St. Robert Bellarmine reacted to Luther's denigration of the visible church by insisting that ecclesial institutions were integral to the very definition of the church: "The church is a gathering of persons which is as visible and palpable as the gathering of the people of Rome, the kingdom of Gaul or the Republic of Venice."[1] It was during the late sixteenth and early seventeenth centuries that the church came to be seen as a *societas perfecta*, a "perfect society." The idea was not that the church was morally perfect but rather that it was completely self-sufficient, possessing all the institutional resources necessary for the fulfillment of its mission. A rather polemical and defensive account of the church would appear, an account that would stress its institutional features. Ecclesiology during this period gave little attention to the church's spiritual origins in the trinitarian missions of Word and Spirit. Defense of the legitimacy of church office and ordained ministry led to an emphasis on the sacrament of holy orders over the sacraments of initiation. In the following centuries, this defensive posture was directed not just against the churches of the Reformation but also against other external forces perceived as threats to the church's mission and very existence.

First, the rise of absolute monarchies in Western Europe from the fifteenth to the nineteenth centuries increasingly subjected the exercise of the church's mission to state control. By the nineteenth century, the time when popes would speak and emperors and monarchs would do their bidding had long passed. Christendom had come to an end and the medieval harmony (maintained in theory if not in practice) between church and state gave way to suspicion and controversy. The emergence of stronger nation-states led their monarchs to place more restrictive limits on the activity of the church within the boundaries of their states.

The rising nationalist consciousness of many churches represented yet another threat. In the late Middle Ages, Catholicism had been torn apart by the Western Schism in which, at one point, there were three claimants to the chair of St. Peter. The crisis was finally resolved by the actions of an ecumenical council, the Council of Constance, leading some to hold that councils possessed inherently greater authority than the pope. This theory came to be known as conciliarism and, at least in its most extreme form, it was condemned by the Council of Florence-Ferrara. From that time on the papacy would remain ever after nervous that the claims to a limited autonomy by national churches and their bishops represented but new forms of the pernicious conciliarist threat. Consequently, in the late seventeenth and eighteenth centuries, the papacy sought to purge the church of such nationalist movements as Gallicanism, Febronianism, and Josephinism, movements that sought to give some autonomy to national churches and their bishops.

The rise of the Enlightenment posed yet another threat to modern Catholicism. By championing the autonomy of human reason, the Enlightenment appeared to call into question the legitimacy of any kind of revealed knowledge. The Bible, church tradition, and the legitimacy of an authoritative church teaching office were all challenged during the age of reason. Intellectual challenges posed by the Enlightenment and later nineteenth-century Romanticism indirectly encouraged the rise of neo-scholasticism as the dominant form of Catholic theological discourse. Neo-scholasticism was a form of theology that emerged in the nineteen and early twentieth centuries and dominated seminary education. It was indebted to certain forms and concepts distantly related to the thought of St. Thomas Aquinas and other thinkers of the scholastic period. These forms of thought, however, were filtered through the lens of sixteenth-century scholastic commentators and were expounded in theology manuals that were often both highly deductive and a-historical in their presentation of the Catholic faith.

The age of reason was also an age of revolution, marked by major revolutionary upheavals in France and North America. The virulent anti-clericalism that came in the wake of the French Revolution and the further revolutions that hit much of Europe in 1848, particularly in Italy, led church leadership to be suspicious of the revolutionary impulse itself, whether in the name of democracy or some other ideological banner.

Fear regarding both the encroachments of the state and the dangers of the nationalist church movements gave rise, in the nineteenth century, to a countervailing ecclesial movement. This movement, known as Ultramontanism (looking "beyond" the "mountains" in obedience to the views of Rome), was bent on the centralization of church authority in the papacy. The impulse toward stronger papal authority found expression in the First Vatican Council's dogmatic constitution *Pastor Aeternus*, which solemnly defined the dogmas of papal primacy (already taught at the Council of Florence-Ferrara) and papal infallibility. Although these teachings on the papacy were very carefully circumscribed, the ultramontane climate in which the teachings were received led to a much more expansive attribution of authority to the papacy than Vatican I had ever intended.

The church's sharply critical stance toward society continued in the late nineteenth and early twentieth centuries. The papacy issued harsh rebukes of significant elements of modern capitalism, socialism, industrialism, and the continued program of state encroachment in church matters. The 1930s brought Catholic condemnations of communism and, more cautiously, fascism. Catholic fears regarding communism would continue up to the eve of Vatican II.

At Vatican II the bishops overcame the defensive Catholic posture that had resulted from centuries of perceived threats to the church and its mission. To say that Roman Catholicism from Trent to Vatican II was marked by a growing defensiveness is not to say that this period was without its own positive features. A number of important church developments and movements would prepare the way for the council. This period saw an unprecedented flourishing of male and female religious orders that reinvigorated the post-Reformation Catholic Church with a renewed energy directed toward both the missionary activity of the church and its work in the fields of education, catechesis, and social outreach.

Nineteenth-century Protestant interest in applying the canons of modern historical scholarship to the study of the Bible caught the interest of Catholic scholars as well. Ernest Renan, Marie-Joseph Lagrange, and Alfred Loisy were all Catholic scholars eager to adopt the tools of higher biblical criticism. Although some of these critical methods met with papal condemnation in Pope Leo XIII's encyclical, *Providentissimus Deus*, the pope did acknowledge the value of a more sophisticated application of linguistic and exegetical tools for biblical study. Fifty years later, Pope Pius XII would dramatically reverse decades of ecclesiastical distrust of modern biblical scholarship with his encyclical, *Divino Afflante Spiritu*. This groundbreaking document, often referred to as the Magna Carta of modern Catholic biblical scholarship, openly encouraged responsible use of the tools of higher biblical criticism.

The nineteenth century also saw the birth of the liturgical renewal movement. The movement began in the early nineteenth century as an attempt to renew the liturgical life of the Benedictine monasteries. However, this essentially conservative monastic reform movement coincided with calls by pastoral theologians like Johann Baptist Hirscher and Anton Graf of the Catholic faculty of Tübingen for major reforms in the liturgy: communion under both species for the laity, Mass in the vernacular, and shorter, more biblically oriented homilies. This impetus for liturgical renewal soon led to a flowering in liturgical scholarship, with important works being published on the history of the liturgy and on ancient liturgical texts. A landmark event occurred in 1909 when Dom Lambert Beauduin, a monk from Maredsous, a foundation of the Beuron monastery, addressed the National Congress of Catholic Action in Malines, Belgium. There Beauduin called for the full involvement of the laity in the liturgical life of the church. Beauduin had a particular gift for popularizing scholarly developments in the study of the liturgy and did much to restore the liturgy to its central place in the life of the whole church. The popular liturgical movement took hold in the United States. Dom Virgil Michel, a Benedictine monk of St. John's Abbey, spent nineteen months in Europe at the monastery at Beuron and returned to found the liturgical studies journal *Orate Fratres* (later *Worship*) and the Liturgical Press.

Around the end of the nineteenth and beginning of the twentieth centuries some Catholic theologians sought to break out of the intellectual straightjacket of the neo-scholastic theology manuals. These theologians, later lumped together and referred to as "modernists," shared a conviction, from a variety of starting points, that there were things to be learned from modernity: (1) its commitment to history as an account of real human change and development; (2) its acknowledgment of human experience as the place where meaning and truth are encountered; and (3) its recognition that all human knowledge, including religious knowledge, is symbolic in character. The attempts of these theologians at a modern reformulation of the Catholic faith were uneven and at times idiosyncratic, but many church historians question whether even these shortcomings merited the sweeping, severe condemnations that issued from Pope Pius X and the Holy Office (formerly the "Holy Inquisition" and now the Congregation for the Doctrine of the Faith) in the first decade of the twentieth century. The "anti-modernist" condemnations created a climate of fear and suspicion that induced a chilling effect on modern Catholic theological scholarship.

It was not until the 1930s that theologians would dare to venture again beyond the safe confines of neo-scholasticism to engage modernity. The French Dominican theologian Marie-Dominique Chenu would insist that the writings of St. Thomas Aquinas must be read within their historical context. He criticized modern neo-scholasticism for its speculative and a-historical grasp of Thomas's thought, often seeking from Thomas answers to questions that the great Dominican doctor had never considered. Other theologians like Karl Rahner, Bernard Lonergan, and Henri Bouillard dared to reinterpret the great Thomistic tradition in conversation with modern philosophical developments. Still other theologians, like another French Dominican Yves Congar, and the French Jesuit Henri de Lubac, looked to recover ancient biblical, patristic, and liturgical sources as a foundation for theological and ecclesiological renewal.

In summary, the Roman Catholic Church of the 1950s could be characterized as a church in which a still dominant stance of reflexive defensiveness was being cautiously challenged by countervailing movements of reform and renewal percolating just below the surface of church life. It would take the peculiar dynamisms of an ecumenical council to bring these movements for reform and renewal to the forefront.

PLANNING A COUNCIL[2]

In 1959, shortly after his announcement of plans for a new council, Pope John XXIII created an initial Ante-Preparatory Commission headed by the secretary of state, Cardinal Domenico Tardini. This commission's work would transpire over three phases: (1) soliciting initial proposals for the agenda of the council from curial officials, bishops, religious superiors (male only), university faculties, and theologians; (2) drawing up a rough outline of topics to be addressed based on the bishops' responses; and (3) proposing membership for the various preparatory commissions that would be assigned the tasks of producing working draft documents. The proposals gathered from the bishops would provide the raw material for the more direct preparation of the council.

The consultative process appeared crippled from the outset when the pope assigned leadership of the Ante-Preparatory Commission to several curial figures: in general these officials were little disposed to take the consultation of the bishops very seriously. The very notion of a consultation, they felt, was a slap in the face to curial leadership;

after all, who better knew the needs of the whole church than those who worked in service of the universal church on a daily basis in the Roman curia? Moreover, the very idea of widespread consultation smacked of a democratic mentality thought to have no place in Christ's church.

In any event, invitations to submit proposals for the council agenda went out to 2,812 bishops, theologians, male religious superiors, theological faculties, and Roman congregations. Of this number, 2,150 replied in some manner, though many responses were short and perfunctory. From these proposals the Ante-Preparatory Commission created a set of documents that grouped into various categories the comments and proposals the commission had received. These documents were quite important, because they would largely determine the agenda for each preparatory commission.

In 1960 Pope John created ten preparatory commissions (most of which would be presided over by the heads of the appropriate Roman dicasteries or curial offices), three secretariats, and a separate Central Preparatory Commission (the pre-conciliar clearinghouse to which all schemata had to be sent for emendation and final approval before they could be submitted as working draft documents for the council itself), which he himself was to head. Each commission was made up of bishops and consultors. The Secretariat for Promoting Christian Unity would later be given the status of a commission, bringing the total number of commissions to eleven.

By early 1962 the preparatory commissions had produced over seventy schemata. In August of that year, the bishops were sent the seven schemata which they were to consider at the beginning of the council. Many bishops complained about receiving the schemata at such a late date and only 10 percent responded with comments.[3] The responses were overwhelmingly negative. Cardinal Paul Emile Léger, the Archbishop of Montreal, drafted an extensive twelve-page letter, which he sent to the pope on September 11, with the accompanying signatures of Cardinals Joseph Frings, Achille Liénart, Julius Döpfner, Leon-Joseph Suenens, and Franz König. In it he complained of the poor quality of the drafts and questioned the attitudes of those responsible for planning the council. Theologians were also allowed to read the schemata and many offered pointed commentaries. Karl Rahner and several other German theologians met with Cardinal Döpfner and other members of the German episcopate to offer an extensive critique of the documents. Yves Congar also distributed detailed criticisms. The German and French bishops commissioned Rahner to draw up a statement rejecting the schemata proposed by the Theological Commission. Dominican theologian Edward Schillebeeckx penned a response on behalf of the Dutch bishops, urging that the first four schemata be completely rewritten. Although the schemata would not be revised prior to the council, as we shall see, many would be completely rejected early in the council.

A BRIEF HISTORY OF
THE DOGMATIC CONSTITUTION ON THE CHURCH
(*LUMEN GENTIUM*)

At the first session of the council, in the fall of 1962, the bishops were greeted with an initial schema on the church prepared by the council's Theological Commission, headed by the prefect of the Holy Office, Cardinal Alfredo Ottaviani. It had been clear from the beginning of conciliar planning that the council would have to attend to a theology of the church. The last ecumenical council, Vatican I, had been suspended because of the Franco-Prussian War before it was able to debate its planned constitution on the church. The council had only been able to promulgate a constitution on the Catholic faith (*Dei Filius*) and a second on the papacy (*Pastor Aeternus*). It was for this reason that the Ante-Preparatory Commission for the planning of Vatican II had expressly charged the Theological Commission with producing a dogmatic constitution on the church.[4]

The Preparatory Schema *De Ecclesia*

The preparatory schema (a draft document) on the church originally consisted of eleven chapters:

Chapter 1: The Nature of the Church Militant

Chapter 2: Church Membership and Necessity of Church for Salvation

It was this draft which was first debated in the closing weeks of the council's first session.[5] The schema was a blend of the neo-scholastic ecclesiology currently being taught in seminaries and the teaching of Pope Pius XII in his encyclicals, *Mystici Corporis* and *Humani Generis*. The tone of the document was reflected in the title of the first chapter, "The Nature of the Church Militant." An essentialist analysis of the church's "nature" and a preoccupation with the visible structures of the church dominated the text. The first chapter largely followed *Mystici Corporis* in identifying the mystical body of Christ with the Roman Catholic Church. The second chapter, on membership in the church, also followed the papal encyclical, limiting true membership in the body of Christ to Catholics. All others, including non-Christians, were, at best, following the pope's terminology, related to the church only by desire (*votum*).

In the third and fourth chapters on the episcopate and presbyterate we see a continued dependence on the thought of Pius XII, as the schema asserted that the bishop's power of jurisdiction proceeded not from ordination but from a juridical mission received from the pope. Such a view had the practical effect of presenting the bishop as if he were a veritable vicar of the pope. The college of bishops, the schema proposed, succeeded the college of apostles but could share in supreme authority over the universal church only "in an extraordinary manner and in devoted subordination to the Vicar of Jesus

Christ on earth, when, as, and to what extent he deems it expedient in the Lord."[6]

The fifth chapter on the "States of Evangelical Perfection" asserted that perfection in holiness was achieved preeminently by those who pursued the evangelical counsels of poverty, chastity, and obedience. There was virtually no consideration of the other 99+ percent of the church who were not called to professed religious life. Indeed, implicit in the chapter is the assumption that those who do not pursue these counsels have accepted the more pedestrian path to holiness provided by the ten commandments and the precepts of the church. The sixth chapter was much more promising in that it offered a quite positive presentation of a theology of the laity that represented a genuine step forward in church teaching. It began with a reflection on the universal priesthood in which all believers participate by virtue of their baptism. The chapter invoked the experience of the Catholic Action movement over the previous several decades and affirmed the rights and the responsibilities of the laity within the church. It also asserted that the laity were called not only to a vocation in the secular realm but also to an active life in the church.

Chapters 7 and 8 dealt with the teaching office of the church in particular and the exercise of ecclesiastical authority in general. Chapter 7 gave considerable attention to the scope and purpose of the papal teaching office, summarizing, in large measure, the teaching of Vatican I. The document expressly mentioned both the primary object of the church's teaching office, namely divine revelation or the deposit of faith, and the secondary object, which is all that is necessary to explain and defend the deposit of faith. The text thereby introduced a distinction that had only been alluded to at Vatican I but was commonly included in many of the dogmatic manuals. The consequence was a significant broadening of the scope of infallibility. Also of note is the inclusion of a passage from Pope Pius XII's encyclical *Humani Generis*, contending that if popes should "explicitly pass judgment on a matter hitherto controverted, it must be clear to all that this matter, according to the mind and will of the same Pontiffs, can no longer be considered a question for public discussion among theologians." The chapter further taught that the pope could, at least in part, "entrust" his magisterium to the Roman curia. Theologians possessed a distinctive authority, but their primary vocation was to explain scripture and church teaching, determine the authority or theological note of various teachings, and defend the faith.

The schema warned of a contemporary "crisis of authority." It equated ecclesiastical authority with divine authority, asserting that resistance to church authority was equivalent to resistance to "God's ordinance." Authority was presented as the exercise of power by "superiors" over "subjects." The schema did admit that those in authority "should not refuse to listen to the views of their subjects or deny room for undertakings either suggested or even spontaneously initiated by their subjects" and that, "in proportion to their learning," church members have the duty to make their views known to church leadership for the welfare of the church. Later in chapter 8 the sense of the faithful is contrasted with public opinion, the former being characterized by a Spirit-guided agreement of the faithful governed by the magisterium. If the first three chapters of this schema were heavily dependent on Pope Pius XII's encyclical *Mystici Corporis*, chapters 7 and 8 drew mainly from his encyclical, *Humani Generis*.

Chapter 9, which concerned the relationship between church and state, was in fact a reworking of a text that had been prepared for the Holy Office a few years earlier.[7] The chapter offered a nuanced version of the "thesis-hypothesis" framework for understanding church-state relations. The "thesis" or ideal situation was one in which civic authority would grant full freedom and full civic support to the practice of the Catholic religion while constraining all religious expressions contrary to the full truth of Catholicism. The "hypothesis" recognized that in reality this was not always possible and that therefore states might find that they serve the common good better by "tolerating" the practice of other religions. Chapter 10 asserted the church's right and obligation to preach the gospel throughout the whole world, and it warned against any state interference in this divinely mandated mission.

The final chapter considered a topic that would remain in the forefront of the council's deliberations, ecumenism. The chapter went beyond the rather meager "ecumenism of return" articulated in Pope Pius XI's 1928 encyclical *Mortalium Animos* by acknowledging the salvific elements found in other Christian communities, and by cautiously affirming the emerging ecumenical movement. Still, one finds in this chapter echoes of Pius XI's fears of "indifferentism," understood as the belief that differences among the Christian churches are ultimately inconsequential.

We should note that another preparatory document on the church, with a strikingly different tone and theological orientation, had been proposed by the Secretariat for Christian Unity (SCU). It displayed more developed biblical foundations and, not surprisingly, was much more open to the emerging ecumenical spirit than was the Theological Commission's schema. The SCU text reflected the views of Cardinal Augustin Bea, president of the secretariat, who had claimed that in some limited sense non-Catholic Christians were indeed members of the body of Christ since their own traditions did possess means of grace. The SCU also avoided the thesis-hypothesis framework in favor of a more positive endorsement of religious freedom. This text was sent on to the Theological Commission for their consideration as they worked on their own draft document on the church, but there is little evidence that any serious effort was made to incorporate any of its themes and motifs into the *De Ecclesia* schema.

Before the council opened, the *De Ecclesia* schema was sent, as were all preparatory schemata, to the Central Preparatory Commission for evaluation and amendment. Unfortunately, the commission was overwhelmed by the many schemata it had received and the announcement in February of 1962 that the council would be opening that coming October. Consequently, the schema on the church, arguably the most important of all the preparatory texts, received only the most cursory of consideration by the Central Preparatory Commission.[8] The schema was not ready for distribution in the summer of 1962 and therefore was not included among the seven schemata that were bound as one volume and sent to the bishops for their advance consideration. Indeed, the bishops did not receive the schema on the church until November 23, near the end of the first session.

Even before debate began, the schema had been subject to scathing criticism by theologians like Schillebeeckx and Rahner. Their written criticisms were quickly distributed and influenced the interventions of several bishops. The debate on the schema was not undertaken until the final days of the first session, December 1–7.[9] Among the seventy-seven bishops who spoke during the debate there were certainly voices heard in favor of the schema, lauding its dogmatic tone and emphasis on the juridical and institutional dimensions of the church. One bishop even called for a greater stress on the Petrine character of the church, going so far as to propose that a fifth mark of the church, *petrinitas*, be added to the Nicene creed![10] It is safe to say, however, that this enthusiasm for the juridical/institutional tone was a minority view. In fact, there was a sense among many of the bishops, even before debate began, that the schema would have to be completely redone.[11] Cardinal Liénart complained about the strict identification of the mystical body with the Roman Catholic Church, echoing some of the earlier concerns of the Secretariat for Christian Unity. Cardinal Döpfner criticized the excessively juridical tone of the text. Archbishop Hermann Volk noted the schema's woefully inadequate biblical foundations and Cardinal Frings complained that there was little reference to the great patristic tradition, East and West. Several bishops pointed out the inconsistency in the schema's assertion that the college of bishops could exercise its ordinary power only in an extraordinary mode of episcopal action.

Perhaps the most significant speech came from Bishop Emile de Smedt, who summed up the concerns of many in attendance when he outlined three fundamental shortcomings: (1) the tone of the document was inappropriately *triumphalist*; (2) the schema reflected a *clericalism* in its pyramidal view of the church, placing the pope at the apex and the laity at the base; (3) the document's vision of the church was excessively *juridical*, lacking an appreciation for the church as mystery. De Smedt also complained of the "pompous style" of the text and objected to the first chapter's reference to the *ecclesia militans*, which he insisted was a medieval view of the church portrayed as an army on the march. Such an image was no longer appropriate, he insisted.

The first session ended without any decision being made on the *De Ecclesia* schema. In February a sub-commission was formed to do further work on the text. This sub-commission was comprised of some of the leading bishops and *periti* (theologians who advised the bishops). Among the bishops were Michael Browne, Paul Emile Léger, Franz König, Pietro Parente, André Charue, Gabriel Garrone, and Joseph Schröffer. Among the *periti* were M.-R. Gagnebet, Andre Naud, Karl Rahner, Gérard Philips, Jean Daniélou, and Yves Congar. Officially this sub-commission was told that they were to work from the existing draft; however, this mandate "was given the broadest possible interpretation."[12] In fact, the sub-commission had at its disposal a number of alternative texts composed by various bishops and theologians. The decision was made to follow a text that had been composed early in the council by the Belgian *peritus* Gérard Philips, while also including some sections from a schema composed by Archbishop Parente. Philips would play a vital role in the entire process, serving as a brilliant theologian and a master facilitator capable of forging compromises between opposing camps.

A brief word needs to be said regarding another crucial development in the council's treatment of the church. Initially it was assumed that there would be one foundational document on the church. However, early in the council the influential Cardinal Suenens of Belgium suggested that the council's agenda be shaped around a basic theological distinction borrowed from trinitarian theology. Near the end of the first session, he proposed that the council consider the church under two aspects: the church *ad intra*, or its inner life, and the church *ad extra*, its relationship to the world. This vision was quite similar to what had emerged at meetings of the Commission for the Lay Apostolate.[13] The decision was made to create a mixed commission comprising members of the Commission for the Lay Apostolate and the Theological Commission charged with creating a second schema to complement the *De Ecclesia* draft already under consideration. This second schema would address the church's relationship to the world. It was a document that would have a particularly tortured history in council deliberations but ultimately would be approved near the end of the council as *Gaudium et Spes*, the Pastoral Constitution on the Church in the Modern World.

The Second Schema

By the summer of 1963 the sub-commission had succeeded in producing what was, in reality, a new schema comprised of four chapters:

Chapter 1: The Mystery of the Church

Chapter 2: The Hierarchical Constitution of the Church and the Episcopate in Particular

Chapter 3: The People of God and the Laity in Particular

Chapter 4: The Call to Holiness in the Church

The change in the first chapter alone was significant. Where the first schema was markedly triumphalist in treating the church "militant," this second schema began with a consideration of the church's mystical origins in the triune life of God. The second chapter contained a number of controversial assertions regarding the supreme authority over the church shared by the whole college of bishops in communion with the pope. The term "collegiality" soon became identified with this claim that all of the bishops, as an episcopal "college," shared authority over the universal church with the pope, who as bishop of Rome was a member and head of this college.

The third chapter was the closest in content to its corresponding chapter in the preparatory schema, combining material on baptism and Christian identity with specific reflections on the role of the laity today. The fourth chapter constituted a considerable reworking of the chapter in the preparatory schema on the states of evangelical perfection. The fundamental criticism directed toward that earlier chapter concerned its tendency to place the secular and spiritual realms in opposition to one another and to stress individual holiness more than the holiness of the whole church. The reworked chapter succeeded in taking into account many of these concerns.

This four-chapter schema was sent on to the bishops in July of 1963 for their consideration in preparation for the second session of the council. However, even as this text was being sent out, a new division of the material was being recommended by Cardinal Suenens in the summer meeting of the Central Commission. The Belgian cardinal proposed that the third chapter, "The People of God and the Laity in Particular," be split and that the material on the people of God be formed into a separate chapter and placed immediately after the opening chapter and *before* the chapter on the hierarchy. This reversal in the orders of the second and third chapters is generally viewed by commentators as of particular importance. It signalled a conciliar move away from past juridical and clerical approaches in favor of the primacy of the whole church, ordained and lay, as the one people of God. Although this proposal met with considerable sympathy at the Central Commission meeting, the change was not made; instead it was decided to put the proposal before the council at the fall session.

Debate on the schema began on September 30, 1963. The focus initially was on the first chapter concerning the church as mystery.

The new theological orientation of the revised chapter made many of the bishops uneasy, accustomed as they were to the clarity of a more neo-scholastic and juridical approach. Nevertheless, many council participants also praised the commission for producing a draft that was much more biblical and pastoral. In fact, some wanted this development to go even further. Cardinal Frings spoke in the name of a number of German and Scandinavian bishops in requesting an even greater development of the church as sacrament. Demands were made for a more explicit connection between the church and the Eucharist, recalling the principle mentioned in the debates on the liturgy constitution: *eucharistia facit ecclesiam* (the Eucharist makes the church). Bishop Giuseppe Gargitter officially proposed what Suenens had already suggested in the meeting of the Central Commission the previous summer, namely, that the chapter on the people of God and the laity be split into two, with the first section being placed as a separate chapter before the chapter on the hierarchy. This proposal was broadly and enthusiastically received. Less well received was a proposal by Cardinal Silva Henriquez of Chile that a previously prepared schema on Mary be incorporated into the present schema on the church. (This would be a topic of considerable controversy in the council's deliberations.) He also called for a further development of the trinitarian origins of the church and the fuller incorporation of the biblical notion of *koinonia*. A request was also made by several bishops from Latin America, the most notable being Archbishop Helder Câmara, that explicit mention be made of the kingdom of God as a central concept in the gospel.[14]

There was some controversy in the debate on chapter 2 (the chapter on the people of God had not yet been officially placed before the chapter on the hierarchy) because of fundamental disagreements regarding the notion of episcopal collegiality. The very term, "college," was new and un-theological, complained some bishops. Many objected to the statement that the church was founded on Peter *and the apostles*. Some bishops felt this put, by extension, the pope on a par with other bishops and undermined his unique status as "rock" of the church. There was also a concern that a commitment to episcopal collegiality would compromise Vatican I's teaching on papal primacy. The Italians and the Spanish were particularly cautious and preferred a much more juridical view of the bishops' relationship to the pope. Several bishops also noted with dismay the paucity of attention given to the presbyterate.

Debate included discussion of the restoration of the diaconate as a permanent and stable ministry in the church. During the initial preparations for the council there were 101 different proposals made regarding the restoration of the permanent diaconate.[15] The topic had been debated by the Central Preparatory Commission in January before the opening of the council. It was not treated at all in the preparatory schema on the church but it did appear in chapter 2 of the second schema. Many bishops, including the American Cardinal Francis Spellman, objected during the conciliar debates that a married diaconate would have an adverse effect on priestly vocations. Other interventions were much more positive, perhaps none more so than a speech offered by Cardinal Döpfner but authored by Karl Rahner. Cardinal Suenens also offered a comprehensive defense of the permanent diaconate, citing biblical, historical, and theological arguments.

The Theological Commission worked throughout the second session to implement some of the changes being called for on the council floor. Two significant decisions were made in the commission regarding the structure of the schema: (1) the chapter on people of God and the laity would indeed be split into two chapters that would sandwich the chapter on the hierarchy; (2) the material on Mary would be incorporated into the schema as a sixth chapter. Since the commission's vote was much more divided on the second matter, it was decided that this issue should be put to a vote before the entire council. Consequently, on October 29 a vote was taken on whether to dedicate a separate document to Mary or to treat her within the document on the church. The vote was quite close, with 1,114 voting to treat Mary in the document on the church and 1,074 voting for a separate document.

In the midst of wide-ranging debates on the chapter on the hierarchy, speeches in favor of the schema's treatment of episcopal collegiality seemed evenly matched by speeches in opposition. It was unclear whether this division reflected a similar division among all the council bishops or simply those who chose to give interventions. The four moderators of the council (Cardinals Julius Döpfner, Giacomo Lercaro, Leon-Joseph Suenens, and Grégoire Agagianian, appointed by Pope

Paul VI to provide guidance and order to the work of the council) decided, with papal approval, to conduct a series of straw votes on several controverted positions in order to more clearly ascertain the sense of the council bishops. The next day the straw vote was taken on five propositions related to the chapter on the hierarchy:

1. That the episcopate was the highest level of the sacrament of orders

2. That every legitimately consecrated bishop, in union with the pope, is a member of the whole body of bishops

3. That the body or college of bishops succeeds to the college of the apostles and that this body in union with its head the pope possesses full and supreme authority in the church

4. That this authority belongs to the college of bishops itself by divine law

5. That the draft should deal with the opportuneness of restoring the permanent diaconate

The results of these votes came as a surprise to many, for while the vote on the treatment of Mary reflected the sense of division that many bishops had felt in the recent debates, the straw votes on these five propositions revealed a remarkable consensus: 98 percent voted in favor of proposition one; 95 percent for proposition two; 84 percent for proposition three; 80 percent for proposition four; and 75 percent for proposition five.[16] These votes constituted, in the minds of many, a crucial turning point in the course of the council. The widespread agreement among the council bishops had been clearly manifested, establishing a discernible momentum and direction for the course of the council.[17]

Council discussions acknowledged the need for a positive description of the laity in the church. A lively exchange was witnessed between Cardinals Leon-Joseph Suenens and Ernesto Ruffini. Suenens argued passionately for making greater use of the biblical category of "charism" as a way of speaking of the gifts given by the Spirit to all the faithful by virtue of their baptism. Ruffini objected to the ambiguity of the term. Several other bishops advocated a theology of the laity grounded in the threefold office of Christ as priest, prophet, and king.

In early November the bishops also debated material presented in a position paper that would eventually be included in the chapter on the people of God. The subject was most delicate, namely the relationship of non-Catholic Christians to the body of Christ, the church. The text of this document claimed that only those who acknowledged the whole structure of the visible Roman Catholic Church (profession of faith, sacraments, and church governance) were incorporated in the fellowship of the church "in the true and absolute sense of the term" (*incorporantur. . . reapse et simpliciter loquendo*).[18] A proposal was made by a representative of the bishops of Indonesia to drop this formulation entirely and to adopt instead the language of full incorporation (*plene incorporantur*), which suggested the possibility of degrees of incorporation into the church.[19]

Discussion of the chapter on the universal call to holiness was dominated by a sense of discomfort regarding the shift away from the preparatory schema's focus on professed religious life. Professed religious life cannot be considered a third way separate from the clergy and the laity, since professed religious are drawn from both. However, the question of whether to treat professed religious life in a separate chapter would be postponed until the third session. As the second session came to a close, the rapidly developing schema now was comprised of six chapters:

Chapter 1: The Mystery of the Church

Chapter 2: The People of God

Chapter 3: The Hierarchical Constitution of the Church and the Episcopate in Particular

Chapter 4: The Laity

Chapter 5: The Universal Call to Holiness

Chapter 6: The Role of the Blessed Virgin Mary, Mother of God, in the Mystery of Christ and the Church

The *De Ecclesia* Schema after the Second Session

In the closing weeks of the second session as well as during the inter-session, the Theological Commission sought to further revise the second draft. At the same time, Pope Paul VI became a tireless advocate for the constitution. In his opening address for the third session he stressed the importance, in particular, of finishing what Vatican I could not, a full consideration of the role of the bishops.

During the 1964 intersession the sub-commission dedicated to the revisions of the schema on the church brought a minor debate to a conclusion. They decided, provisionally, that the chapter on holiness be separated into two chapters, one on the universal call to holiness and the second on professed religious life. A final decision on the matter would be put before the council bishops during the next session.

In May of 1964 Paul VI sent to the Theological Commission some suggestions on the matter of episcopal collegiality that reflected his general support of the teaching but also his caution about its potential divisiveness. He also asked the commission to integrate into the schema on the church an independent text that considered the heavenly church and veneration of the saints. The text had been the inspiration of Pope John XXIII and had been drafted by a Jesuit, Paolo Molinari. This mandate was accepted with something less than full enthusiasm, as many on the commission were concerned that the schema on the church was already becoming quite lengthy.[20] The chapter, provisionally titled "The Eschatological Nature of Our Calling and Our Union with the Heavenly Church," would be placed before the chapter on Mary. This placement did have the merit of better situating the Marian chapter within an eschatological consideration of the communion of saints.

The text on Mary was the subject of considerable revision. The commission was given the task of reducing the originally independent schema on Mary to one chapter. It also had to find a middle ground between two distinct theological perspectives. The first perspective presented a more Christocentric view of Mary and the privileges that rightly accrued to her in light of her unique role in the economy of salvation. Advocates of this perspective eagerly sought a solemn definition on Mary as mediatrix of graces. The second perspective was grounded in a more biblical foundation and sought to connect Mary more closely to the church. Advocates of this second position were concerned that too much emphasis on Marian doctrine and practice would further impede the ecumenical imperative of the council.

The history of the drafting of this chapter is a fascinating story in itself, highlighted by a protracted battle between Gérard Philips, who revised the original text from a more biblical perspective, and the Franciscan theologian Carl Balič, who had authored the original text. The result was a compromise text that retained much of Philips's biblical material while referring cautiously to Mary as mediatrix, a reference that was nevertheless vigorously protested by some members of the Theological Commission. The text carefully avoided, however, any reference to Mary as co-redemptrix.

Finally, on July 3, 1964, Pope Paul VI had the completed schema on the church, now comprising eight chapters, sent to the council fathers for their consideration. The eight chapters were thematically paired: the first two chapters explored the church's transcendent and historical dimensions; the second pair developed the organic structure of the church; the third pair addressed the sanctification of the church and the special role of vowed religious; the fourth pair concluded with a consideration of the eschatological dimension of the church.

Chapter 1: The Mystery of the Church

Chapter 2: The People of God

Chapter 3: The Hierarchical Constitution of the Church and the Episcopate in Particular

Chapter 4: The Laity

Chapter 5: The Universal Call to Holiness

Chapter 6: Religious

Chapter 7: The Eschatological Nature of Our Calling and Our Union with the Heavenly Church

Chapter 8: The Blessed Virgin Mary, Mother of the Church

Final Schema: Approval and Promulgation

Voting on the first chapter, "The Mystery of the Church," occurred early in the third session. The bishops had before them a chapter that included, as a result of further revisions between sessions, a new statement presenting the mission of the church as one to "proclaim and to spread among all peoples the Kingdom of Christ and of God and to be, on earth, the initial budding forth of that kingdom" (*LG*, 5). This important statement constituted a break with the ecclesiological tendency to identify the church and the kingdom of God, instead placing the church in service of God's reign. Unfortunately, this text was added at too late a date to exert any influence on the overall document.

A second addition to the chapter was perhaps the most significant single word change in the history of all the council documents. Where the earlier text had quoted Pope Pius XII's assertion that the church of Christ "is (*est*) the Catholic church," article 8 now said that the church of Christ "subsists in" (*subsistit in*) the Catholic church. This much debated change suggested that the church of Christ was at least in some manner to be encountered in non-Catholic Christian communities as well. This chapter was overwhelmingly approved.

As the bishops prepared to vote on the second chapter they were given a report providing the rationale for having placed the chapter on the people of God in front of the chapter on the hierarchy. The chapter now before them included further refinements in the treatment of the proper relationship between the common priesthood of the faithful and the ministerial priesthood. The final text read:

> Though they differ from one another in essence and not only in degree, the common priesthood of the faithful and the ministerial or hierarchical priesthood are nonetheless interrelated: each of them in its own special way is a participation in the one priesthood of Christ. (*LG*, 10)

Not all bishops were happy with this formulation. For some the difficulty lay with the use of the word *essentia* in this passage. Bishop Antonio Jaramillo of Colombia had proposed changing the *essentialiter* to *sacramentaliter*, which would communicate more accurately that the distinction between the common priesthood of the baptized and the ordained priesthood was derived from their respective sacramental consecrations.[21] It was inevitable that use of the word *essentia* would lead many to read in this text a metaphysical distinction between the two priesthoods when it is not at all clear that this was the intention of the council.[22]

There were also numerous interventions by bishops who did not wish to affirm the full priestly identity of the baptized for fear of compromising the distinctive identity of the ordained. These bishops suggested that the baptized possessed only an "interior," "inchoate," "spiritual," or "mystical" priesthood. Yet, in the end, these proposals were rejected as the bishops affirmed unambiguously the equal dignity of the two "priesthoods," rooted as they were in the one priesthood of Christ. Once again, what the council wished to avoid is clearer than what it wished to say positively. It does appear that the text was crafted specifically to avoid presenting the common priesthood as of a lesser order; the ordained priesthood was not to be seen a fuller or more intense participation in the priesthood of Christ.[23]

This affirmation of the priesthood of all believers had already appeared in the preparatory schema, *De Ecclesia*. As this chapter began to move toward its final form, the affirmation of the priesthood of all believers was placed in a more comprehensive theological framework. The council asserted that the whole people of God participate not only in the priesthood of Christ but also in the prophetic and kingly offices of Christ.[24] Refinements would also be made concerning the manner in which various groups of people (non-Christians, Jews, people of good will, etc.) were related to the church. This chapter would be approved during this session, but would still require some twenty-four additional changes to the text to be made by the Theological Commission.

Although chapter 3 on the hierarchy was not to be subject to further debate on the council floor, it would receive considerable attention behind the scenes. Even before the opening of the third session the pope had received a lengthy letter from some leading prelates vigorously opposed to the "new" doctrine on collegiality found in the chapter. A series of thirty-nine distinct votes was held on individual sections of the chapter. Given the passion and energy expended by the opponents of the chapter, it is all the more amazing that each of the sections on the episcopate and episcopal collegiality passed overwhelmingly. Only the votes on the permanent diaconate garnered significant dissent, with a slimmer majority approving the two central provisions of the text: (1) the right of episcopal conferences to determine whether to restore the diaconate in their region and (2) opening up the permanent diaconate to mature married men. After the chapter on the hierarchy was approved, it was left to the Theological Commission to consider the attached *modi* (proposed amendments) and propose final revisions.

Chapter 4 on the laity, of all the chapters, probably changed the least with respect to the original preparatory schema. However, additional material had been included that sought to offer a positive definition of the laity and their place in the church. Following the framework laid out in chapters 2 and 3, the theology of the laity was also considered with respect to the laity's unique participation in the threefold office of Christ: priest, prophet, and king/shepherd. This chapter was also overwhelmingly approved.

The council next formally ratified the Theological Commission's decision to create a separate chapter on religious life out of material originally located in the chapter on the universal call to holiness. Both chapters 5 and 6 were then quickly approved with little further controversy.

Since the material in chapter 7 on the eschatological character of the church, unlike the other chapters, had not been previously discussed by the entire conciliar assembly, two days of open debate were dedicated to this chapter. Some criticized the text for its excessively individualistic focus, others for its lack of a pneumatology (a theology of the Holy Spirit). Cardinal Suenens gave a provocative address in which he complained of the high percentage of canonized saints who were professed religious and noted as well the high percentage who were western European. His proposal that the locus of the canonization process shift from the Vatican to regional episcopal conferences fell on deaf ears. In light of these and other criticisms, Yves Congar was asked by the sub-commission to draft a text that would address more comprehensively the eschatological nature of the church itself.[25] As a consequence, the title of the chapter was eventually changed to read, "The Eschatological Nature of the Pilgrim Church and her Union with the Heavenly Church." This change reflected a pronounced shift in the tone of the document. We are now far from neo-scholastic understandings of the church as a "perfect society" with their focus on static church institutions; this text presented the church itself as "pilgrim," awaiting its perfection at the end of history. As pilgrim, the church must submit to necessary and ongoing reform and renewal. This chapter too received an overwhelming vote of approval.

Somewhat predictably, given the history of contentious debate in the council regarding the role of Mary, the final Marian chapter met with diverse criticism. Much of the dispute focused on the inclusion in the text of the title "mediatrix." Some, including the influential Cardinal Bea, advocated deleting the reference altogether, as many of the Protestant observers had warned of its problematic character for ecumenical relations. Others suggested keeping the title but including it among a number of other Marian titles of use in Marian piety (e.g., advocate, helper) as a way of minimizing its doctrinal significance. The second strategy received crucial papal support, including the pope's recommendation that the text include an unambiguous assertion of the unique mediation of Christ. A decision was also made not to accede to the pope's request to include in the chapter heading the title of Mary as "Mother of the Church."[26] This title was opposed by the Theological Commission as ecumenically problematic; it was of fairly recent provenance in the Western tradition and foreign to the East. The final chapter headings read then as follows:

Chapter 1: The Mystery of the Church

Chapter 2: The People of God

Chapter 3: The Hierarchical Constitution of the Church and the Episcopate in Particular

Chapter 4: The Laity

Chapter 5: The Universal Call to Holiness in the Church

Chapter 6: Religious

Chapter 7: The Eschatological Nature of the Pilgrim Church and Its Union with the Heavenly Church

Chapter 8: The Blessed Virgin Mary, Mother of God, in the Mystery of Christ and the Church

There is one final coda to the history of the Dogmatic Constitution on the Church. In spite of the clear majority of bishops who supported the theological tenor of the controversial third chapter on the hierarchy, Pope Paul VI was convinced that a moral unanimity among the bishops was prudentially advisable on this matter in order to prevent enduring divisions among the bishops. In consequence, members of the Theological Commission prepared extensive responses to a number of the *modi* proposed by the minority bishops concerning the council's treatment of episcopal collegiality. The council was then informed that a revised distillation of these responses would be attached to the third chapter "by higher authority," meaning, presumably, the pope. This text sought to clarify that (1) the use of the term *collegium* with regard to the bishops is not meant to suggest a society of equals, (2) although the offices of teaching and governing are conferred at episcopal ordination, they cannot be made "ready for action" without further canonical or juridical determination from the pope, (3) the college of bishops is a true college only in union with its head, the pope, and (4) the pope, as head, may act either personally or collegially in his exercise of supreme authority while the college can exercise its supreme authority only intermittently in strictly collegial activity.

The authorship of this text, which was referred to as a *Nota Explicativa Praevia*, has long been shrouded in mystery. Its attachment to the chapter on the hierarchy was intended as a reassuring response to the concerns of those bishops who retained deep reservations regarding the chapter's teaching on collegiality. Predictably, these bishops cheered the attachment of the *Nota* to the chapter. Equally predictably, this maneuver was protested by many more bishops and council theologians, who saw it as an attempt to undermine the theological import of chapter 3. Many also resented that the *Nota* would not itself be subject to a vote.

In spite of this controversial nod to the minority concerns, the final version of the constitution received solemn approval on November 21, 1964 with only five negative votes. The history of the document, from preparatory schema to its final form, represents one of the most remarkable shifts in ecclesiology ever found in an ecclesiastical document. It is worth summarizing some of the principal developments in Catholic ecclesiology evident in the final text.

Central Developments in the Schema on the Church

- The document begins with the church's theological foundations in the triune life of God.

- The chapter on the people of God precedes the chapter on the hierarchy, highlighting the priority of church unity and the equality of all the church's members.

- In affirming the universal priesthood of all believers, the constitution retrieves an ancient but long-neglected biblical insight.

- The text acknowledges that non-Catholic Christians are incorporated (even if not "fully") in the life of the church.

- The principle of collegiality is affirmed, granting that the bishops share with the bishop of Rome supreme power and authority exercised in service of the universal church.

- The positive role of the laity in the life of the church is affirmed.

- The document insists that all Christians are called to the perfection of charity and holiness.

- The pilgrim character of the church is affirmed and its need for reform and renewal acknowledged.

- Mary is more fully connected to the church.

A BRIEF HISTORY OF THE DECREE ON THE PASTORAL OFFICE OF BISHOPS IN THE CHURCH (*CHRISTUS DOMINUS*)

The Decree on the Pastoral Office of Bishops in the Church is often overlooked when discussing the most significant conciliar documents. However, the topic it addressed, the episcopate, was a very high priority for many at the council. Most agreed that theological reflection on the office of the bishop had been eclipsed by theological considerations of the papacy. Leading figures at the council were determined to address this lacuna.

For much of the first millennium, the ministry of the bishop had been central to the life of the church. Both individually and together in regional synods, the bishops were the principal ministers of unity in the church. Virtually all church crises were addressed and resolved, not by the pope, but by regional gatherings of bishops and eventually by universal gatherings, often initiated by the emperor in order to address issues dividing the church (and consequently, the Roman empire!). It is only in the second millennium that the papacy began to displace the college of bishops as the principal ministry in service of the unity of the church.

The gradual weakening of episcopal authority from the eleventh to the sixteenth centuries did not go unnoted. The Council of Trent addressed this situation, with council fathers engaging in a lively debate regarding the authority and ministry of the bishop. Accounts of the debates at the Council of Trent reveal a movement, largely encouraged by the Spanish bishops, to resolve some questions regarding the relationship between the primacy of the pope and the authority of bishops.[27] The Spanish bishops complained of a steady erosion of episcopal authority in the face of increasing interventions by Roman officials and the preferential treatment given to religious orders. The first matter of debate concerned whether the office of bishops existed by divine institution or was established by the pope. The Spanish bishops wanted the council to assert clearly that Christ himself instituted the office of the bishop. The bishops also debated the origins of the episcopal powers of orders and jurisdiction. Although all agreed that the power of orders was given at episcopal consecration, many thought that the bishop received the power of jurisdiction from the pope. Bonaventure Kloppenburg writes of the practical effect of this view of orders:

> According to this conception, the bishop was a priest who had received a special jurisdiction from the pope, a head of a diocese, a kind of governor and administrator who, in the measure that he had received jurisdiction, could more or less exercise an immediate and ordinary pastoral function. All the power he had he had by favor of the Holy See, which could restrict or entirely remove jurisdiction that had been freely given. In other words, and in practice, this kind of bishop was

not a vicar of Christ but a vicar of the pope, who thus seemed to be really the only authentic successor of the Apostles.[28]

Again, many bishops objected to this theory. They held that while the pope may *assign* a particular jurisdiction to a bishop, the source of the power of jurisdiction, the power to pastor a flock, comes from episcopal consecration itself. In spite of vigorous debate, these matters were left unresolved.

Three centuries later, at the First Vatican Council, there was again an attempt to address the authority of the bishop. An early draft of a document on the church was rejected by the bishops for a number of reasons, one of which was its insufficient treatment of the office of the bishop. The document was sent back to committee for reworking with only the material on the papacy going forward for conciliar debate. Before there was any opportunity to revise and reconsider the material sent back to committee, the council was suspended. Vatican I's teaching on the papacy thus stood alone without any accompanying consideration of other aspects of the church. In consequence, the teaching of Vatican I was widely misread as granting the pope virtually unfettered authority, rendering him the veritable "first bishop" of every diocese. The conciliar teaching was in fact much more measured, but this subtlety was lost on many who read *Pastor Aeternus*. Bismarck, the chancellor of Germany, for example, had read the constitution to mean that the pope could assume episcopal rights of every diocese, that episcopal jurisdiction was absorbed by papal jurisdiction, and therefore that the bishops were mere instruments of the pope. The German bishops felt compelled to respond formally to the chancellor:

> According to [the] teaching of the Catholic church, the pope is bishop of Rome but not bishop of another diocese or another town.... But as bishop of Rome he is at the same time pope, that is, the pastor and supreme head of the universal Church, head of all the bishops and the faithful and his papal power should be respected and listened to everywhere and always, not only in particular and exceptional cases. In this position the pope has to watch over each bishop in the fulfillment of the whole range of his episcopal charge. If a bishop is prevented, or if some need has made itself felt, the pope has

the right and the duty, in his capacity as pope and not as bishop of the diocese, to order whatever is necessary for the administration of that diocese.... The decisions of the Vatican Council do not offer the shadow of a pretext to claim that the pope has by them become an absolute sovereign and, in virtue of his infallibility, a sovereign more perfectly absolute than any absolute monarch in the world.[29]

In March of 1875, Pope Pius IX gave formal approval of the German bishops' declaration.[30] In England, John Henry Newman would feel compelled to offer a similar clarification of the council's teaching in his famous *Letter to the Duke of Norfolk*. Several decades later Pope Leo XIII would again insist that the bishops

are not to be looked upon as vicars of the Roman Pontiffs; because they exercise a power really their own, and are most truly called the ordinary pastors of the people over whom they rule.[31]

In spite of these clarifications, after Vatican I many of the Latin seminary manuals would propose a vision of the church that highlighted papal prerogatives and the centralization of authority in the papacy. One ecclesiology manual, for example, written in 1891 by Domenico Palmieri, bore the following title, *Tractatus de Romano Pontifice cum Prolegomena de Ecclesia* (*Tract on the Roman Pontiff with an Introduction on the Church*). As the title of this manual indicates, in many instances, considerations of the church were preoccupied with the papacy. There were, of course, many exceptions to this papocentrist tendency, but as the church moved toward Vatican II, Catholic ecclesiology seemed to suffer, if not from any fundamental defect, then certainly from a pronounced imbalance in its treatment of the relationship between papal authority and episcopal authority.

This imbalance was uppermost on the minds of those who undertook preparations for Vatican II. Many were aware that the council needed to consider some important issues: (1) the relationship of the bishops to the pope and the degree to which they shared his supreme authority over the church; (2) the extent to which the episcopate existed by divine institution; (3) whether the power of jurisdiction was conferred at episcopal consecration; (4) whether episcopal consecration was properly sacramental; (5) the need to highlight a more pastoral rather than juridical view of the bishop's office.

In spite of the widely shared conviction that this topic was of critical importance, preparations for conciliar treatment of the office of the bishop suffered under several handicaps, foremost of which was the decision to treat the disciplinary and doctrinal aspects of the office of the bishop separately.[32] The Preparatory Commission on Bishops and the Governance of Dioceses was charged with treating disciplinary matters pertaining to the episcopate (e.g., questions of jurisdiction, the role of episcopal conferences, the relationship between bishops and the pope, the retirement of bishops), largely with a view toward the eventual reform of the code of canon law. The Theological Commission, on the other hand, was to consider doctrinal matters related to the episcopate. This separation of the disciplinary and doctrinal dimensions of the episcopate was unfortunate and resulted in a much weaker decree on the bishops than might have otherwise been possible.

The Preparatory Commission on Bishops and the Governance of Dioceses sent seven schemata on to the Central Preparatory Commission. These seven schemata were reworked into two documents: "On the Bishops and the Government of Dioceses" (*De Episcopis ac de Diocesium Regimine*) and "On the Care of Souls" (*De Cura Animarum*). Although the first was briefly debated in 1963, the second never came up for debate and was ultimately incorporated into a later version of the first document. Let us consider the course of the development of the final decree in more detail.

The First Schema

The schema "On Bishops and the Government of Dioceses" that the bishops debated in the fall of 1963 had already gone through a series of revisions in the preparatory phase. This process of revision was undertaken not by the full commission but by what Klaus Mörsdorf referred to as a "rump commission" consisting of a few experts and commission members chosen by Cardinal Paolo Marella, then head of the Commission on Bishops.[33] In fact, most of the specific revisions were made under the direction of Bishop Giovanni Carli, widely thought to be opposed to any substantive reconsideration of the theology of the episcopate.[34] This revised text was to be discussed by the full membership of the Commission on Bishops before being sent on to the council bishops. However, Cardinal Marella cancelled the planned meeting of the full commission scheduled for April of 1962 (indeed every meeting of the full commission scheduled during the preparatory period was ultimately cancelled!), thus preventing the commission members from debating the text prior to its being sent on to the council bishops. It is difficult to avoid the conclusion that both Marella and Carli were zealously protecting a text that largely reflected the *status quo* regarding the office of the bishop.

In any event, as submitted for council debate, the schema consisted of the following five chapters:

Chapter 1: The Powers of the Bishops

Chapter 2: The Coadjutor and Auxiliary Bishops

Chapter 3: The National Episcopal Conference

Chapter 4: The Suitable Boundaries of the Dioceses and Ecclesiastical Provinces

Chapter 5: The Erection of Parishes and Their Suitable Boundaries

Also included in the draft were two appendices, the first listing the faculties to be granted to both diocesan and titular bishops and the second concerning the Roman curia and its relationship to the bishops. Most noteworthy in the second appendix were a number of proposals for curial reform.

In the course of just over a week of debate during the second session, some important issues were raised and rather pointed criticisms of the schema surfaced.[35] As we saw earlier, a lively debate on episcopal collegiality had already transpired with respect to the schema on the church, a debate that culminated in the famous straw vote in late October of 1963 that had approved, in principle, the notion of episcopal collegiality. Consequently, several bishops voiced concerns that this principle was not reflected in the schema on bishops, while others felt in-depth discussion of this topic was premature given the fact that no final decision had been made on collegiality.

The schema, at this point, reflected a largely juridical approach to the bishop's office, with very little consideration of the developing theology of the episcopate evident in the revised schema on the church. Many bishops expressed their desire for a strong assertion of the rights of individual bishops, particularly over against the authority of the Roman curia. Cardinal Bernard Alfrink of Utrecht insisted that the curia served not only the pope but also the college of bishops. From an ecclesiological perspective, he argued, the Roman curia must not be seen as superior to the bishops but in service of their ministry.

Over the course of these debates, a few interventions merit special note.[36] Melkite Patriarch Maximos IV Saigh drew on the experience of the Eastern churches with permanent synods, offering them as a model for the creation of a synodal body to assist the pope in governance of the universal church. This echoed a number of similar proposals that had been floated by various bishops who were looking for ways to enhance the participation of the bishops in decisions involving the universal church. At one point, a letter requesting the creation of a synod was sent to the pope with the signatures of some five hundred bishops.[37]

The Melkite patriarch also introduced the long neglected distinction of ancient provenance concerning the various offices held by the pope. The pope is, first of all, the bishop of a local church, Rome, and only because he is bishop of Rome is he also the primate of Italy, the patriarch of the West, and pastor of the universal church. The neglect of these necessary distinctions had led, in the second millennium, to an inflation of papal authority. The West, the patriarch contended, had failed to recognize that not all exercises of church authority by the bishop of Rome were properly papal exercises; in some instances, for example, the pope was acting as patriarch of the West, making decisions that could not be considered applicable to the Eastern churches. We will return to these issues when we consider the Decree on the Catholic Churches of the Eastern Rite.

A second intervention of particular significance was presented on October 30, 1963, by Cardinal Frings. Frings offered a clear and

pointed attack on the Roman curia, criticizing in general its centralization of authority and in particular abuses of the Holy Office,
"whose procedure in many respects is no longer suited to our age,
harms the Church, and is scandalous to many."[38] He objected to the
first appendix listing faculties granted to the bishops. The very use of
the term "faculties" suggested something conceded by the pope,
rather than realities proper to the ministry of the bishop. Better to
assume that a bishop is granted through ordination those powers necessary for the exercise of his office, he contended, and list only those
exceptional powers to be reserved to the pope. He also criticized the
elevation to the episcopate of curial officials, a practice that transformed the episcopate from a ministry of service to an honorific.

It was not long before this provocative intervention was met with
an equally impassioned response from Cardinal Ottaviani. He vigorously defended the Holy Office, identifying it with the authority of the
pope himself. He also insisted that the straw vote on episcopal collegiality should not carry any weight in the council's deliberations.
Indeed, Ottaviani went so far as to question the decision of the council
moderators to conduct the series of straw votes in the first place. These
exchanges suggest the considerable weight the council bishops gave to
the various issues associated with the theology of the episcopate.

During the council's discussion of the chapter on auxiliary and
coadjutor bishops, some council members addressed the possibility of
the retirement of bishops and whether making episcopal retirement
mandatory would render the appointment of coadjutor bishops (bishops with right of succession) unnecessary. It was noted that at present
there were more titular bishops (bishops who were given "title" to a
now non-existent church because they were either auxiliaries, coadju-
tors, or bishops serving in a Vatican post) than diocesan ones. Cardinal
Döpfner even questioned the wisdom of having dioceses so large that
multiple auxiliary bishops were necessary; better to divide these dioceses up, allowing for one bishop per diocese, in keeping with ancient
custom. Yet in the debates concerning the chapter on diocesan boundaries, there was considerable disagreement regarding what constituted
the optimum size of dioceses. At the time of the council, significant
disparities in the size of dioceses existed from nation to nation. For
example, Germany was then comprised of 22 dioceses while Italy had
288![39]

We must also note the debates regarding the treatment of episcopal conferences, that is the organization of bishops into regional groupings in order to achieve some pastoral purpose. The draft had envisioned making episcopal conferences legally binding intermediary institutions between the papacy and the local bishop. This proposal was widely criticized, with many questioning the advisability of granting significant legislative powers to these conferences. Those in favor of granting significant powers to the conferences generally saw this as a concrete avenue for pursuing a much needed decentralization of church authority. Those opposed were committed to protecting the prerogatives of the individual bishop.

During the council's deliberations, then theologian and *peritus* Joseph Ratzinger gave a much discussed lecture on episcopal collegiality and used the theological status of episcopal conferences as a test case.[40] Ratzinger was committed to a retrieval of the patristic ecclesiology of communion. In his lecture he criticized a narrow and primarily juridical view of collegiality that saw its sole expression limited to the formal acts of the whole college of bishops in communion with its head, the bishop of Rome. Instead, he hearkened back to the more fluid notion of collegiality manifested in the regional synods of the early church. This view called for a more elastic understanding of collegiality correlated to the ecclesiological principle of communion. Every relationship between one bishop and another was considered an expression of the *communio ecclesiarum*, the spiritual communion among the churches. This is why, he contended, the participation of three bishops was deemed sufficient at episcopal consecration. To those who held that collegiality could be applied only to the entire episcopate, Ratzinger, echoing the views of another theologian, the Dominican Jerôme Hamer,[41] responded that every exercise of collegiality need not be an exercise of the *suprema potestas*, the supreme power and authority that was properly attributed only to the whole episcopate. On this point Ratzinger wrote at the time:

> We should rather say that the concept of collegiality, besides the office of unity which pertains to the pope, signifies an element of variety and adaptability that basically belongs to the structure of the Church, but may be actuated in many ways. The collegiality of bishops signifies that there should be in the

Church (under and in the unity guaranteed by the primacy) an ordered plurality. The bishops' conferences are, then, one of the possible forms of collegiality that is here partially realized but with a view to the totality.[42]

In spite of his eloquent argumentation, the council would content itself with only a few muted references to episcopal conferences.

Soon after the second session drew to a close it became clear that the bishops were not going to be able to address the second schema, "On the Care of Souls." They decided to incorporate the most important material from this draft into the further revisions of the schema, "On the Bishops and the Governance of Dioceses." In January of 1964 these revisions gave rise to a new schema, titled "On the Bishops' Pastoral Office in the Church." This text was much improved, with a diminishment of the juridical tone that dominated the earlier draft on episcopal governance, and with more attention to the theology of the episcopate that had emerged in chapter 3 of the Dogmatic Constitution on the Church. Included in chapter 1 was a proposal for a central group of bishops to assist the pope in his pastoral leadership of the universal church. Absent, however, was any theological justification for the role of episcopal conferences, which were instead justified on historical and pragmatic grounds.[43]

Second Schema

In April of 1964 a new draft was sent to the Central Commission and, after being further revised, was then sent on in May to the council members, with the following structure:

Preface

Chapter 1: The Relationship of Bishops to the Universal Church

Chapter 2: Bishops and Their Particular Churches or Dioceses

Chapter 3: The Cooperation of Bishops for the Common Good of Many Churches

This schema was debated only briefly in the third session. The debate was still handicapped by the fact that one crucial doctrinal question had not yet been addressed, namely whether jurisdiction was conferred by episcopal consecration or by the pope. In spite of this, the controversial material in chapter 1 that affirmed the doctrine of episcopal collegiality remained untouched. Only four days were given to debate of the text. Several French bishops proposed strengthening the relationship between a bishop and the priests of his diocese, and there was a quite vigorous discussion of the principle of exemption that gave professed religious communities limited autonomy with regard to the internal workings of their communities. Among the various interventions offered during this time of limited debate, perhaps the most provocative was that of Bishop Carli, himself a member of the Bishops' Commission, who continued to object to the inclusion of the material on collegiality. He viewed this new direction as theologically imprudent and claimed that it risked obscuring the bishop's primary relationship to his particular church.[44] After the debate, the bishops voted on each of the three chapters, with only the third chapter receiving full approval. Thus it was left to the Bishops' Commission to make further revisions of the text in light of the various criticisms and specific recommendations.

In the end, the final text could not be considered in the closing days of the third session, and would be approved only in the final session. Controversy would continue to surround the text. Key conciliar figures, such as the secretary general of the council, Archbishop Pericle Felici, insisted that the schema's teaching on episcopal collegiality was inopportune and should be dropped in favor of a treatment of more properly pastoral concerns related to the bishops' office.[45] Although Felici's efforts to eliminate the decree's treatment of collegiality failed, it is regrettable that the final text was not able to take into account later refinements of chapter 3 of *Lumen Gentium*. In any event, in the fall of 1965 votes were taken on the amended sections of the schema, followed by a vote on the whole schema, which was overwhelmingly approved on October 28, 1965.

A BRIEF HISTORY OF THE DECREE ON
THE CATHOLIC CHURCHES OF THE EASTERN RITE
(*ORIENTALIUM ECCLESIARUM*)

The four centuries prior to Vatican II were characterized by an almost inexorable movement toward greater uniformity in church discipline, liturgy, and theology. Nevertheless, along the ecclesial periphery of Roman Catholicism stood a number of Eastern Catholic churches, each with its own unique history and all of which had retained, more or less successfully, distinct canonical, liturgical, and theological traditions that distinguished them from the Latin church.[46] These churches have a complicated history. Some, like the Maronite Catholic Church and the Syro-Malabar Catholic Church, proudly claim origins in the earliest centuries of Christianity. Others were born out of a dubious Catholic policy that treated Eastern Orthodox Christians as the object of Catholic missionary endeavors in which churches with liturgical, theological, and spiritual resonances with Orthodoxy were established to "win over" converts. This practice, long since renounced in the Catholic Church, remains even today a serious bone of contention with the Eastern Orthodox, who refer to Eastern Catholic churches disparagingly as "Uniate churches." These Eastern Catholic churches often claim a very painful history. Despised by the Orthodox, they also suffered a pattern of forced latinization by Roman Catholic church leadership. The scandalous treatment of the Eastern Catholics here in the United States by Latin bishops is one of the sadder chapters in the history of American Catholicism.

As preparations began for the Second Vatican Council, a decision was made to divide up responsibilities for ecumenical issues between two preparatory commissions: the Secretariat for Christian Unity was to deal with relations with Protestantism while the Commission for the Oriental Churches was to address relations with both the Orthodox and the Eastern churches in communion with Rome. This assignment was unfortunate, as the Commission for the Oriental Churches was much less zealous than the Secretariat for Christian Unity and did relatively little to establish relations with the Orthodox churches and negotiate the invitations for observers.[47] The commission was at least marginally more successful at treating questions related to the Eastern Catholic churches. It produced one schema on Christian unity with the Eastern Orthodox and numerous short schemata,[48] each of which was envisioned as a chapter for one larger document. Of note was an extended discussion of the role of patriarchs, including such questions as whether Eastern patriarchs should be made cardinals and whether Latin and titular patriarchs should be suppressed. Unfortunately, when the draft was sent on to the Central Preparatory Commission, material was added that cast the role of the patriarch in a decidedly Latin perspective, claiming that the patriarch's authority could be seen only as a participation in what was properly papal authority. Most of the rest of these schemata dealt with disciplinary matters (e.g., the proper minister of confirmation, the problem of mixed marriages, the need for a common dating of Easter). Some material from the schema on Christian unity was combined with the other short schema to form one document, *De Ecclesiis Orientalibus*, ("On the Oriental Churches"). The remainder of the material from the schema on Christian unity would eventually be combined with other schemata to form the Decree on Ecumenism.

When the council began in the fall of 1962, *De Ecclesiis Orientalibus* was given to the newly created Conciliar Commission on Oriental Churches. This commission included episcopal representatives from nearly all of the major Eastern Catholic churches. The revised draft was then sent to all of the bishops for comment in the spring following the first session. Comments and proposed amendments were considered as the commission continued reworking the text throughout most of the second session and over the course of the following spring. This work during the second intersession occasioned complaints from leading figures on the commission, like Patriarch Maximos, who was concerned that the work was done largely by those commission members residing in Rome to the exclusion of consultation with other members. In any event, the size of the schema was dramatically reduced. The much compressed version was sent to the bishops in late spring of 1964. Finally, debate on the schema began on October 15, 1964.

One can identify important improvements as the draft moved through its various revisions, and many of the interventions during the debate lauded the text for its ringing affirmation of the legitimacy of the Eastern Catholic churches, the equality of all the churches *sui iuris*, and the autonomy of the Eastern patriarchs. Given the Latin church's poor track record where treatment of the Eastern Catholic churches was concerned, these affirmations took on new significance. On November 21, 1964, the document, now titled "The Decree on the Catholic Churches of the Eastern Rite," was officially approved by the council. The continuous pressure to reduce the size of the document and the limited opportunities for further revision after the conciliar debate limited its potential contribution to the renewal of the church (it is the third shortest of the conciliar documents).

In Part One I have set the subject matter of these three documents in a broader historical context. I have also offered a very brief outline of the historical development of the documents. I have called attention to some of the more significant issues that were under debate and have noted important shifts that occurred over the history of these documents. In Part Two, diachronic analysis of the historical development of these texts will give way to a more synthetic analysis that focuses on their final form and identifies the emergence of consistent themes.

PART II

Major Points

Having explored in Part One the textual history of *Lumen Gentium*, *Christus Dominus*, and *Orientalium Ecclesiarum*, we are now in a position to bring that diachronic reading together with a more synchronic consideration of the final form of these texts. The focus will turn to an examination of emergent themes and a consideration of how these themes were prepared for, complemented, or further developed by other conciliar documents. The emergent themes will be treated under three headings: (1) theological foundations of the church, (2) unity and catholicity in the church, and (3) the structures and exercise of church leadership.

THEOLOGICAL FOUNDATIONS OF THE CHURCH

Yves Congar had often written of the Gregorian reforms of the eleventh century as a decisive turning point in the history of the church.[1] Several popes in the eleventh century were concerned with the increased influence of secular princes on the ministry of bishops. In order to protect the proper autonomy of the church and its mission, Pope Gregory VII insisted that the pope had authority over all ecclesiastical offices and, for that matter, over secular princes themselves. He made sweeping claims to virtually absolute papal authority and called for canon lawyers to begin assembling various legal texts in support of these claims. What Gregory set in motion was a gradual yet inexorable shift from a church whose foundation lay in theology and sacramental practice to a church whose foundation lay in canon law. It would be no coincidence that the popes of the following three centuries would be predominantly canon lawyers. Gregory's reforms almost certainly helped preserve the autonomy of the church, but, as William Henn has observed,

> one may wonder whether the juridical means used to achieve this end may not have overshadowed the desired effect. The desired freedom was won, but the fundamental "sacramentality" of the church was somewhat forgotten in the face of the overriding insistence that the church is a juridically structured society.[2]

In spite of periods of tremendous theological creativity, henceforward for almost nine hundred years the dominant framework for understanding the church would be that of law and jurisdiction rather than theology.

This may explain the profound disappointment with which the preparatory schema on the church was received by the bishops at Vatican II. Many on the eve of the council believed that the Catholic Church was in need of a broad rediscovery of its sacramental and theological foundations. Pope Pius XII's encyclical, *Mystici Corporis*, had offered an important step toward a renewed theology of the church, yet many council bishops were convinced that the pope's encyclical marked an important starting point, not an end point, for such a theology.

The council produced no systematic treatises on the church. No document produced by the convoluted process of committee drafting and redrafting could ever pass muster as a truly systematic treatise. Yet these documents did offer a substantial retrieval of ancient theological insights. The first chapter of *Lumen Gentium* explored the spiritual origins of the church in the trinitarian missions of Word and Spirit. The council quoted St. Cyprian of Carthage who asserted that the church is "a people made one with the unity of the Father, the Son and the Holy Spirit" (*LG*, 4). The innermost reality of the church, its participation in the triune life of God, shifted from background to foreground.[3] According to the council, the church shares in the mystery of God to the extent that it participates in God's saving work on behalf of humankind. The church is not an autonomous entity; rather, its very existence depends on its relationship to God through Christ and in the Spirit. Through Christ and by the power of the Spirit believers are invited to participate in the divine life of God through their participation in the life of the church (*LG*, 2). The divine communion of trinitarian persons is mirrored in the spiritual communion that abides in the church, for, the council wrote, Christ established the church as "a communion of life, charity and truth" (*LG*, 9). This trinitarian theology of the church is further developed by way of a number of biblical and patristic images and theological concepts. We need to consider these in more detail.

Church as Sacrament

At least since the Protestant Reformation, Catholic ecclesiology had been preoccupied with defending the essential character of the visible, institutional structures of the church. St. Robert Bellarmine had compared the church with the Republic of Venice.[4] The church could be viewed much like a civil society insofar as it possessed all that was necessary for the achievement of this society's particular end, the salvation of souls. In his encyclical *Mystici Corporis*, Pope Pius XII retrieved a long neglected theology of the church as the mystical body of Christ. Yet in doing so he limited his reflections to the visibility and institutional integrity of the church. What was needed was a new basis for affirming the necessity of the church's institutional structures without making them ends in themselves, and without eclipsing the spiritual dynamism of the church.

The council accomplished this by taking advantage of the seminal contributions of the liturgical movement and the return of many theologians to biblical and patristic sources. The 1950s and early 1960s saw the publication of several important systematic treatises by figures like Edward Schillebeeckx, Otto Semmelroth, and Karl Rahner on the sacramentality of the church.[5] Drawing on these theological developments, the council affirmed that the church was not simply an administrator of seven sacraments. The church itself was sacramental insofar as it was an effective and graced sign before the world of God's saving love. This theme was first proposed in the Constitution on the Sacred Liturgy, *Sacrosanctum Concilium*: "For it was from the side of Christ as He slept the sleep of death upon the cross that there came forth the wondrous sacrament of the whole Church" (*SC*, 5). Already in the first paragraph of *Lumen Gentium* the council taught that

> the Church is in Christ like a sacrament or as a sign and instrument both of a very closely knit union with God and of the unity of the whole human race.... (*LG*, 1)

Later, in article 9, the document states:

> God gathered together as one all those who in faith look upon Jesus as the author of salvation and the source of unity and peace, and established them as the Church that for each and all it may be the visible sacrament of this saving unity.

By describing the church as sacrament, the council acknowledged the necessity of the church's visible structures. Just as the sacramental nature of the Eucharist demanded bread and wine, so too the church as sacrament required a visible reality. Yet in the Eucharist, bread and wine ultimately become effective symbols of something else—real communion with Christ. So too the affirmation of the church's sacramental character reminds us that the visible and institutional dimension of the church—its law, offices, ritual actions—must be valued not as ultimate realities but as mediations of God's saving action. Rather than simply juxtaposing the visible with the invisible, the sacramentality of the church asserts that the church's visible humanity opens out into God's saving presence. Moreover, it is not just the institutional dimension of the church that participates in its sacramentality. Ultimately, the church consists not of structures and laws but of believers. The church is a *congregatio fidelium*. The whole church, saints and sinners alike, share in the sacramentality of the church, insofar as the witness of each believer's life participates in the corporate sign value of the whole church.

Body of Christ

The council continued to employ the mystical body theology that was found in Pius XII's encyclical. Throughout the documents we find a vigorous christological affirmation: the church *is* the mystical body of Christ. As the council affirmed in the opening words of *Lumen Gentium*, "Christ is the Light of nations" (*LG*, 1). These christological affirmations must not be overlooked. "The church has saving power not because she possesses good institutions or laws, nor because she is well organized and up-to-date, but because Christ acts in and through her."[6]

We should not overlook the council's continuity with the teaching of *Mystici Corporis*, but there is no mistaking the ways in which *Lumen Gentium* also went beyond Pius XII. First, it considered the church as mystical body within a chapter that explores other complementary biblical metaphors for the church: both sheepfold and flock, God's field to be cultivated, vine and branches, the building of God constructed with living stones, God's holy temple, spotless spouse. Second, *Lumen Gentium* considered the church as mystical body, not only as regards the visibility of its institutional structures, but as a spiritual communion comprised of people from every nation, whose "soul" is the Holy Spirit. The body of Christ is built up, the council asserted, by the diversity of the church's members and gifts (*LG*, 7). The council's teaching evokes important insights from St. Paul's use of the body as a metaphor for the church.

Paul's whole ecclesiology presupposed an organic view of the church that suggested not just the complementarity and diversity of its members but also their shared life.[7] To be a member of the church meant to draw life and sustenance from communion with God and one another. For Paul, life in Christ meant life in the body of Christ, the church. The church was no mere aggregate of individuals. Rather, by baptism into the Christian community one participated in a new reality; one was a new creation. As Yves de Montcheuil put it, "It is not Christians who, in coming together, constitute the Church; it is the Church that makes Christians."[8]

Third, the council completely sidestepped the question of who was or was not a member of the body of Christ, preferring to speak of degrees of incorporation into the church of Christ. We will return to this topic below. Finally, the council recalled the vital relationship between the eucharistic body of Christ and Christ's body the church. This had been a consistent theme of the early church writers. St. Augustine, in one of his most famous sermons on the Eucharist, said:

Since you are the Body of Christ and His members, it is your mystery that is placed on the Lord's table, it is your mystery that you receive.... Be what you see, and receive what you are.[9]

In the Eastern church St. John Chrysostom wrote:

For what is the bread? It is the body of Christ. And what do those who receive it become? The Body of Christ—not many bodies but one body. For as bread is completely one, though made up of many grains of wheat, and these, albeit unseen, remain nonetheless present, in such a way that their difference is not apparent since they have been made a perfect whole, so too are we mutually joined to one another and together united with Christ.[10]

In article 7 of *Lumen Gentium* the council recovers this ancient eucharistic vision of the church:

Really partaking of the body of the Lord in the breaking of the eucharistic bread, we are taken up into communion with Him and with one another. "Because the bread is one, we though many, are one body, all of us who partake of the one bread." In this way all of us are made members of His Body, "but severally members one of another."

This eucharistic ecclesiology would, in turn, lead the council to affirm the theological significance of the local church. If each celebration of the Eucharist is a matter not only of Christ's sacramental presence on the altar but also of his ecclesial presence in the gathered community, then each eucharistic local church must be more than a subset of the universal church; it must be the body of Christ "in that place."

The Church as Communion

The understandings of church as sacrament and body of Christ were integrated, in the council's teaching, with a recovery of the ancient biblical concept, *koinonia*. In the New Testament the Greek term is found in the writings of Paul, in the Acts of the Apostles, and in the Johannine literature, each with distinct resonances. There is both a vertical dimension in which *koinonia* denotes one's fellowship with God in Christ (1 Cor 1:9; 1 John 1:3–7), and a horizontal fellowship with members of the church (1 Cor 10:16–17; Acts 2:42). This biblical notion of *koinonia*, translated as *communio* in Latin, would play a central role in the developing ecclesial self-understanding of the early church. Vatican II explicitly employed *koinonia-communio* language in a number of passages.

Attending to the vertical dimension, the council taught that it is through the mediation of Christ's church, by the power of the Spirit, that we are drawn into the triune life of God. By the power of the Holy Spirit, God the Father restores life to those who were dead through sin. "By the power of the Gospel [the Spirit] makes the Church keep the freshness of youth. Uninterruptedly He renews it and leads it to perfect union with its Spouse" (*LG*, 4). In that same article we find attention to the horizontal dimension: "the Spirit leads the church into all truth and unites it in communion and ministry...."[11] In the church believers experience the life of communion into which all humanity is invited. Beyond passages such as these, the concept of communion can be said to undergird all of the council's ecclesiology. Even where the term does not appear, there are numerous passages that bring into sharp relief the relational dimension of the church, the way in which the church is built up sacramentally rather than juridically, and the necessary interplay of unity and diversity in the church.

The People of God

Figuring prominently in the chapter on the people of God is the theme of divine election; the church is God's people not through any merit of its own but only as the consequence of God's free initiative. Each Christian belongs to God's people not in virtue of any distinguishing rank but solely because of this election. The council wrote:

> For those who believe in Christ, who are reborn not from a perishable but from an imperishable seed through the word of

the living God, not from the flesh but from water and the Holy Spirit, are finally established as "a chosen race, a royal priesthood, a holy nation, a purchased people...who in times past were not a people, but are now the people of God." (*LG*, 9)

In this second chapter of the constitution we have neither a theology of the laity nor a theology of the clergy but rather a theology of the whole Christian faithful, the *christifideles*, equal in dignity and called to a common discipleship through baptism. This theme informs the entire constitution. In the chapter on the laity the bishops invoked that equality of all the Christian faithful that is a consequence of their common identity as God's people:

[I]f by the will of Christ some are made teachers, pastors and dispensers of mysteries on behalf of others, yet all share a true equality with regard to the dignity and to the activity common to all the faithful for the building up of the Body of Christ. For the distinction which the Lord made between sacred ministers and the rest of the People of God bears within it a certain union, since pastors and the other faithful are bound to each other by a mutual need. (*LG*, 32)

Chapter 2 of *Lumen Gentium* further develops the common identity of the whole Christian faithful by a meditation on each believer's participation in Christ's threefold office as priest, prophet, and king/shepherd.

All Christians, by virtue of their baptism, share in the priesthood of Christ and all are called to render their entire lives "a living sacrifice, holy and pleasing to God" (*LG*, 10). This common priesthood, the council taught, differs "in essence and not only in degree" from the ministerial priesthood, yet both share equally in the one priesthood of Christ. The recovery of the ancient theology of the priesthood of the baptized is all the more remarkable since it was a theme that for centuries had been so strongly identified with the theology of the Luther and other reformers.

The whole Christian faithful share as well in Christ's prophetic office insofar as they must give witness to Christ in all that they do. Yet their responsibility lies in more than Christian witness. God's

Word has been given to the whole Christian people and not exclusively to the pope and bishops. All the members of the church must share, each in their proper way, in the task of receiving God's Word. The council taught that the whole Christian faithful, "from the bishops down to the last of the lay faithful," share in a "supernatural discernment in matters of faith." This spiritual gift is often referred to by the Latin term, *sensus fidei*. The people of God "adheres unwaveringly to the faith given once and for all to the saints, penetrates it more deeply with right thinking, and applies it more fully in its life" (*LG*, 12; see also *LG*, 35). It is this capacity that allows a believer, almost intuitively, to sense what is of God and what is not.

This teaching must be read in conjunction with the council's Dogmatic Constitution on Divine Revelation, *Dei Verbum*, which teaches that all the faithful participate in the development of tradition:

> For there is a growth in the understanding of the realities and the words which have been handed down. This happens through the contemplation and study made by believers, who treasure these things in their hearts through a penetrating understanding of the spiritual realities which they experience, and through the preaching of those who have received through episcopal succession the sure gift of truth. For as the centuries succeed one another, the Church constantly moves forward toward the fullness of divine truth until the words of God reach their complete fulfillment in her. (*DV*, 8)

The council asserted that the whole people of God share in that infallibility which Christ gave the church inasmuch as, when they are in agreement on a matter of faith and morals, they cannot err. It follows from this that the bishops' obligation to fulfill their unique teaching office by "teaching only what has been handed on, listening to it devoutly, guarding it scrupulously and explaining it faithfully in accord with a divine commission and with the help of the Holy Spirit" (*DV*, 10), means that they must also listen to the insights and testimony of all the faithful.

This exposition of the believers' share in Christ's priestly and prophetic office was followed by a much less developed meditation on their share in Christ's kingly office which is described, somewhat vaguely, as undertaking all that is necessary to prepare for the coming of God's kingdom on earth.

Temple of the Holy Spirit

For much of the history of Western ecclesiology, the role of the Holy Spirit has been eclipsed by a certain *Christomonism*, that is, a tendency to consider the church almost exclusively in relation to Christ, with little consideration of the role of the Holy Spirit. In this mode, baroque or post-Tridentine treatments of the church would focus on Christ's decisive role in founding the church, instituting the sacraments, and calling forth the apostles. Pentecost and the ongoing presence of the Spirit in building up the church and guiding it through history received little attention. This had long been the objection of Orthodox theologians, and it was a point made time and again by Yves Congar.[12] This makes the council's rediscovery of the church's pneumatological foundations all the more significant. The council's pneumatology is evident in its treatment of the *sensus fidei* that we have already discussed above, and in its consideration of the biblical understanding of charism.

The council's teaching on the *sensus fidei* demonstrated the bishops' conviction that the whole church is animated by the Spirit and that, through the Spirit, it is the whole church that receives divine revelation. It was the council's renewed attention to pneumatology that saved it from the temptations of what might be called an ecclesiastical Gnosticism, that is, the tendency to think that saving knowledge is given to us only through ecclesiastical structures such as the magisterium. The council's affirmation of the role of the Spirit in bringing each believer to a recognition of the saving truth of Christ does not deny the distinctive role of the apostolic office of the bishops to testify to the apostolic faith. It does remind us that the apostolic faith abides, by the power of the Spirit, in the whole church.

Since the Protestant Reformation, Christianity had suffered through an ongoing polemic between Protestant and Catholic scholars over whether the early church was founded primarily on stable church offices (the hierarchical structure of the church) or on charisms given to all believers. The Second Vatican Council took decisive steps toward overcoming this impasse. Where St. Paul described the body of each believer as a temple of the Holy Spirit (cf. 1 Cor 3:16; 6:19), the bishops applied this image to the entire church. They wrote:

> The Spirit abides in the church and in the hearts of the faithful as in a temple. In them the Spirit prays and bears witness to their adoption as children. The Spirit leads the church into all truth, unites it in communion and ministry, builds it up and directs it through a diversity of hierarchic and charismatic gifts, and adorns it with Her fruits. (*LG*, 4)[13]

In this text, "hierarchic gifts" refers to stable church office and "charismatic gifts" refers to those many charisms that the Spirit distributes among all the faithful. Charism and office cannot be opposed to one another, since both have the Spirit as their origin. The council acknowledged that church office could not exist unless it was animated by the Holy Spirit and charisms could not survive unless they submitted to an ordering that sought the good of the whole church.

By appealing to the biblical concept of charism, the council was able to affirm the indispensable role of all the faithful in building up the church and assisting in the fulfillment of the church's mission in the world. The bishops wrote:

> It is not only through the sacraments and the ministries of the Church that the Holy Spirit sanctifies and leads the people of God and enriches it with virtues, but, "allotting his gifts" to everyone according as He wills, He distributes special graces among the faithful of every rank. By these gifts He makes them fit and ready to undertake the various tasks and offices which contribute toward the renewal and building up of the Church. (*LG*, 12)

Although few if any at the council could have anticipated the flourishing of lay ministries that would occur in the decades after the council, it is this pneumatological theme that provided a helpful theological framework for interpreting that later post-conciliar development.

This renewed attention to both charism and the *sensus fidei* represents but two instances of the expanded role the council gave to the work of the Spirit in the life of the church. This constitutes one of the most overlooked contributions of the council.

The Laity

A brief story captures the common understanding of the laity in many ecclesiastical circles in the nineteenth and early twentieth centuries. In the mid-nineteenth century John Henry Newman, an eminent Catholic thinker and convert from Anglicanism to the Roman Catholic communion, had had the temerity to suggest that the bishops might find merit in consulting the lay faithful, even on matters of doctrine. His view was met with derision by one of the leading members of the Roman curia, a Msgr. George Talbot. Talbot contended that Newman's provocative views made him "the most dangerous man in England." Talbot wrote in a letter: "What is the province of the laity? To hunt, to shoot, and to entertain. These matters they understand, but to meddle with ecclesiastical matters they have no right at all."[14] Talbot's attitude was hardly the exception in many ecclesiastical circles, yet in the early and mid-twentieth century, contemporary events were calling some to question the adequacy of Talbot's view.

The Catholic Action movement emerged, first in Western Europe and then in the United States in the 1930s, 1940s, and 1950s, as a lay movement committed to lay participation in the apostolate of the hierarchy in order to revitalize the Christian roots of Western civilization. One French branch of the movement, the Young Christian Workers, stressed the evangelization of the workplace and a way of evaluating contemporary life in the light of the gospel through a three-step process first proposed by the Belgian Cardinal Joseph Cardijn: observe—judge—act. In the United States the Christian Family Movement used a similar approach to reinvigorate the life of the family. Catholic Action was given vigorous support by Pope Pius XI. The burgeoning liturgical movement had also been emphasizing the active participation of the laity in the liturgical life of the church. Theologians like Yves Congar, Marie-Dominique Chenu, Jean Daniélou,

Gérard Philips, and Karl Rahner had all been exploring the role of the laity in their writings.

This search for a more positive treatment of the laity was reflected in the preparatory draft on the church, which asserted, with a boldness uncharacteristic of the rest of the document, that the laity had not only obligations but also rights in the church, and that they were "to participate actively in the saving work of the church." It would be refined in the final version of *Lumen Gentium*, chapter 4; in the Decree on the Apostolate of the Laity; in the Constitution on the Sacred Liturgy; and in the Pastoral Constitution on the Church in the Modern World. The principal features of this emerging theology can be summarized briefly.

The council taught that the laity have a right and responsibility to be actively involved in the church's apostolate (*LG*, 30, 33). They are equal sharers in the threefold office of Christ who is priest, prophet, and king (*LG*, 34–36). They are called to full, conscious, and active participation in the liturgy, a participation that is demanded by the very "nature of the liturgy" (*SC*, 14). Pastors must acknowledge the expertise, competency, and authority of the laity and gratefully accept their counsel (*LG*, 37). The council encouraged laypersons to pursue advanced study in theology and scripture (*GS*, 62). Finally, it is the laity who are to take the initiative in the transformation of the temporal order (*LG*, 31; *GS*, 43).

In spite of these significant advances, the council's treatment of the laity was not completely consistent. Giovanni Magnani has asserted that there are two different views of the laity evident in the council documents, a contrastive view and an intensive view. The contrastive view of the laity is so named because it seeks to *contrast* the identity of the laity with that of the clergy, treating each as complementary categories of membership in the church.[15] This contrastive view is evident in *Lumen Gentium* 31, which defines the laity as "all the faithful except those in holy orders and those in the state of religious life specially approved by the Church." This text then states that

What specifically characterizes the laity is their secular nature. ...The laity, by their very vocation, seek the kingdom of God by engaging in temporal affairs and by ordering them according to the plan of God. They live in the world, that is, in each and in all of the secular professions and occupations. They live in the ordinary circumstances of family and social life, from which the very web of their existence is woven. They are called there by God that by exercising their proper function and led by the spirit of the Gospel they may work for the sanctification of the world from within as a leaven. In this way they may make Christ known to others, especially by the testimony of a life resplendent in faith, hope and charity.

This same view largely informs the Decree on the Apostolate of the Laity, which also seeks to locate the distinctiveness of the laity in their "secular nature" (*AA*, 4, 29). However, according to Magnani, this contrastive view of the laity stands in tension with a more *intensive* approach to a theology of the laity. By "intensive" he means an approach that presents the laity, not as radically distinct from the clergy (or professed religious), but as a more intensive realization of the situation of all the Christian faithful, including those who are ordained and who belong to professed religious life.[16] Neither *Lumen Gentium* 31 nor the Decree on the Apostolate of the Laity was attempting to offer a formal definition of the laity. This is confirmed in Bishop Wright's report on behalf of the sub-commission regarding *Lumen Gentium* 31 in which he noted that the text should not be read as an "ontological definition" but merely as a "typological description."[17] Already in *Lumen Gentium* 30, the first article of the chapter on the laity, the council had written that

> everything that has been said above concerning the People of God is intended for the laity, religious and clergy alike. But there are certain things which pertain in a special way to the laity, both men and women, by reason of their condition and mission.

The starting point for a consideration of the laity is found in chapter 2 in the presentation on the theological status of the whole people of God.

The council's consistent assertion of the fundamental equality of all the Christian faithful helps explain why even the texts that speak of the "distinctive" or "special" characteristic of the laity never present these characteristics as exclusive to them.[18] *Lumen Gentium* 31 admits that the ordained may also engage in "secular activities." Similarly, *Gaudium et Spes* 43 notes that "secular duties and activity" belong to the laity, "though not exclusively to them."

It is possible to discern, over the course of the council, a subtle and halting shift in the council's way of relating the church to the world. This is reflected in the evolving use of the "leaven" metaphor. The metaphor is generally used in reference to the role of the laity in transforming the world from within. It is only in the pastoral constitution, arguably the most mature document of the council, that it is the church itself, comprised of all the Christian faithful, who are "leaven and the very soul for human society as it is to be renewed in Christ and transformed into God's family" (*GS*, 40).[19] Later in that same article the council members wrote of the mission of the church to heal and elevate the dignity of the human person, to strengthen human society and to help humanity discover the deeper meaning of their daily lives. "Thus through each of her individual members *and the whole community*, the church believes she can contribute greatly toward making the human family and its history still more human" (*GS*, 40; emphasis is mine).[20] This passage suggests that the attitudes and actions of all members of the church, including the clergy and professed religious, have social and political import. The life witness of the layperson is but a more intensive realization of the evangelical imperative incumbent upon all Christians to give testimony of God's saving love to the world.

Pilgrim Church

Yet another shift in the ecclesiological vision of the council is evident in chapter 7 of *Lumen Gentium*. This chapter originally was concerned with the communion of saints, the veneration of relics, and a traditional treatment of eschatology (that realm of theological discourse concerned with our final destiny and that of the entire cosmos). When

Yves Congar reworked the chapter at the behest of the Theological Commission, the focus shifted to the eschatological character of the church itself. By conceiving of the church not just as a collection of individual pilgrims but as itself pilgrim, the council adopted a tone of eschatological humility, a conviction that, while the church was confident it was headed in the right direction as guided by the Spirit, it had not yet arrived. The council wrote:

> The Church, to which we are all called in Christ Jesus, and in which we acquire sanctity through the grace of God, will attain its full perfection only in the glory of heaven, when there will come the time of the restoration of all things. (*LG*, 48)

We are a people *on the way* who have the promise of God's presence and guidance but who still await the consummation of God's plan. In a similar way, *Dei Verbum* had, in its description of the development of tradition, presented the church, not in full possession of the truth but as moving "forward toward the fullness of divine truth until the words of God reach their complete fulfillment in her" (*DV*, 8).

By placing the church in this eschatological framework, it was now possible to acknowledge the need for ongoing reform. If the church as pilgrim has not yet arrived at its final fulfillment, then there is more work to be done. Earlier in the constitution the bishops had acknowledged this ongoing need for renewal:

> While Christ, holy, innocent and undefiled knew nothing of sin, but came to expiate only the sins of the people, the Church, embracing in its bosom sinners, at the same time holy and always in need of being purified, always follows the way of penance and renewal. (*LG*, 8)

The council returned to the question of church reform and renewal again in the Decree on Ecumenism:

> Christ summons the Church to continual reformation as she sojourns here on earth. The Church is always in need of this, in so far as she is an institution of men [and women] here on

earth. Thus if, in various times and circumstances, there have been deficiencies in moral conduct or in church discipline, or even in the way that church teaching has been formulated—to be carefully distinguished from the deposit of faith itself—these can and should be set right at the opportune moment. (*UR*, 6)

When one considers the arrogant triumphalism of the preparatory draft on the church, this more historically conscious and sober attitude regarding the ongoing need for church reform becomes all the more striking.

Mary and the Church

The concluding chapter of *Lumen Gentium*, like many of the texts that were finally promulgated at Vatican II, was something of a compromise document in that its authors were seeking to incorporate two theological strands of Marian reflection. The first is often referred to as a Christocentric model insofar as it considers Mary primarily in terms of her relationship to her son and her decisive role in salvation history. This approach is particularly evident in the first half of the chapter. In article 53 we read:

Redeemed by reason of the merits of her Son and united to Him by a close and indissoluble tie, she is endowed with the high office and dignity of being the Mother of the Son of God, by which account she is also the beloved daughter of the Father and the temple of the Holy Spirit. Because of this gift of sublime grace she far surpasses all creatures, both in heaven and on earth. (*LG*, 53)

The text briefly mentions some of the traditional titles associated with Mary, yet the bishops expressly rejected the proposal of more than four hundred bishops that the council solemnly define a Marian title.

The second half of the chapter develops, however briefly, a more ecclesio-centric view of Mary, considering her primarily in her relationship to the church. Christians, the council explains, now turn their eyes to Mary who shines forth to the whole community of the elect as the model of virtues. Piously meditating on her and contemplating her in the light of the Word made man, the Church with reverence enters more intimately into the great mystery of the Incarnation and becomes more and more like her Spouse. (*LG*, 65)

Although these two approaches did not sit easily alongside one another, the final text did better reflect more recent developments in Marian studies. In particular, the chapter gave a prominent role to scripture. Although the text briefly mentioned several traditional Marian titles (e.g., auxiliatrix, mediatrix), they were not developed in any depth and many of the other titles open to misinterpretation (e.g., coredemptrix and dispensatrix of graces) were avoided entirely. Thus, this chapter reflected an important development in its attempt to root Mary's place, however preeminent, firmly within the church.

While acknowledging the important theological advances evident in this chapter on Mary, we must also point out that the text has been criticized for an underdeveloped pneumatology. German theologian Heribert Mühlen has observed that, at key points, attributes are credited to Mary (e.g., helper, advocate) that ought more properly be attributed to the work of the Holy Spirit in the economy of salvation.[21] This mistake can result in a displacement of the proper role of the Holy Spirit in the life of the church.

The themes we have considered in this first section serve as a foundation for the council's consideration of any of a number of important particular issues. From this treatment of the council's emerging ecclesiological vision, we now turn to the first of two central issues addressed throughout the documents of the council, namely, how to conceive the church's unity and catholicity.

THE UNITY AND CATHOLICITY OF THE CHURCH

The church of Jesus Christ is both one and many. Its unity is grounded in two realities. First, it is the recipient of the one revelation of God in Christ. Second, through the power of the Holy Spirit, as St. Paul emphasized, the church *is* the one body of Christ. At the same time, this one church possesses a mission that is universal. Over the centuries Christians have recognized that this unity manifests itself in history not as a rigid uniformity—although such uniformity has at certain periods presented itself as the only acceptable form of unity—but as a unity realized in diversity.

Looking back to the churches of the New Testament, we find a startling diversity in practice and even belief among the many churches. Compared to our own era, the possibilities for travel and communication across great distances were much more limited. It was inevitable that local churches would develop with a much higher degree of autonomy. Yet there is little evidence to support the idea that individual churches thought of themselves merely as independent congregations who could freely choose or decline to enter into compact with other congregations. Underlying their diversity and relative autonomy was an at least incipient conviction regarding the spiritual unity of all the churches. Moreover, even as those early Christians tended to view the world through critical eyes, with significant exceptions, Christians realized that it was not their lot to simply escape their world, but rather to bring the gospel to the world.

The second century of Christianity saw an increased awareness of this interplay between unity and diversity, identity and mission. It was during this period that church leaders began to describe the church as both one and "catholic." The latter term was first used by St. Ignatius of Antioch: "[W]herever the bishop appears, there let the people be; as wherever Jesus Christ is, there is the Catholic church."[22] In the introduction of the second-century document, *The Martyrdom of Polycarp*, we find this passage:

> The Church of God dwelling as a pilgrim at Smyrna to the Church of God in pilgrimage at Philomelium, and to all the congregations of the Holy and Catholic church in every place. May the mercy and peace and love of God the Father and of our Lord Jesus Christ be multiplied.[23]

The meaning of "catholic" in these two ancient texts is not completely clear, as some scholars see the term emphasizing the purity and authenticity of the Christian faith, and others its extension and comprehensiveness. Whatever its particular meaning, this catholicity was present in the church by virtue of the gift of revelation that was given in its fullness in Christ. The "whole" of the faith was already encountered in the gift of Christ. Etymologically, the Greek word *katholikos* carries multiple senses, perhaps the most dominant being, "pertaining to the whole." Catholicity, then, would suggest a sense of both fullness and inclusivity or comprehensiveness. This fullness or comprehensiveness was realized not in the abstract but in the local churches where Christianity was lived. By the fourth century St. Augustine would use the term to refer to the sense of the churches spread throughout the world yet in communion with one another.[24] What we find is an ancient and enduring conviction that an authentic spiritual communion existed among the churches.

For much of the first millennium the delicate balance between the autonomy of the local churches and the unity of all the churches in one spiritual communion would be maintained through the communion manifested among the bishops within and between various regions. This communion among the churches was realized in many ways. When Christians traveled they often took with them a letter of commendation from their bishop and offered it to the bishop of the church in the geographic locale they were visiting. If the local bishop accepted the letter, the visitor would be allowed to participate in the Eucharist.[25] The acceptance of the letter of commendation was a tacit acknowledgment of the communion between the two churches. A second expression of the communion among the churches can be found in the early practice of the bishops of a given region gathering in a synod. At these gatherings the bishops would deliberate on matters of common concern, often regarding disciplinary matters but not infrequently addressing more doctrinal concerns as well. The early "ecumenical councils" were in fact little more than regional synods, generally convened at the instigation of the emperor, which dealt with matters of import for the universal church. As their solutions were gradually accepted by the church universal, their "ecumenical status" (from the Greek word *oikoumene*, meaning "the inhabited world") would be acknowledged in subsequent centuries. By the fourth century the various patriarchal sees (Rome, Constantinople, Antioch, Alexandria) would play a growing role, with the bishop of Rome gaining significant authority in the West. This understanding of catholicity realized in and through the communion of churches would continue through the Middle Ages.

Beginning in the second millennium, after the formalization of the festering division between the Western and Eastern churches, the bishop of Rome gradually became the center and focus of unity among the churches of the West. From the eleventh century on one can trace a development toward a more pyramidal view of the church in the West. Even as local churches would maintain a marked autonomy in their daily affairs, claims for a centralizing papal authority would grow and in the Middle Ages there would emerge a corporatist conception of the unity of the church, a conception that understood local churches to be largely subsets of a more monolithic universal church. After the crisis of the Reformation, the Catholic Church would embark on a program to root the unity of the church in an unprecedented uniformity at the level of liturgy, church discipline, and theology. This uniformity would reach its apex in the mid-twentieth century pontificate of Pope Pius XII. Throughout much of the modern period, catholicity would remain limited to a sense of the geographic reach of the church and, again, its visible unity. With important exceptions (most notably the nineteenth-century Tübingen school) catholicity was practically collapsed into the marks of unity and apostolicity, that is, visible union with and obedience to the apostolic see of Rome.

The need to reconsider the necessity of strict ecclesial uniformity became a topic of concern during the very first session of Vatican II. The council's rediscovery of the patristic sense of the church's unity and catholicity is evident in a number of the council's documents. The liturgy constitution affirmed the theological integrity of the local church and a legitimate cultural diversity that might find expression in liturgical celebrations (*SC*, 37). *Lumen Gentium* explicitly celebrated the catholicity of the church as manifested in the diversity of the church's members:

> In virtue of this catholicity each individual part contributes through its special gifts to the good of the other parts and of

the whole Church. Through the common sharing of gifts and through the common effort to attain fullness in unity, the whole and each of the parts receive increase. (*LG*, 13)

The experience of catholicity as a unity in diversity raised a fundamental ecclesiological question: Since diversity in church life is most evident in comparing the distinctive practices of various local churches, how are we to understand the relationship between the local church and the universal church?

The Relationship between the Local Church and the Universal Church

The question of the relationship between the universal church and the local churches was first addressed in the opening session of the council during the debates on the schema on the liturgy. The Constitution on the Sacred Liturgy took important steps toward recovering the ancient theological integrity of the local church under a bishop's pastoral leadership:

> Therefore all should hold in great esteem the liturgical life of the diocese centered around the bishop, especially in his cathedral church; they must be convinced that the pre-eminent manifestation of the Church consists in the full active participation of all God's holy people in these liturgical celebrations, especially in the same eucharist, in a single prayer, at one altar, at which there presides the bishop surrounded by his college of priests and by his ministers. (*SC*, 41)

The diocese was no longer to be viewed as a mere administrative subset of the universal church. Neither was the bishop to be seen as a vicar or delegate of the pope. Rather, the theological integrity of the local church was manifested whenever the people of God of a particular church gathered around its bishop in the celebration of the Eucharist.

At this point we must note a certain ambiguity in the documents' use of terminology to describe the local church. The council tended to use the term "particular church" in reference to dioceses and "local church" in reference to regional groupings of churches, but it was not always consistent.[26] In the wake of the council a number of theologians sought to develop more conceptual rigor in the use of these terms.[27] The difficulty is that, in the popular life of the church and in much post-conciliar ecclesiological reflection, the term "particular church" has not been broadly accepted. In this volume, I will use the more popularly accepted term, "local church," while admitting that the term can be employed in a variety of ways.

Central to the recovery of an ancient theology of the local church was the council's retrieval of a eucharistic ecclesiology. This is evident in *Lumen Gentium* 26:

> In any community of the altar, under the sacred ministry of the bishop, there is exhibited a symbol of that charity and "unity of the mystical Body, without which there can be no salvation." In these communities, though frequently small and poor, or living in the Diaspora, Christ is present, and in virtue of His presence there is brought together one, holy, catholic and apostolic Church. For "the partaking of the body and blood of Christ does nothing other than make us be transformed into that which we consume."

Local churches were not "branch offices" of some corporate superstructure; they were unique manifestations of communion within the one church of Christ.

The interpenetration of the local and universal dimensions of the one church of Christ was also articulated in *Lumen Gentium* 23, which asserted that it was in and from these local or particular churches that there "comes into being the one and only Catholic Church."

The Decree on the Pastoral Office of Bishops in the Church, *Christus Dominus*, articulated a similar view:

> A diocese is a portion of the people of God which is entrusted to a bishop to be shepherded by him with the cooperation of the presbytery. Thus by adhering to its pastor and gathered together by him through the Gospel and the Eucharist in the Holy Spirit, it constitutes a particular church in which the

one, holy, catholic, and apostolic Church of Christ is truly present and operative. (*CD*, 11)

Taken collectively, these conciliar texts represented a move away from that pre-conciliar, universalist ecclesiology that saw the diocese as little more than an administrative subset of the universal church. As the famous Protestant ecumenist Jean Jacques von Allmen put it, the local church "is wholly Church, but it is not the whole Church."[28] In the council documents we have an undeveloped but nevertheless significant shift toward an ancient vision of the universal church as a *communio ecclesiarum*, a communion of churches. This ecclesiological vision is reflected in the following diagram. The outermost circle represents the universal church; the larger circles represent dioceses, within which are local parishes, surrounding the cathedral church:

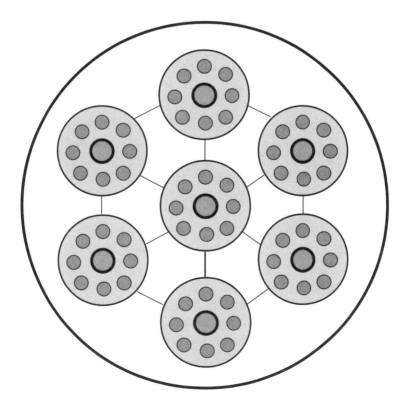

This diagram suggests something of how the local and universal dimensions of the church mutually inform each other. There is no access to, or experience of, the universal church except within a local church. Conversely, there is no participation in a local church that is not, at some level, also a communion with the church universal. The council's presentation of the local church and its relation to the universal church, however brief, constituted nothing less than what Joseph Komonchak has called a "Copernican revolution in ecclesiology."[29]

The "mutual interiority" of the local and universal churches also illuminates further the church's catholicity. One must avoid thinking of the church's catholicity as if that described only the church as a whole. Rather, if the universal church is realized in and through each local church, then it is not just the whole communion of churches that is catholic, but catholicity describes each local church.

The Eastern Catholic Churches

The council's interest in various expressions of unity in diversity was further exhibited in its treatment of the Eastern Catholic churches. Buried in the consciousness of the post-Tridentine Catholic Church was the reality of a longstanding diversity manifested in the Eastern Catholic churches in communion with the bishop of Rome. Many of the bishops who attended the council had had little if any practical contact with these Eastern churches and knew next to nothing of their distinctive theological and liturgical heritage. Though numerically overwhelmed (there were at the council only about 130 bishops from the Eastern Catholic churches), the Eastern bishops were able to make their presence felt and helped redirect the course of the council in important ways. Often it was the practical interactions the Western bishops had with their Eastern brothers that helped them recognize the diversity that had always been present in the church, however much it had been muted and even suppressed in the West. One should not underestimate the practical impact of the conciliar practice of celebrating daily Mass during the council sessions, on a rotating basis, in the different liturgical rites of the church. For many of the bishops, this was their first exposure to the already existing diversity of liturgical rites in the church. On November 28, 1962, Archbishop Asrate Yemmeru of Addis Ababa celebrated, with the entire episcopal assembly, the Ethiopian rite. I quote here Xavier Rynne's account:

> The rite itself was extremely ancient, going back in outline at least to the fourth century, but with many later additions and ceremonies of a distinctly African flavor. It was characterized by a constant dialogue between the celebrant and the faithful, and by a moving simplicity and solemnity. The language was classical Ethiopian or Gheez. As the book of Gospels was being enthroned, the spirited chanting of the seminarians and priests belonging to the Ethiopian College on Vatican Hill behind St. Peter's—they also chanted the mass—was accompanied by the deep rhythms of African drums, the ringing of bells, and the shaking of tambourines, causing the New York *Journal American* to headline its story: "African drums boom in Vatican rite."[30]

Although handicapped by rules and practices that reflected the ornamental rather than the integral place of the Eastern churches in Western consciousness (rules that required that all council affairs be conducted in Latin and that the Eastern patriarchs be given a lower rank in liturgical processions than the cardinals), the Eastern bishops did have a considerable impact in heightening the council's recognition of ecclesial diversity. Their distinctive gifts were recognized in chapter 2 of *Lumen Gentium*:

> [W]ithin the Church particular Churches [Eastern Catholic churches] hold a rightful place; these Churches retain their own traditions, without in any way opposing the primacy of the Chair of Peter, which presides over the whole assembly of charity and protects legitimate differences, while at the same time assuring that such differences do not hinder unity but rather contribute toward it. (*LG*, 13)

A similar pronouncement is found in chapter 3 in a passage that explicitly acknowledges that the Eastern churches, while preserving the unity of faith and the unique divine constitution of the universal Church, enjoy their own discipline, their own liturgical usage, and their own theological and spiritual heritage. Some of these churches, notably the ancient patriarchal churches, as parent-stocks of the Faith, so to speak, have begotten others as daughter churches, with which they are connected down to our own time by a close bond of charity in their sacramental life and in their mutual respect for their rights and duties. This variety of local churches with one common aspiration is splendid evidence of the catholicity of the undivided Church. (*LG*, 23)

Respect for the equal dignity of the Eastern churches was, as one would expect, affirmed in *Orientalium Ecclesiarum*. There the council reasserted the rich catholicity manifested in the Eastern churches.

The decree insisted on the need to preserve the distinctive heritage of these churches. *Orientalium Ecclesiarum* 6 responded to the lamentable policy of "Latinizing" the Eastern churches with a strategy of "Easternization." This strategy called for a systematic return "to their ancestral traditions" and a purging of Western practices that had obscured the distinctive contributions of the Eastern churches.[31] In fact, an easily overlooked advance lay in the decree's repeated reference, not to distinct Eastern liturgical *rites*, but rather to unique Eastern Catholic *churches* that possessed a "rite," which was now understood as a distinctive patrimony to include not only liturgy but also customs, spiritual practices, theology, church discipline, and cultural heritage. Thus it might be the case that more than one church *sui iuris* (the Latin phrase designates a church that possesses its own limited canonical autonomy) would share a common "rite." Five distinctive rites are generally acknowledged to exist among the Eastern churches: Alexandrian, Antiochene, Armenian, Chaldean, and Constantinopolitan. These rites are shared by twenty-one distinct Eastern churches *sui iuris*. Here we have an implicit admission of a diversity that goes beyond the liturgy. This in turn justifies granting to these *churches* their own hierarchy and particular methods of governance:

[T]he Churches of the East, as much as those of the West, have a full right and are in duty bound to rule themselves, each in accordance with its own established disciplines, since all these are praiseworthy by reason of their venerable antiquity, more harmonious with the character of their faithful and more suited to the promotion of the good of souls. (*OE*, 5)

The decree recognized the institution of the patriarchate in the East (*OE*, 7–11) and acknowledged the possibility that new patriarchates might be created. There is mention of the permanent synods of bishops that often played a role in episcopal selection. Perhaps more unexpected was the council's unambiguous support of a number of the distinctive sacramental and liturgical practices of the East, including the role of the priest as the ordinary minister of confirmation (*OE*, 14) and—most surprising of all—the legitimacy of one's Sunday obligation being fulfilled, not only through the Divine Liturgy (the Mass) but also by participation in the Divine Office (the celebration of an Eastern form of the liturgy of the hours often known as the Cathedral Office).

In spite of these important advances, the decree was not without its shortcomings. For example, the document tended to view all of the Eastern churches through the lens of the Byzantine tradition and was too little cognizant of the plurality of traditions that existed within the Christian East.[32] Robert Taft, noted expert on Eastern Catholicism, offers the following summary assessment:

> The text remained, perforce a *Latin* document *about the East*, the document of a monolithic, basically Western Church with several minority satellite communities enjoying a special status and special rites, rather than a Catholic document about a single communion of several sister Churches, each one an equally 'particular' Church.[33]

Nevertheless, *Orientalium Ecclesiarum* brought new prominence to the place of the Eastern churches in the Roman Catholic communion and thereby enhanced the council's teaching on the catholicity of the church.

Unity with Other Christian Churches and Ecclesial Communities

One of the most remarkable features of the council's emerging ecclesiological vision was its willingness to consider the unity and catholicity of the church not only within the scope of Roman Catholicism but also from the perspective of all Christianity. It must be recalled that for most of the second millennium, Roman Catholicism had understood itself to be in complete historical continuity with the church of the New Testament. As divisions emerged within the Christian tradition, the Roman Catholic perspective was generally to interpret these splits from within the framework of either heresy (e.g., Cathari/Albigensians, Waldensians, the sixteenth-century reformers, the Jansenists) or schism (e.g., the Orthodox churches of the East and the Old Catholic Church which emerged in the late nineteenth century). Catholic thought, at least as officially articulated in ecclesiastical statements, was not open to any acknowledgment of shared membership in the body of Christ on the part of non-Catholic Christians. The so called branch theory, first articulated within Anglicanism in the nineteenth century, was officially condemned in a letter of the holy office to Anglican bishops in 1864.[34] This view helps explain initial Catholic suspicion of the ecumenical movement as it emerged in the early twentieth century. In 1928, Pope Pius XI, in his encyclical, *Mortalium Animos*, condemned indifferentism, which for him meant "indifference" to the unique claim of the Roman Catholic Church to be the one, true church of Jesus Christ here on earth. Pius XI gave expression to what has been called a Catholic "ecumenism of return" when he wrote:

> The union of Christians cannot be fostered otherwise than by promoting the return of the dissidents to the one true Church of Christ, which in the past they so unfortunately abandoned; return, we say, to the one true Church of Christ which is plainly visible to all and which by the will of her Founder forever remains what he himself destined her to be for the common salvation of human beings.[35]

Fifteen years later, Pope Pius XII issued an important encyclical, *Mystici Corporis*, that reasserted Pius XI's absolute identification of the mystical body of Christ with the Roman Catholic Church. Pius XII admitted that non-Catholic Christians are in "a certain relationship with the Mystical Body of the Redeemer" by an "unconscious desire and longing," but he insisted that they still could not be considered truly members of Christ's church.[36] As we saw in Part One, this ecclesiological perspective informed, to a considerable extent, the council's preparatory draft on the church. This brings into sharp relief the shift that is evident in the council's treatment of Catholicism's relationship with other Christian traditions.

Although Catholics had generally not been allowed official participation in ecumenical meetings,[37] many bishops who attended the council had developed cordial relationships with leaders of non-Catholic churches even before the council. Theologians like Yves Congar, often considered the father of Catholic ecumenism and the author of several groundbreaking ecumenical studies, were invited to the council as theological advisers and played a key role in the drafting of council documents. Pope John XXIII himself had said from the beginning of his pontificate that he wished the council to address the sad divisions that existed within Christianity. His ecumenical sensitivities had been heightened by experience he gained from diplomatic posts in both Bulgaria and Turkey before his elevation to the papacy. In his January 25, 1959 allocution announcing the council, Pope John mentioned two general aims for the council, the edification of the whole Christian faithful and a "renewed cordial invitation to the faithful of the separated Churches to participate with us in this feast of grace and brotherhood [the upcoming council], for which so many souls long in all parts of the world."[38] The Secretariat for Christian Unity, created by Pope John in 1960, was responsible for inviting non-Catholic observers to the council, and did a remarkable job of giving those observers access to draft documents being considered by the council. The secretariat also funneled the responses of the observers to the appropriate conciliar drafting committees.

Two passages in *Lumen Gentium* merit consideration here. First, in an earlier version of chapter 1 we find a passage drawn from Pius XII that plainly asserted that the Roman Catholic Church "*is* the mystical body of Christ."[39] The bishops realized that this formulation was no longer tenable. After all, the Catholic Church already recognized the validity of trinitarian water baptism in other Christian traditions. Was not one of the effects of baptism to bring the believer into communion in Christ? Consequently, they agreed to a single word change that reflected their rejection of the strict identification of the Catholic Church and the body of Christ. The final text would now read:

> [t]his Church constituted and organized in the world as a society, *subsists in* the Catholic Church, which is governed by the successor of Peter and by the Bishops in communion with him, ...although many elements of sanctification and of truth are found outside of its visible structure. (*LG*, 8; emphasis mine)

The substitution of the verb "subsists" was crucial. The council acknowledged that although the church of Christ has always existed in history, and continues to do so in the Roman Catholic Church, the church of Christ can be encountered beyond the boundaries of Roman Catholicism.[40]

In the second chapter of *Lumen Gentium* on the people of God, the bishops discussed further the vexing question of the relationship of non-Catholic Christians to the church of Christ. As was noted in Part One, an early draft stated that only Roman Catholics who acknowledge the whole structure of the visible Roman Catholic church (profession of faith, sacraments, and church governance) are incorporated in the fellowship of the church "in the true and absolute sense of the term." This passage was changed to read that those who accept the Roman Catholic Church and its entire structure and all the means of salvation "are fully incorporated" into the church of Christ. This modest change in language suggested that there were degrees of incorporation into the body of Christ such that even if one were not a member of the Roman Catholic Church one could, in some sense, belong to the body of Christ. The council taught that the church is "linked with (*coniunctum esse*) those who, being baptized, are honored with the name of Christian" (*LG*, 15). In the Decree on Ecumenism the bishops asserted again that those "who believe in Christ and have been truly baptized are in communion with the Catholic Church even though this communion is imperfect" (*UR*, 3). No longer would the church hold, as it seemed to in the teaching of Pope Pius XII, that other Christians could be saved only in spite of their non-Catholic identity. Rather the council admitted that some and even very many of the significant elements and endowments which together go to build up and give life to the Church itself, can exist outside the visible boundaries of the Catholic Church: the written word of God; the life of grace; faith, hope and charity, with the other interior gifts of the Holy Spirit, and visible elements too. (*UR*, 3)

This explains why both *Lumen Gentium* 15 and *Unitatis Redintegratio* 3 can speak of non-Catholic Christian "churches and ecclesial communities."

Finally, in *Lumen Gentium*, articles 16 and 17 consider the ways in which Jews, Muslims, those who belong to other world religions, and even those who "have not yet arrived at an explicit knowledge of God" yet "with His grace strive to live a good life" are in some sense "related" (*ordinantur*) to the church as well. This teaching would find further development in *Nostra Aetate*, the Declaration on the Relation of the Church to Non-Christian Religions.

These brief passages would open the floodgates of ecumenical and interreligious dialogue in the decades following the council and we will consider their reception in Part Three. However, it is left for us to consider a final set of issues that preoccupied the minds of the council bishops, namely questions of church office and the exercise of ecclesiastical leadership.

CHURCH OFFICE AND THE EXERCISE OF LEADERSHIP

In Part One we outlined the historical context surrounding the treatment of church office in chapter 3 of *Lumen Gentium* and in *Christus Dominus*. The inability of Vatican I to produce a comprehensive document on the church had led to a papocentrism in the period between the two councils. Not surprisingly then, the council's attention was directed toward the need for a more coherent theology of the episcopate, with regard to the role of both the individual bishop and the entire college.

A proper grasp of the council's teaching on ecclesiastical leadership must begin, not with the council's teaching on holy orders, but with its teaching on baptism. *Sacrosanctum Concilium* reminded us, not only in its call for the reform of the rites of initiation but also in its focus on the whole worshiping assembly, that our primary identity as Christians is not as lay or cleric but as members of the baptized called to participate in the life and worship of the church. Article 14 of the constitution referred to the full participation of the baptized in the liturgy as both a right and an obligation. This focus on the primacy of baptism was further developed in *Lumen Gentium*, in particular in its consideration of the church as people of God and temple of the Holy Spirit. The decision to place the chapter on the people of God before the chapter on the hierarchy expressed a profound ecclesiological principle: we must begin with what unites us—faith and baptism—before we can consider what distinguishes us (e.g., ordination). This does not deny, of course, that Christians may be further "ordered" in service of the church by sacramental ordination. It does mean, as Bishop Franjo Seper of Zagreb noted at the council, that the ordained do not cease being members of the people of God after ordination; the obligations that are theirs by virtue of baptism and confirmation still remain.[41] We might recall a remark of Cardinal Suenens: "A pope's finest moment is not that of his election or consecration, but that of his baptism."[42]

This focus on baptism helps us interpret a term employed by the council, "hierarchical communion" (*communio hierarchica*).[43] The council described spiritual communion in the church as "hierarchical," presumably as a safeguard against the danger that notions of communion might degenerate into secular understandings of liberal democracy. It is a problematic expression.[44] The danger is that by describing the church as a *hierarchical* communion, one can end up returning to the hierocratic, pyramidal view of the church that developed in the thirteenth century.

Yet perhaps the term "hierarchical" can be retained if it is carefully purged of those pyramidal and patriarchal conceptions.[45] When the Constitution on the Sacred Liturgy referred to the "hierarchic and communal nature of the liturgy," it did not have in mind a return to a pyramidal ecclesiology. The liturgy is hierarchical, not in the sense of a chain of command or a pyramidal structure, but in the sense that the liturgy manifests the church as an *ordered* communion with a great diversity of ministries and Christian activities that together build up the life of the church.[46] The church of Jesus Christ, animated by the Spirit, is now and has always been subject to church ordering as it receives its life from the God who, in Christian faith, is ordered in eternal self-giving as a triune communion of equal persons. So chapter 3 of *Lumen Gentium* begins by asserting that Christ established a variety of offices for the building up the church (*LG*, 18). In that chapter it attends in particular to the ministries of bishops, priests, and deacons.

The Office of the Bishop

The council reversed an almost thousand year tradition of centering the theology of ordained ministry on the priesthood. From the eleventh century onward, it had become common to see the priesthood as the summit of ordained ministry; bishops were often viewed as priests who had been granted greater jurisdictional authority. Vatican II returned to the vision of the first millennium in which the primary locus of ordained ministry was not the ministry of the priest but that of the bishop. The liturgy constitution placed the bishop at the center of the liturgical life of the diocese. It asserted, moreover, that the most profound manifestation of the local church was encountered at diocesan liturgies presided over by the bishop (*SC*, 41).

The ministry of the bishop was given its most in-depth theological consideration in chapter 3 of *Lumen Gentium*. The chapter begins with the assertion that, by the will of Christ, bishops are successors to the apostles in serving as the shepherds of the church (*LG*, 18). In article 21 we find the doctrinal core of the council's teaching on the episcopate:

> [B]y episcopal consecration the fullness of the sacrament of Orders is conferred, that fullness of power, namely, which both in the Church's liturgical practice and in the language of the Fathers of the Church is called the high priesthood, the supreme power of the sacred ministry. But episcopal consecration, together with the office of sanctifying, also confers the office of teaching and of governing, which, however, of its very nature, can be exercised only in hierarchical communion with the head and the members of the college.

Christus Dominus repeats this teaching:

> Bishops, sharing in the solicitude for all the churches, exercise this episcopal office of theirs, which they have received through episcopal consecration, in communion with and under the authority of the supreme pontiff. (*CD*, 3)

For much of the second millennium it had been a theologically open question whether episcopal consecration was truly sacramental. These texts plainly asserted that it was and that all three offices or functions (*munera*)—sanctifying, teaching, and governing—were conferred at episcopal ordination. The council thereby rejected the view that the power of jurisdiction (which would incorporate the functions of teaching and governing) was only conferred on the bishop by the pope after consecration. The text did specify, however, that the offices conferred in episcopal consecration could be exercised only by a bishop in communion with both the other bishops and with the head of the college, the bishop of Rome. This latter point was reiterated in the *Nota Explicativa Praevia*. The three functions or offices may be conferred at episcopal consecration, but they are not "fully ready to act" without a further canonical determination by the appropriate church authority. This new teaching did much to dismantle the post-Tridentine tendency to view the bishop as vicar of the pope. Indeed the council explicitly rejected this view, writing:

> The pastoral office or the habitual and daily care of their sheep is entrusted to them [the bishops] completely; nor are they to be regarded as vicars of the Roman Pontiffs, for they exercise an authority that is proper to them, and are quite correctly called "prelates," heads of the people whom they govern. (*LG*, 27)

This signaled an abandonment of the centuries old "concessions system" in which the pope *conceded* certain faculties (e.g., regarding marriage and penal law) to bishops for five-year terms. The canonical assumption of this system was that the faculties were proper to the pope but could be conceded or delegated to the individual bishops. Instead, Vatican II assumed that these faculties were proper to the bishops and instead referred to certain cases that were to be "reserved" to the pope (*CD*, 8).

According to the teaching of the council, preeminent among the bishop's responsibilities as pastor of the local church was the ministry of preaching and teaching (*CD*, 12). Bishops are to be "preachers of the faith, who lead new disciples to Christ" (*LG*, 25). They are to teach with an authority endowed to them by Christ. Consequently, although they do not individually teach with the charism of infallibility, when they teach on faith and morals the faithful must give a religious assent to their teaching.[47] In fulfilling this vital ministry, the bishop must take care to understand the difficult issues and questions of the time so that he may present the faith of the church as timely and relevant to contemporary human concerns (*CD*, 13).

In both *Lumen Gentium* and *Christus Dominus*, the council consistently affirmed the *pastoral* character of the bishop's office. The bishops were to be much more than administrators.

> They should, therefore, constantly exert themselves to have the faithful know and live the paschal mystery more deeply through the Eucharist and thus become a firmly-knit body in the unity of the charity of Christ. "Intent upon prayer and the ministry of the word," they should devote their labor to this end that all those committed to their care may be of one mind in prayer and through the reception of the sacraments may grow in grace and be faithful witnesses to the Lord. (*CD*, 15)

The bishops should not be aloof or distant from their people; rather, they should "stand in the midst of their people as those who serve," seeking to know the particular conditions and concerns that define the lives of their flock (*CD*, 16). Even the determination of the boundaries of particular dioceses ought to be made with the welfare of the people of God uppermost in mind (*CD*, 22–24).

The council's placement of the bishop at the center of the local church stands in a certain tension with the council's teaching that the first effect of ordination is to introduce the bishop into the college of bishops, even before he has been assigned to a local church (*LG*, 22). Although the council made great gains in recovering the early church's assumptions regarding the necessary relationship between episcopal ordination and pastoral charge to a local church, it did not completely extricate itself from an alternative view of the college of bishops as existing separate from and above the communion of churches. This leads us to a more direct consideration of the council's teaching on episcopal collegiality.

Episcopal Collegiality

The council's teaching on episcopal collegiality is a good example of conciliar teaching contributing to a substantive development in doctrine. The extent of this development, however, was obscured somewhat in chapter 3 of *Lumen Gentium* by an excessive caution. In the very first article of this chapter the council repeated the teaching of Vatican I on both papal primacy and infallibility. The flow of the chapter is hobbled by a determination to anticipate and forestall at every turn any construal of the teaching as a rejection of Vatican I.[48] This concern was a natural consequence of the protracted struggles and heated debates over the doctrine of episcopal collegiality addressed in this text. Throughout the text we find repeated assurances of the unfettered authority of the pope over the college of bishops, passages clearly aimed at the nervous minority group of bishops concerned about the doctrine.

Papal Primacy and Episcopal Collegiality

The council recalled the bond of communion shared among bishops and with the bishop of Rome that was attested to in the ancient tradition and reflected in the gathering of bishops at synods and councils. The council taught that although the college of bishops has no authority on its own apart from communion with its head, the pope, nevertheless, the college shares with the bishop of Rome, and never apart from him, "supreme and full power over the universal church" (*LG, 22*).

This assertion of shared power and authority over the universal church represented the heart of the teaching on collegiality. It overcame a centuries long tendency to pit the college of bishops against the pope in a kind of zero-sum relationship—to assert the authority of the bishops was to take it away from the papacy, and vice versa. The council moved beyond this opposition primarily by placing the pope *within* the college of bishops as its head. Consequently, even when the pope exercises his authority apart from the explicit cooperation of the bishops, his actions must presuppose an enduring communion between the pope and the college within which the pope always stands as head.

As we pointed out in Part One, many bishops and *periti* complained that the force of the council's teaching on episcopal collegiality was weakened by the *Nota Explicativa Praevia* that had been attached to *Lumen Gentium* without the approval or even debate of the council. In paragraph 3, the *Nota* seemed to be returning to a neo-scholastic position, describing the distinction between the pope alone and the pope with the college as "two inadequately distinct subjects" of supreme authority in the church. The difficulty with the teaching of the *Nota* was that it appeared to stand at odds with the theological force of the council's teaching that the pope never truly acts "alone"; as pope he is always head of the college and therefore remains in spiritual communion with the college.

In spite of certain inconsistencies, *Lumen Gentium* offers a new framework for relating the ministry of the pope to that of the college of bishops. For example, in article 25 the council reaffirms Vatican I's teaching on papal infallibility. But this reaffirmation comes only *after* the text has asserted the infallibility of the whole college of bishops, an infallibility that may be exercised either when the bishops are dispersed throughout the world but are in agreement on a matter of faith and morals as a teaching to be held as definitive (often referred to as the infallibility of the ordinary universal magisterium), or when gathered together in ecumenical council.[49]

Collegiality and the Communion of Churches

The exposition of the council's teaching on collegiality in *Lumen Gentium* appears to develop along two different trajectories. Articles 20–22 treat the topic of episcopal collegiality within a "universalist" ecclesiological framework that begins with the bishops' membership in the college and the college's share, with and subordinate to the pope, in supreme authority over the whole church. Within this trajectory each bishop's relationship to a local church goes unmentioned. In article 23, however, we see a different way of conceptualizing the college of bishops, namely by beginning with each bishop's relationship to his particular church: "This collegial union is apparent also in the mutual relations of the individual bishops with particular churches and with the universal Church." If articles 20–22 presented the college of bishops more as an administrative governing board presiding over the universal church, article 23 presents the college of bishops in relation to the communion of churches:

> The individual bishops, however, are the visible principle and foundation of unity in their particular churches, fashioned after the model of the universal Church, in and from which churches comes into being the one and only Catholic Church. For this reason the individual bishops represent each his own church, but all of them together and with the Pope represent the entire Church in the bond of peace, love and unity. (*LG*, 23)

Unfortunately, these two different versions of episcopal collegiality, one setting the college over the church, and the other seeing the college as a concentrated manifestation of the universal church, were never really reconciled in the council documents.[50]

Institutional Expressions of Collegiality

If the council's teaching on collegiality was of historical importance, the council was reluctant to prescribe in any detail specific structures that would give this doctrine concrete expression. Immediately preceding the council, Cardinal Bernard Alfrink of Utrecht had already called for a permanent body of bishops to assist in the government of the universal church loosely based on the model of the permanent synods of the Eastern churches. Various versions of this idea were proposed during council debates and many bishops considered a formal request for the creation of a permanent body of bishops to collaborate with the pope in shared pastoral ministry over the whole church. This would constitute a concrete institutional structure reflecting the important ecclesiological conviction voiced at the council that the college of bishops, under the headship of the bishop of Rome, possesses supreme authority over the whole church. As we saw in Part One, this proposal was offered by Patriarch Maximos IV, Melkite patriarch of Antioch. That such proposals were given such a muted expression in *Christus Dominus* 5 reflected the fact that Pope Paul VI had, before the council ended, already promulgated *Apostolica Sollicitudo*, establishing the world synod of bishops. However, in contravention of the hopes and requests of many bishops, the synod was established not as a permanent body but only as an intermittent synodal gathering of representative bishops possessing only consultative authority.

The council also presented regional associations of bishops, referred to as episcopal conferences, as limited participations in collegiality. Though gatherings of bishops on a regional level do not share in the authority given to the entire college, the bishops recalled the importance of ancient synods in the life of the early church and recommended that, in keeping with that tradition, conferences of bishops be formed on a national or regional basis. As we saw earlier, the council had already granted authority to these conferences in the Constitution on the Sacred Liturgy (*SC*, 22). *Christus Dominus* avoided, by and large, the tricky question of what precise authority and ecclesial status were to be given to these episcopal conferences, but it did acknowledge their pastoral importance and recognized that episcopal conferences were in keeping with the ancient tradition of regional bishops meeting in synods (*CD*, 36).

Subsidiarity

The bishops' thinking on primacy, collegiality, and the relationship between the local and universal church appears to have been guided, at several points, by what was already being referred to as the principle of subsidiarity. First articulated in a church document by Pope Pius XI in his encyclical *Quadragesimo Anno*, the principle had several levels of application. First, it asserted the primacy of the individual person over other associations. Second, it affirmed the priority of smaller social groupings over larger, more complex groupings (e.g., the state). And finally, it asserted the obligation of larger associations to assist the smaller when necessary.

Pope Pius XII extended the principle's sphere of application when he observed in 1946 that this principle, "valid for social life in all its grades" was valid "also for the life of the church without prejudice to its hierarchical structure."[51] As applied to the life of the church, the principle has two dimensions, one positive and the other negative. Positively, subsidiarity affirms the obligations of more comprehensive church entities to assist both smaller communities and individual persons in the realization of their proper goals. Negatively it precludes, under ordinary circumstances, those large or more comprehensive church structures from interfering in the affairs of individuals or smaller communities. We might formulate the ecclesiological application of this principle as follows: *The realization of the legitimate Christian goals of individual persons and local Christian communities must be supported by "higher" or more comprehensive levels of church life, such that the "lower" or less comprehensive levels of personal and communal life must have primary responsibility for addressing particular ecclesial issues. Only when these issues appear insoluble at the lower level and/or threaten the faith and unity of the church universal should one expect intervention from higher levels of church life.*

The first theologian to explore the ecclesiological implications of this principle in any depth was the canon lawyer Wilhelm Bertrams.[52] In 1957 Bertrams argued that the principle diminishes in its applicability when issues are related more directly to the supernatural mission of the church and increases in applicability when concerned with organizational and administrative issues.

Although the principle of subsidiarity was never explicitly applied to the church in the conciliar documents,[53] a number of bishops appealed to the principle in their interventions, particularly during the second session, and it did seem to inform the council's teaching.[54] The most obvious instances are found in the liturgy constitution where significant authority that had once been exercised by Vatican dicasteries was granted to episcopal conferences in *Sacrosanctum Concilium* 22, 36, 39–40, and 44.[55] The substance of the principle is also presupposed in *Lumen Gentium* 27, which acknowledges the ordinary power of the bishops, and insists that this ordinary episcopal power can be "regulated" or "circumscribed" only "for the advantage of the Church or of the faithful." Here the context seems to be the facilitation of the relationship between primacy, on the one hand, and the authority of the local bishop(s) on the other. As a formal principle for considering the relationship between the universal church and the local church, subsidiarity was a theme that would garner considerable attention in the post-conciliar period.

Reform of the Curia

Finally we must note the council's call for a reform of the curia and a reconsideration of its relationship to the bishops. During the council itself, there were numerous calls for curial reform. Some suggested the creation of a special council of bishops that would assist the pope in the pastoral care of the church universal. Others suggested that a special congregation be created within the curia which would consist of representative bishops and would have authority over the other congregations. The council pointedly described the responsibility of the curia as that of acting in the name of the pope and with his authority "for the good of the churches and *in the service of the sacred pastors*" (*CD*, 9, emphasis mine). The decree on the bishops' office called for a clearer description of the responsibilities of the various curial offices, a more international membership, and increased representation of diocesan bishops in the various Vatican congregations. Although the suggestions for reform included in *Christus Dominus* lacked detail, a more specific set of proposals was to be sent on to Pope Paul VI for consideration in a more substantive post-conciliar reform of the curia.

The Office of the Priest-Presbyter

Because of the considerable attention given to the office of the bishop, theological reflection on the presbyterate was somewhat neglected at the council. *Christus Dominus* itself defined the office of the priest-presbyter in relation to the bishop's own office:

> All presbyters, both diocesan and religious, participate in and exercise with the bishop the one priesthood of Christ and are thereby constituted prudent cooperators of the episcopal order. In the care of souls, however, the first place is held by diocesan

priests who are incardinated or attached to a particular church, for they have fully dedicated themselves in the service of caring for a single portion of the Lord's flock. In consequence, they form one presbytery and one family whose father is the bishop. (*CD*, 28)

Lumen Gentium also taught that priests were collaborators with the bishop and, with him, constituted one priesthood to be lived out in pastoral care of the people of God.

As we saw earlier, one of the most pervasive structuring principles in the council's ecclesiology was the incorporation of the *tria munera* schema, the threefold office of Christ as priest, prophet, and shepherd/king. The council taught that all the baptized are sharers in the threefold office of Christ (cf. *LG*, 10–13, 31; *AA*, 2). This represented a significant widening of the application of the *tria munera* which, prior to the council, had been limited, by and large, to the clergy. The council also held that the baptized and those who are both baptized and ordained have a share in the *tria munera* which is essentially different. However, the nature of this "essential" distinction was not always clear. The council taught that by reason of his ordination the priest was uniquely configured to the one priesthood of Christ:

They exercise their sacred function especially in the eucharistic worship or the celebration of the Mass by which acting in the person of Christ and proclaiming His Mystery they unite the prayers of the faithful with the sacrifice of their Head and renew and apply in the sacrifice of the Mass until the coming of the Lord the only sacrifice of the New Testament namely that of Christ offering Himself once for all a spotless Victim to the Father. (*LG*, 28)

This unique priestly configuration to Christ is reaffirmed in the Decree on the Ministry and Life of Priests, *Presbyterorum Ordinis*:

Wherefore the priesthood, while indeed it presupposes the sacraments of Christian initiation, is conferred by that special sacrament; through it priests, by the anointing of the Holy

Spirit, are signed with a special character and are conformed
to Christ the Priest in such a way that they can act in the person of Christ the Head. (*PO*, 2; see also *PO*, 13)

This teaching, that the priest acts "in the person of Christ, head of the
church," is taken more or less directly from Pope Pius XII's 1947
encyclical on the liturgy, *Mediator Dei*.

At the same time, the council avoided referring to the priest as an
alter Christus. This expression had its origins in the seventeenth-
century French school of priestly spirituality associated with Sts.
Pierre de Bérulle, Jean Eudes, and Vincent de Paul.[56] The French school
viewed the priest as representing Christ through the priest's interior
holiness and the offering of the holy sacrifice of the Eucharist. In this
line of thought, the entire theology of the priesthood was reduced to
one essential moment, that when the priest pronounces the words of
institution in the Eucharist. The priest represented Christ not in his
action or service on behalf of the kingdom, but in his very being. This
spirituality was spread worldwide by the Oratorians, Vincentians, and
Sulpicians who staffed numerous seminaries throughout the world.
Indeed, for much of the first half of the twentieth century, priests were
nourished on a classic expression of this spirituality in Dom Marmion's
Christ—The Ideal of the Priest.[57]

The christological view of the priesthood presented in the council
documents is much broader and richer. The priest's acting "in the person of Christ" does not refer only or even primarily to the priest's
power to "confect the Eucharist" and absolve sins, but to his entire
pastoral ministry as a proclaimer of the gospel and a shepherd of the
people of God (in collaboration with his bishop). This much more
pastoral consideration of the office of the priest was reflected in the
council's decision in *Presbyterorum Ordinis* to use the Latin term *presbyter* rather than the more cultic term *sacerdos*.

Alongside this more christological view of the priesthood we can
find in the council documents another more pneumatological conception of priestly ministry. We saw earlier the important acknowledgment of those charisms that the Spirit has bestowed upon all the
Christian faithful. In several passages the council also suggested a possible theology of ordained pastoral leadership within a community

animated by many charisms. It asserted that the pastoral leadership of the ordained need not compete with the exercise of the many gifts and charisms of the faithful. Each required the other. The council insisted that those ordained to pastoral leadership were not to absorb into their own ministry the entire task of building up the church on their own. Indeed, it was an essential aspect of their ministry that they recognize, empower, and affirm the gifts of all God's people. In the Decree on the Apostolate of the Laity the council held that, having received charisms from the Spirit through baptism,

> there arise for each believer the right and duty to use them in the Church and in the world for the good of men [and women] and the building up of the Church, in the freedom of the Holy Spirit who "breathes where He wills." This should be done by the laity in communion with their brothers [and sisters] in Christ, especially with their pastors who must make a judgment about the true nature and proper use of these gifts not to extinguish the Spirit but to test all things and hold for what is good. (*AA*, 3)

The Decree on the Ministry and Life of Priests likewise asserted the responsibility of the priest to affirm and nurture the gifts of the faithful:

> While trying the spirits to see if they be of God, priests should uncover with a sense of faith, acknowledge with joy and foster with diligence the various humble and exalted charisms of the laity. (*PO*, 9)

These passages situate presbyteral ministry not above but within the Christian community. The ordained minister is responsible for the discernment and coordination of the charisms and ministries of all the baptized. Yet by baptism and confirmation all the faithful are empowered by the Spirit to participate in the life and ministry of the church. As was the case with the council's presentation of two different versions of episcopal collegiality, the council bishops were not able to fully integrate these two conceptions of the priesthood, the christological and the pneumatological.

The Office of the Deacon

Finally we recognize the brief but important consideration given to the diaconate in the council documents. The brevity of its treatment should not deceive us; the call for the restoration of the diaconate "as a proper and permanent rank of the hierarchy" was momentous. The council taught that the deacon was ordained not into the priesthood but into "a ministry of service" (*LG*, 29). The bishops acknowledged a broad range of ministries proper to the diaconate including baptism, distribution of communion, the witness to and blessing of marriages, preaching, and so on. In the Decree on the Catholic Churches of the Eastern Rite the council acknowledged a stable diaconate as belonging to the ancient tradition of the Eastern churches and recommended its reestablishment (*OE*, 17).[58]

The call for the restoration of the permanent diaconate represented an initial step toward the dismantling of the then-dominant view of permanent ministries as constituting a kind of ecclesiastical ladder. The life of the early church was rich with a great diversity of ministries.[59] By the Middle Ages, however, these various ministries were no longer seen as vital to the life of the church but solely as stepping stones for hierarchical advancement. For example, a candidate for the priesthood in the Roman rite would have to move up the ecclesiastical ladder of porter, lector, exorcist, acolyte, subdeacon, and deacon before being ordained a presbyter. Many of these ancient ministries were reduced to nothing but a formality.

The restoration of the diaconate as a permanent ministry recalls a much more ancient tradition, a time when each of these ministries was valued for its own sake. "Promotion" was then a matter of the church recognizing that the gifts an individual exercised in a given ministry might justify that person's being called to a new ministry of ecclesial leadership. For example, in the early centuries, bishops were frequently chosen from the ranks of the diaconate without first being ordained to the presbyterate.

A second contribution of Vatican II's restoration of the permanent diaconate was the church's recognition that celibacy need not be a condition for ordained ministry. By allowing married deacons—not as a dispensation from the law but as part of the permanent ordering of the community—the council rightly understood a distinction often lost in the church's current view of presbyteral and episcopal ministry, namely, the distinction between ministerial service to the church (am I called to ordained ministry?) and the concrete manner in which one might live out the universal call to holiness (am I called to the single life, the public witness to evangelical celibacy, or the vowed life of marriage?). In its restoration of the permanent diaconate to married persons, the council was, in effect, saying that it was possible to respond to an ecclesial call to ordained ministry while fulfilling the universal call to holiness through the vowed life of marriage.

The ecclesiological shifts enacted in the council documents, as we have seen, were enormous. Without ignoring the obvious continuity in tradition—no one at the council thought they were creating a "new church"—there can be no denying the important new directions or "micro-ruptures" undertaken by the council. Still, these shifts were not always consistent, and on important issues, as we have seen, there are enduring tensions in the conciliar texts. The bishops were often much clearer about that which they wished to move away from than they were regarding the new vision they wished to explore. Consequently, the council documents cannot be read as if they were hermetically sealed texts whose meaning is obvious, indisputable, and immune to further development. The four decades since the council have witnessed the church doing what it has always done in the wake of a council—critically receiving the teaching of the council in its doctrinal pronouncements, in theological reflection, and in the concrete pastoral life of the church. It is to this critical reception and ongoing implementation of conciliar teaching that we will turn in Part Three.

PART III

POST-CONCILIAR RECEPTION AND IMPLEMENTATION

We now stand some four decades removed from the Second Vatican Council. From this vantage point it is possible to evaluate how and to what extent the council's teaching has been received in the church's developing self-understanding, its pastoral practice, and its ecclesiastical structures. We should not be surprised to find post-conciliar developments reflecting both an uneven reception of conciliar teaching and conflicting interpretations of the council. As John Henry Newman observed over a century ago, "it is uncommon that a Council not be followed by great confusion."[1] In order to consider this process of reception, I will continue to work from a consideration of fundamental conciliar themes proposed in Part Two.

THEOLOGICAL FOUNDATIONS OF THE CHURCH

The council offered less a systematic treatise than an evocative vision of the church, a vision that was a combination of historical retrieval and pastoral imagination. Over the past four decades much of this vision has seeped into the ecclesial consciousness of the post-conciliar church.

The Church as the People of God

In the early decades after the council no image captured the imagination of Catholics like that of the church as the new people of God. In chapter 2 of *Lumen Gentium* the council emphasized the constitutive role of baptism and taught that all the Christian faithful participate, in a way proper to their baptism, in the threefold ministry of Christ as priest, prophet, and shepherd/king. Renewed emphasis on the dignity of the baptized was aided, in no small part, by the implementation of the liturgical and sacramental reforms called for in the Constitution on the Sacred Liturgy, *Sacrosanctum Concilium*. That document's call for the full, conscious, and active participation of all the faithful brought sweeping reforms in the celebration of the liturgy. In the last twenty years, some voices in the church have called key elements of that liturgical reform into question. It is hard to deny, however, the positive ecclesial effects that the council's emphasis on liturgical participation have realized. If the Sunday liturgy is the fundamental ritual enactment of the church, then we should not be surprised to find that it is changes in the liturgy that have had the greatest impact in implementing the council's vision of the church.

The revised rites of Christian initiation that emerged in the wake of the council offer yet another feature of the liturgical reform that enhanced the church's consciousness of itself as the people of God. At least in the United States, one could argue that no pastoral initiative has been as effective at parish renewal as the Rite of Christian Initiation for Adults (RCIA). The RCIA has communicated, not only to those seeking membership in the church but to the entire Catholic Christian community, the full meaning and significance of one's baptism and one's baseline identity as a disciple of Jesus. The RCIA moved beyond more cognitive approaches to admission into the church (reflected in the pre-conciliar practice of private instruction with a priest) to highlight the need for wholistic personal conversion and both the rights and considerable obligations of Christian baptism. In the U.S. church it is no coincidence that the most active and committed members of a parish are frequently those who have gone through the RCIA process either as candidates, catechumens, or sponsors.

We should also note the critical reception of this understanding of the church in Latin America. There the seminal event of conciliar reception was the Medellín Conference convened by CELAM (the Spanish acronym of the Episcopal Conference of Latin America) in 1968. The focus of Medellín was on the implications of the Pastoral Constitution on the Church in the Modern World and the Decree on the Mission Activity of the Church.[2] Medellín helped sanction a broader theological and pastoral movement to "read the signs of the times" and respond appropriately as a Christian community.

Another key event in the reception of the council's teaching on the church as the people of God was the promulgation of the new Code of Canon Law in 1983. This new code was intended as a codification of the teaching of the Second Vatican Council. As such it was a mixed success. Although the documents of the council are frequently cited in the code, and important conciliar themes do appear, Eugenio Corecco contends that the project to revise the code of canon law came too soon after the close of the council. The commission charged with the revision "lacked the necessary distance from the conciliar event and, instead of undertaking a work of comprehensive comparative interpretation of the conciliar texts, preferred to make a selection."[3] Most of the canonists who served on the commission had themselves been trained prior to the council, rendering it difficult for them to take sufficiently into account the new ecclesiological vision presented by the council. Consequently, in spite of significant advances, the new code too often failed at a deeper level to reflect adequately the council's ecclesiology. For example, Book II of the new code is dedicated to the church as the people of God yet it does not succeed in grasping the full ecclesiological and canonical implications of seminal conciliar insights regarding the common priesthood of all believers and the *sensus fidei*.[4]

In the realm of post-conciliar theology, ongoing reflection on the council's teaching on the church as the people of God was continued in the journal *Concilium*, founded in the wake of the council by Karl Rahner, Edward Schillebeeckx, Hans Küng, and others to further the spirit of the council. Although attentive to "the return to the sources" that had been so fruitful for the council itself, theologians associated with *Concilium* tended to privilege the council's work of *aggiornamento*, bringing the church "up to date" through a careful "reading of the signs of the times." This trajectory of theological reflection celebrated the value of dialogue within the Catholic Church, in relations with other Christian traditions, in interreligious encounters and, finally, in the church's engagement with the world. The call for dialogue drew on *Lumen Gentium*'s positive evaluation of Catholicism's relationship to other Christians, to persons of other faiths, and to all people of good will in its chapter on the people of God (*LG*, 14–17). Also important for this emerging theology of dialogue was *Gaudium et Spes*'s presentation of the church's essentially dialogical relationship to the world, the council's important positive statements on the value of other religions in *Nostra Aetate* (the Declaration on the Relation of the Church to Non-Christian Religions), and Pope Paul VI's first encyclical, *Ecclesiam Suam*.

The popularity of the conciliar image of the church as the people of God led, in some circles, to calls for greater participation of all Catholics in church decision-making. Responsible scholarship noting democratic processes and structures that have long been part of the church's tradition[5] were mixed with more provocative and theologically problematic calls for a "constitutional convention."[6] Other movements have built on a sense of the church as the whole people of God to empower the baptized to voice their opinions and concerns to church leadership. These movements include, in the United States, Call to Action, born out of the 1976 Call to Action Conference convened by the American bishops as a way to seek input from the laity, and, in Western Europe, We Are Church, founded in 1996 in the wake of a 1995 church referendum in Austria calling for sweeping church reform.

Some of these calls for church reform grounded their agenda in Vatican II's vision of the church as the people of God. This led to criticisms that, under the banner of "people of God," many of these movements had imported liberal democratic understandings that could not be easily reconciled with the church's own theological foundations. Consequently, as the church approached the twentieth anniversary of the close of Vatican II in 1985, one could detect the beginnings of a shift in the interpretation of the council by some theologians and church leaders. Analyses of the council's teaching tended to highlight, not the church as the people of God, but rather the council's incipient ecclesiology of communion.

The Church as *Communio*

Important ecclesiological studies had called attention to the importance of the theological concept of communion even prior to Vatican II. Elements of a communion ecclesiology can be traced to the writing of the nineteenth-century Catholic Tübingen theologian, Johann Adam Möhler. It was explored in important pre-conciliar historical studies by influential theologians such as Yves Congar and Henri de Lubac.[7]

Dennis Doyle has carefully analyzed a number of distinctive versions of "communion ecclesiology." According to Doyle, in spite of their significant differences, these various versions tend to share four elements: (1) a retrieval of an ecclesial vision presupposed by the churches of the first millennium; (2) a stress on spiritual fellowship/communion with God and other human beings over juridical structures and processes; (3) an emphasis on the need for visible church unity symbolically expressed in the celebration of the Eucharist; and (4) the promotion of a healthy interplay between unity and diversity.[8]

In the first decade after the council the concept of communion received relatively little attention. In the 1980s, however, this began to change. A renewed interest in communion ecclesiology was particularly evident in the 1985 extraordinary synod of bishops convened by Pope John Paul II to assess the state of the church's implementation of conciliar teaching. At that synod some bishops voiced concerns regarding overly ideological readings of the "people of God" image.[9] Some complained that this image of the church was being employed to create an opposition between the hierarchy and a "people's church." Consequently, the Final Report of the synod expressly avoided considering the church as the people of God, and favored a retrieval of the conciliar teaching on the church as mystery, sacrament, and communion.[10] However, apart from the synod's own concerns, the 1980s and 1990s saw the emergence of a huge body of theological literature that began to explore the biblical notion of *koinonia/communio* as a basis for ecclesiological reflection. One instance of this was the emergence of the theological journal, *Communio*, which was created as an alternative to *Concilium* by Henri de Lubac, Hans Urs von Balthasar, and Joseph Ratzinger. These theologians shared a concern that the council's commitment to ecclesial renewal through a "return to the sources" had been eclipsed by the post-conciliar stress on *aggiornamento* and the reform of external church structures. They were wary of the *Concilium* theologians' emphasis on dialogue, which they feared underplayed the distinctive revelation that Christians have received in Christ. They complained that the "*Concilium* school" risked embracing an unacceptable, Enlightenment-inspired view of dialogue in which conversation partners are expected to bracket out their own convictions. At the risk of over-generalization, one might say that the *Communio* theologians tended toward a more neo-Augustinian view of both the human person as fundamentally enslaved by sin and in need of grace, and of society as fallen. In this perspective, the church's mission to the world should be characterized less as dialogue and more as a sacrament of universal salvation before the world. They would cite Augustine and other patristic sources as a justification for privileging the biblical view of the church as the body of Christ over that of people of God.

Yet many post-conciliar studies in communion ecclesiology would not share all or even most of the concerns of the founders of *Communio*. Internationally respected ecclesiologists such as Jean Marie Tillard, Hervé Legrand, and Hermann Pottmeyer all explored the potential for a communion ecclesiology that built upon a profound biblical and patristic tradition for understanding the church. They tended to privilege the ancient view of the universal church as a communion of communions and used this framework to criticize centralization of church authority in the Vatican. None of these ecclesiologists set "people of God" and "*communion*" in opposition; rather, they placed them in a complementary relationship.

The Church as Sacrament

To some extent, the conciliar treatment of the church as sacrament, along with that of the church as the body of Christ, was taken up within the framework of the church as communion in many post-conciliar studies. However, there are at least two fairly significant post-conciliar developments in theological reflection on the sacramentality of the church that are worth mentioning.

The first was developed in Leonardo Boff's controversial exploration of ecclesiological themes in a liberationist key, *The Church, Charism and Power*. Boff called attention to the pronounced Christomonism of Catholic ecclesiology prior to the council. This one-sided emphasis on the church's relationship to Christ placed artificial limits on the church's structure and limited its ability to respond to changing ecclesial contexts.[11] It also failed to recognize that the Pauline affirmation that the church is Christ's "body" refers to the risen or pneumatic body, a body that transcends physical boundaries. Thus, the reach of the cosmic Christ becomes the reach of the church:

> If the pneumatic (risen) Christ knows no limitations, neither may his body, the Church, confine itself to the limitations of its own dogma, its rituals, its liturgy, or its canon law. The Church has the same boundaries as the risen Christ; and these dimensions are cosmic in nature. Its functions and mysteries, its structures and services must always be open to the Spirit that blows where it will, as a dynamic force in the world. Therefore, all people of faith, in the Spirit, must be members of the church and must have their place within its visible structures. No one is outside of the Church because there is no longer an "outside," because no one is outside of the reality of God and the risen Christ. Yet individuals may elect to reject this reality.[12]

Boff offered a theological vision of the church as a sacrament of the Spirit in order to free the church from past institutional constraints and unleash the power of the charisms of all God's people. Not surprisingly, this ecclesiology has come under considerable criticism. Doyle, for example, scores Boff for falling into the same trap as Hans Küng, that of opposing charism to institution and underplaying the mystical dimension of the church.[13]

The second theological development regarding the sacramentality of the church is found in the writing of Pope John Paul II, who followed *Gaudium et Spes* in interpreting the sacramentality of the church from the perspective of the church's mission in the world. In his encyclical on mission, *Redemptoris Missio*, the pope went beyond the conciliar documents by explicitly considering the relationship between the church as sacrament and the church as seed of the kingdom of God. He wrote:

> The many dimensions of the kingdom of God do not weaken the foundations and purposes of missionary activity, but rather strengthen and extend them. The Church is the sacrament of salvation for all humankind, and her activity is not limited

only to those who accept her message. She is a dynamic force in humankind's journey toward the eschatological kingdom, and is the sign and promoter of gospel values. (*RM*, 20)

Combining the two themes of church as sacrament of salvation and church as seed and sign of the kingdom suggests that one see the church as a sacrament of the kingdom of God. This connection offered a promising trajectory for a Catholic missiology that proceeds from the sacramentality of the church itself. According to Pope John Paul II, the mission of the church goes beyond itself to make present and illuminate fundamental gospel values already at work in the world.

The Church as Temple of the Holy Spirit

In Part Two we discussed the council's recovery of pneumatology, a theology of the Holy Spirit. We highlighted two instances where the renewed appreciation for the role of the Spirit in the life of the church was most significant: (1) the council's acknowledgment of the *sensus fidei*, the supernatural instinct for the faith that the Spirit offers all believers and (2) the council's affirmation of the charisms of all the baptized.

The *sensus fidei* became a popular topic in post-conciliar Catholic ecclesiology. Many studies reflected on the significance of the council's affirmation of this supernatural instinct of the faith given to all the baptized, as well as on the cognate concept of the *sensus fidelium*. The latter term refers to that which the whole people of God in fact believes. When all the baptized are united in a shared belief, when there is a *consensus fidelium*, in other words, the council taught that what they believed cannot be in error. In the decades since the council, many theologians have called for a more developed reflection on this concept. If it is true that all the faithful have the capacity to hear God's Word and to share actively in the "traditioning" process of the church, then should there not be an effort on the part of church leadership to consult the faithful?

In a number of significant historical studies, ecclesiologists noted that over a century before the council, John Henry Newman, one of the great Catholic thinkers of the nineteenth century, had said much the same thing. In his famous essay, *On Consulting the Faithful in Matters of Doctrine*,[14] Newman dared to suggest that there might be some value in the bishops consulting the faithful, even on matters of doctrine, precisely because the same Spirit that guided the bishops in their teaching office also gave witness to the apostolic faith in the graced insight of all the baptized. He broke with the tendency in Catholic thought, at least since the sixteenth century, to divide the church into two different groups, the teaching church (*ecclesia docens*) and the learning church (*ecclesia discens*). For Newman, the whole church participated in the handing on of the faith.

In the decades after the council there has also been considerable attention given by theologians to a concept closely related to the sense of the faithful—the "ecclesial reception" of church teaching. Since the Protestant Reformation and Luther's championing of his slogan *sola scriptura*, Catholic theology has offered vigorous defenses of a notion of tradition as a dynamic process by which the one faith testified to in scripture continues to grow and develop in the life and teaching of the church. These theologies of tradition attend to the distinctive ways in which the one faith has been "handed on" (the root meaning of the Latin verb, *tradere*) from generation to generation. Theologies of reception have pointed out that, in fact, the handing on of the faith is a complex reciprocal process in which those who "receive" that which is handed on make it their own and, in doing so, add new spiritual insight to the dynamic, living tradition of the church. This act of reception, much like the exercise of the *sensus fidei*, might be likened by analogy to our appreciation of a fine work of art. When we encounter a piece of art like a beautiful sculpture, it has an effect on us; we receive the art from our own particular perspective. Our own life story, our storehouse of life experiences, inclines us to understand the work of art in a particular way. The work of the artist is completed in our viewing (or, regarding other artistic media, our hearing, touching, or reading) the work. These new developments lead one to ask: how have these insights into the role of the *sensus fidei* and the processes of ecclesial reception been implemented in post-conciliar church teaching and ecclesiastical structures?

The 1983 Code of Canon Law, in canon 212, explicitly affirms the rights of the faithful to make known their needs and desires and to share their insight with church leaders. In keeping with this fundamental right, the code provides several consultative structures oriented toward input from the Christian faithful.[15] For example the code encourages the creation of diocesan pastoral councils (c. 511) and the convocation of diocesan synods (cc. 460–68); in both instances lay participation is envisioned. However, these structures are only recommended by the code, whereas diocesan presbyteral councils are mandated (c. 495).

There is another structure mandated by the code that, in principle, could offer an important venue for consultation of the faithful, and that is the parish visitation. The Code of Canon Law requires that the bishop or a proxy visit all parishes in their diocese over a five-year period (c. 396, §1). Of course, structures for consultation are not limited to these canonical provisions. In many dioceses one finds various boards and commissions created to oversee important dimensions of the church's ministry and mission and many of these boards and commissions have significant lay representation.

In the 1980s, the American bishops modeled a promising consultative process in the way in which they went about producing two seminal pastoral letters, the first on war and peace, and the second on the economy. The promulgation of each of those documents was preceded by extensive listening sessions and open hearings in which the views of experts were considered at great length. The bishops took seriously the assumption of both Vatican II and Paul VI that all God's people, and not only the hierarchy, must engage in the central processes of ecclesial discernment. In the late 1980s the American bishops began the process of formulating a new pastoral letter on women. They initiated that process by employing the same methodology (e.g., widely distributed drafts and listening sessions) used with regard to their two earlier pastoral letters on social issues. Midway in the process, however, the bishops were notified by the Vatican that the overall process being employed was unacceptable and had to be abandoned. Presumably, the widespread consultation and revision process was thought to be setting a dangerous precedent for episcopal leadership. Subsequent episcopal documents promulgated by the conference have not used the earlier methodology. Yet many ecclesiologists consider that procedure to be a model of collaboration between the bishops and the people. There is a sense among many church commentators that attempts to implement this important conciliar teaching have, to a large extent, been hamstrung.

Others have claimed that this disappointment stems from an insufficiently theological understanding of the meaning of the *sensus fidei*. They point out that the spiritual sense of the faith given to each believer in baptism must be cultivated within the life of the church. One would assume, they suggest, that Catholic Christians who have cultivated their spiritual instincts through the faithful practice of their Catholic faith will exercise a more developed insight than "lapsed" Catholics. Consequently, some have criticized appeals to polling data on the grounds that such polls seldom distinguish between active, practicing Catholics and inactive Catholics. Recourse to polls may be helpful, but they are not sufficient for assessing the true sense of the faithful.

The second example of the council's pneumatological ecclesiology lies in its consideration of charisms. This theme has received considerable attention in a number of post-conciliar ecclesiological projects. The work of Hans Küng, Edward Schillebeeckx, Leonardo Boff, Gotthold Hassenhüttl and, more recently, Roger Haight, have all sought to develop an ecclesiology from below that makes "charism" the constitutive starting point for understandings of ministry and order in the church.[16] These projects seek to transcend the post-Reformation opposition of charism and church office. Both charism and church office depend on the prior action of the Holy Spirit in the church. As we shall see later, this rediscovery of a theology of charism will provide a fruitful theological foundation for assessing the post-conciliar emergence of lay ministries.

The Laity

In Part Two we discussed some tensions that were present in the council's tentative exploration of a theology of the laity. Although few theologians since the council have attempted a constructive theology of the laity,[17] numerous dimensions of the experience of the laity in the life of the church have been explored in countless books on spirituality and ministry.[18] The theological treatments of the laity that have emerged since the council have tried to understand more fully the council's somewhat ambiguous teaching on the laity's theological status. The two different strands of thought discussed in Part Two, one a contrastive view of the laity and the second an intensive view, have continued since the council. These two strands are distinguished by their differing views of what the council meant by rooting a theology of the laity in the "secular character" of the lay vocation.

Those advocating a more contrastive view reject the claim that the secular character of the laity refers primarily to a sociological datum. It is not merely an expression of the fact that the vast majority of the laity live their lives "in the world." Rather, this secular character has a theological/ontological significance, defining the laity in an essential way in virtue of their unique and distinctive share in the church's mission in the world through their immersion in temporal affairs (e.g., the family and the workplace).[19] In 1997 the Vatican published a controversial document issued jointly by eight Vatican offices. The document, "Some Questions Regarding Collaboration of Non-ordained Faithful in Priests' Sacred Ministry,"[20] presupposed this ontological view of the secular character of the lay vocation and was reluctant to grant a proper role to the laity in the ministerial life of the church save as a concession to pastoral necessity. Indeed, the document seems to return to a pre-conciliar theology of "two realms," the sacred and the secular, and sees the laity's proper place limited to the secular.[21]

Yet the more intensive view of the laity can also be found in post-conciliar documents. Pope Paul VI, for example, seemed to adopt this approach when he noted that the whole church

> has an authentic secular dimension, inherent to her inner nature and mission, which is deeply rooted in the mystery of the Word Incarnate, and which is realized in different forms through her members.[22]

Pope John Paul II emphasized this as well in his 1987 post-synodal apostolic exhortation, *Christifideles Laici* :

> Certainly all the members of the Church are sharers in this secular dimension but in different ways. In particular the sharing of the lay faithful has its own manner of realization and function, which, according to the Council, is "properly and particularly" theirs. Such manner is designated with the expression "secular character." (*CL*, 15)

Although both popes go on to affirm the secular character of the laity by placing it in the context of the church's own secularity in virtue of its mission in the world, they avoid absolutizing the secular status of the laity as the contrastive view does. John Paul II does express a concern regarding abuses that obscure the unique ministry of the ordained, but he willingly affirms that there are ministries grounded in holy orders and ministries grounded in baptism and confirmation (*CL*, 23). We will return to the question of lay ministry in the section on ecclesiastical leadership, but as a general observation we must acknowledge a certain lack of consensus in the church today regarding both a theology of the laity and the status of lay ministries vis-à-vis the ministry of the ordained.

The Pilgrim Church

One of the many original contributions of the council was its reflection on the church within an eschatological frame of reference. No longer was the church presented as the *societas perfecta*, the perfect society in firm possession of divine truth and hovering serenely above the vicissitudes of human history, waiting for the world to acknowledge the church's divine origins. The church was not just a church of pilgrims; it was a pilgrim church, a church that would not achieve its perfection until the consummation of human history. This affirmation of the pilgrim status of the church opened new avenues for considering ecclesial reform and renewal. Indeed, the program for reform and renewal that emerged from the council was filled with promise. In hindsight, the hope for ecclesial reform engendered by the council may have been unrealistic.

In the early years after the council much of the energy for reform was directed toward the revision of the liturgical and sacramental rites of the church. The revision of the Code of Canon Law, completed in 1983, marked yet another noteworthy effort at institutional reform, as did the 1988 apostolic constitution *Pastor Bonus*, which was directed toward the reform of the Roman curia. The ministry of catechesis was called to renewal in content and methodology in the 1971 *General Catechetical Directory*. That document was eventually superseded by the *General Directory for Catechesis* in 1997. Conciliar teaching was brought to bear on Catholic higher education as well in the 1990 apostolic constitution *Ex Corde Ecclesiae*. The *Directory for Ecumenism*, which appeared in two parts in 1967 and 1970, was followed by a revised directory in 1993. This directory was created in order to ensure that the ecumenical teachings of the council were reflected in the church's ecumenical policies and practices. Programs for priestly and diaconal formation were issued with a view to implementing conciliar teaching in the processes of formation for ordained ministries.

In spite of these important developments, the many and diverse hopes for an ambitious program of institutional reform and renewal were not realized. Too often, the bureaucratic institutions themselves in need of reform (e.g., the Roman curia) were the institutions charged with the task of implementing the council's program for reform. Moreover, the rationale that was presented for ecclesial reform frequently relied on a far too selective and superficial grasp of conciliar teaching.

The mixed success of this agenda for ecclesiastical reform has engendered different responses. Some, hopeful for a more far-reaching and ambitious reform, have become jaded and even resentful at the bureaucratic shell game that many programs of renewal resembled. Other commentators have suggested that the time for church reform is over. They believe that the program of institutional reform has distracted the church from its primary mission of evangelization in the world.

Perhaps nowhere was the fruit of the council's teaching on the church's pilgrim status more profoundly realized than in Pope John Paul II's call for a purification of the church's memory. John Paul II demonstrated a singular commitment to seek forgiveness for the failings of Christians past and present. Luigi Accattoli documents over ninety instances in which John Paul II asked forgiveness for the failings of Christians.[23] Over the course of his remarkable pontificate, John Paul II offered apologies for the Galileo affair, crimes of anti-Semitism, abuse of women, and crimes against non-Catholic Christians, among others. This remarkable program achieved its most dramatic expression on the First Sunday of Lent during the Jubilee year when Pope John Paul II presided over a solemn liturgy that included the participation of key cardinals from within the Roman curia. This liturgy was officially titled, "Confession of Sins and Asking for Forgiveness." In the liturgy key church officials asked forgiveness for the past sins of Christians.

There were some voices in the church that quietly expressed discomfort over this papal program. They were concerned that these formal apologies might suggest that the church itself had, in a sense, sinned. In response to these concerns, the International Theological Commission undertook a study of the question. The result was a report titled, *Memory and Reconciliation: The Church and the Faults of the Past.*[24] Unfortunately, the document relied very little on the conciliar image of the church as pilgrim, preferring instead to speak of the relationship between "Holy Mother Church" and "her sinful children." Within this framework, the commission insisted, one must distinguish between the holiness *of* the church, which is unaffected by human sin, and holiness *in* the church, which can be compromised by the sinfulness of the church's members. The document firmly rejected any claim that the church was itself sinful in virtue of the sin of its members.

This theological perspective has itself been subjected to critique. Francis Sullivan, in a careful evaluation of the document, admitted that obviously the church cannot be sinful in the sense that it is itself the subject of a sinful act, since properly speaking only individuals can sin.[25] Yet it is one thing to acknowledge that individual Christians have sinned and do sin, and it is another to grasp the full significance of individual Christian leaders sinning in actions undertaken, not just individually, but in the name of the church. When church leaders have called for the torture of Jews, the slaughter of innocents in the crusades, or the burning of "heretics" at the stake, these sinful deeds cannot be interpreted as merely private acts but must be seen as acts undertaken "in the name of the church." This suggests that the church ought properly to ask for forgiveness not only for the sins of the "sons and daughters of the church" but also for the sins of individual Christians undertaken *in the name of the church.*

Mary and the Church

Assessing the post-conciliar reception of the council's treatment of Mary is tricky. When considering Marian devotion, it is certainly the case that the traditional Marian piety of many Catholics continued largely unaffected by the council. However, in much of Western Europe and in North America, an undeniable waning of traditional devotional practices has occurred. There are different theories regarding the reason for this diminishment in Marian devotion. Some either credit or blame the teaching of the council.[26] Yves Congar claimed that the council's determination to place Mary in the context of her relationship to the church inevitably diminished the theological rationale for devotions grounded in a more "isolated Mariology."[27] Stefano de Fiores suggests that the council's teaching on the hierarchy of truths relativized Marian doctrine.[28] Pope Paul VI put his finger on yet another significant factor, one that cannot be credited to the council, one way or another. In his 1974 apostolic exhortation *Marialis Cultis*, which many regard as the most balanced and mature ecclesiastical document on Mary since the council, the pope pointed to a basic difficulty for many today regarding Marian devotion:

> the discrepancy existing between some aspects of this devotion and modern anthropological discoveries and the profound changes which have occurred in the psycho-sociological field in which modern man lives and works. The picture of the Blessed Virgin presented in a certain type of devotional literature cannot easily be reconciled with today's life-style, especially the way women live today. In the home, woman's equality and coresponsibility with man in the running of the family are being justly recognized by laws and the evolution of customs. In the sphere of politics women have in many countries gained a position in public life equal to that of men. In the social field women are at work in a whole range of different employments, getting further away every day from the restricted surroundings of the home. In the cultural field new possibilities are opening up for women in scientific research and intellectual activities. (*MC*, 34)

However, in that same document, Paul VI also noted a significant opportunity offered by the council's more biblically grounded portrait of Mary:

> The modern woman will note with pleasant surprise that Mary of Nazareth, while completely devoted to the will of God, was far from being a timidly submissive woman or one whose piety

was repellent to others; on the contrary, she was a woman who did not hesitate to proclaim that God vindicates the humble and the oppressed, and removes the powerful people of this world from their privileged positions (cf. Lk. 1:51–53). The modern woman will recognize in Mary, who "stands out among the poor and humble of the Lord," a woman of strength, who experienced poverty and suffering, flight and exile (cf. Mt. 2:13–23). These are situations that cannot escape the attention of those who wish to support, with the Gospel spirit, the liberating energies of humankind and of society. And Mary will appear not as a Mother exclusively concerned with her own divine Son, but rather as a woman whose action helped to strengthen the apostolic community's faith in Christ (cf. Jn. 2:1–12), and whose maternal role was extended and became universal on Calvary. These are but examples, but examples which show clearly that the figure of the Blessed Virgin does not disillusion any of the profound expectations of the men and women of our time but offers them the perfect model of the disciple of the Lord.... (*MC*, 37)

This more biblical foundation has been fruitfully pursued by liberation theologians like Ivonne Gebara and Maria Clara Bingemer.[29] Critical, historical retrievals have also been employed by feminist theologians like Elizabeth Johnson in her book *Truly Our Sister*.[30] In her work, Johnson deliberately distances herself from more symbolic approaches to Mary:

She has been symbolized to such an extravagant degree divorced from her own life history—symbol of the maternal face of God, of the eternal feminine, of the disciples, of the idealized church—that approaching her as an actual human being surprises us with the discovery that she too struggled, that her own life's journey, in Vatican II's poetic phrase, was a pilgrimage of faith, including sojourning in faith's dark night.[31]

Johnson situates Mary within the framework of a theology of the communion of saints established in her earlier work, *Friends of God and*

Prophets.[32] In that work she challenged the patronage model that has dominated Catholic understanding of this doctrine since the early centuries of the church, a model built on the feudal relationship between the nobility and the peasant class. Johnson retrieved from the earlier centuries of the church a theological vision of the communion of saints grounded in companionship and the solidarity of the saints with the living. This demythologization of Mary as theological symbol and retrieval of a historical portrait of Mary has been embraced by many feminist theologians, but it has not been without its critics. Indeed, it would be a mistake to assume that criticism of Johnson's approach is limited to the complaints of Catholic traditionalists. Noted sociologist of religion Andrew Greeley hardly counted among the voices of the Catholic right, has decried the symbolic reductionism found in some modern forms of Marian studies.[33] Charlene Spretnak has similarly complained, from a perspective generally sympathetic to the broader ecclesiological reforms of the council, of the loss of the more cosmological symbolism of Mary that follows from Johnson's approach.[34]

Another avenue of Marian studies that wishes to affirm a historical retrieval of Mary without losing the symbolic is found in Latino/a theologies of Mary, particularly those that attend to devotion to *La Virgen de Guadalupe.* Jeanette Rodriguez, for example, highlights ways in which the cult of *la Virgen* has been symbolically empowering for an oppressed people.[35]

A quite different post-conciliar exploration has entailed less a historical retrieval of Mary than a typological one that builds on the council's explicit association of Mary and the church. This was developed by the Swiss theologian Hans Urs von Balthasar, who saw in Mary a type of the church's receptivity to God's saving initiative.[36] Von Balthasar articulated a "Marian principle" that emphasized the church's properly receptive relationship to Christ.

Finally, we must consider the fruits of the council's determination to be ecumenically sensitive in its presentation of Marian teaching. The work done in retrieving a biblical portrait of Mary has, not surprisingly, been positively received in ecumenical circles. One notable instance of this is the recent document to come out of the Anglican–Roman Catholic International Commission (ARCIC), "Mary: Grace and Hope in Christ."[37] In that document, for the first time, there is the suggestion that the Marian dogmas need not be an obstacle to church reunion.

As we have seen, virtually every significant ecclesiological theme explored during the council has received considerable attention and development in the decades since the council. Not all of these developments can be easily reconciled with one another. Communion ecclesiology, for example, has been developed in quite different ways by Joseph Ratzinger and Jean Marie Tillard. More striking however, is the disparity between the ample theological development of these themes and the far less successful implementation of these developments in church structures and practices. This mixed record may, ironically, be the result of a determination to press forward with ecclesiastical reforms before there was time for sufficient theological reflection to grasp the full ecclesial implications of conciliar teaching. Thus by 1985, a mere twenty years after the council, the vast majority of post-conciliar reform in canon law, liturgy, the Roman curia, and religious education had already been accomplished. As Catholic ecclesiology continues to mature, we may hope for a future revisiting of these structures and policies from the perspective of a more robust and differentiated reception of the council's ecclesial vision.

THE UNITY AND CATHOLICITY OF THE CHURCH

Perhaps no theological problematic received more attention during the council deliberations than, on the one hand, how to affirm church unity without yielding to a rigid and sterile uniformity, and, on the other hand, how to celebrate a legitimate and invigorating ecclesial diversity without dissolving into a church fractured by division.[38] This debate centered, more often than not, on the relationship between the local and the universal church. As we saw in Part Two, the council made important contributions to a new understanding of the relationship between the local and universal church, but its presentation was not always consistent. Consequently, it should not surprise us that the post-conciliar reception of this teaching has been particularly complex.

The Development of Theologies of the Local Church

In one of the most famous assessments of the enduring significance of Vatican II in all the post-conciliar literature, Karl Rahner contended that Vatican II marked the beginning of the church's "discovery and official realization of itself as *world-Church*."[39] This was the case not only because of the large number of native-born bishops from outside Western Europe and North America who participated in the council, or because of the council's positive appreciation of the role of culture in the expression of the Christian faith, but because the council had moved to a new appreciation of the local church as the place where the universal church was concretely realized. The council rejected any notion of the local church as a mere branch office of the universal church; the local church was the historical "eventing," if you will, of the church universal. This theology of the local church suggested that each local church not only receives from the universal church but also offers to the church universal its own particular gifts and insights as the geographical and cultural site in which the gospel is always being proclaimed, received, and lived out.

Nowhere was the council's renewed emphasis on the local church received more quickly than in the church of Latin America. The CELAM meeting at Medellín in 1968 marked a landmark attempt to combine the council's commitment to "read the signs of the times" with its renewed emphasis on the local church. This constituted a crucial step in the implementation of conciliar teaching as regional church leaders began to address their own geo-political situation in the light of the gospel. It was out of this attention to local context that there emerged in this region a "preferential option for the poor."

"Local theologies" began to emerge in Africa and Asia as well. In both instances they were marked by a trend toward an inculturation of the Christian faith that dared to ask how that faith was to be lived within local cultures previously untouched by Western Christianity. Emerging consciousness of the theological significance of these regional churches led to new theological reflections by both local theologians and local church leadership that have challenged the overly Westernized formulations of the faith that were first brought to their continents. These regional churches have contributed much to the universal church over the last several decades as they struggled to come to grips with their minority status in regions dominated by other religious traditions. They have worked to distinguish between what is essential and unchanging in church dogmatic statements and sacramental practice and that which may admit of new formulations and customs. They have dared to ask whether celibacy must remain a prerequisite for ordination to the priesthood in cultures where celibacy is not revered. They have asked whether central sacramental rituals and symbols can be seen as seeds to be planted in a particular culture and allowed to bloom in new forms. In the last fifteen years the church of Asia, in particular, has led the way in exploring the challenges and possibilities of interreligious dialogue.[40]

Returning for a moment to Latin America, theological reflection on the reality of the local church was taken in a new direction as the result of a new modality of the local church, often referred to as *communidades de base*. These "basic Christian communities" flourished sometimes within and sometimes in tandem with traditional parochial church structures.[41] The communities were comprised of local Christians who gathered together for prayer, reflection on scripture, and analysis of their social context. In this regard, they could be said to resemble certain pre-conciliar lay movements constituted by small faith sharing communities (e.g., Catholic Action, the Christian Family Movement) influenced by the Cardijn method: "observe—judge—act."[42] What was distinctive in these communities was the way in which they read the scriptures through the interpretive lens of their own experience of suffering and injustice. Scripture was not appealed to for abstract truths but for a vital faith response to the concrete experience of these believers. The base communities would spread throughout much of Latin America in the 1970s and 1980s. Although the changing character of the episcopate in Latin America has led to diminished support for this ecclesial movement, many such communities continue today.

A similar phenomenon, often referred to as "small Christian communities," also emerged in Africa. In 1973 the bishops of East Africa made these communities a central part of their pastoral strategy.[43] These communities were generally more fully incorporated into parish life than in the Latin American context but they shared with their Latin American counterparts a critical reflection on their particular social context.

Finally, we should point out that small Christian communities have also flourished in the United States. Sometimes these have been encouraged as part of larger pastoral renewal programs (e.g., *Renew* or the Paulist program, *Disciples in Mission*) and other times they have emerged "from below" in response to the felt need of Catholics for a more intentional experience of Christian community.[44]

These small faith communities have had a mixed reception from church leadership. They were explicitly welcomed by Pope Paul VI in his apostolic exhortation, *Evangelii Nuntiandi*. In that document, one of the most influential of Paul VI's pontificate, he distinguished between those legitimate base communities that lived in communion with the larger church and that were the fruit of a desire "to live the church's life more intensely" and those base communities that were characterized by "a spirit of bitter criticism of the church" (*EN*, 51). Yet some Vatican officials warned that these communities could not be considered local churches in themselves; at best it could be said that they contained "elements" of a local church, since they were not constituted as eucharistic communities under the presidency of a bishop. This viewpoint has occasioned considerable ecclesiological debate.

Liberation theologians have generally insisted on the real ecclesiological significance of these communities, affirming that they merit the title "local churches." Leonardo Boff, in his book *Ecclesiogenesis*, wrote:

> We must face the new experiences of church in our midst. We in Brazil and Latin America are confronted with a new concretization of church, without the presence of consecrated ministers and without the eucharistic celebration. It is not that this absence is not felt, is not painful. It is, rather, that these ministers do not exist in sufficient numbers. This historical situation does not cause the church to disappear. The church abides in the people of God as they continue to come together, convoked by the word and discipleship of Jesus Christ. Something *is* new under the sun: a new church of Christ.[45]

Boff contended that for all of the real advances of the council in its renewed ecclesiology of the local church, the council treatment was inadequate insofar as it still defined the church in terms of the ministry of the bishop and the celebration of the Eucharist. However, Boff's own theology of the local church is a bit muddled. On the one hand, he noted that each local church (and by this he included basic Christian communities) was not wholly the church because it did not, in its life, exhaust the whole mystery of salvation. He admitted that base communities would still ideally be under the leadership of the local bishop (as are the majority of these communities in his own country, Brazil) and would be able to celebrate the Eucharist.[46] On the other hand, he seemed to view the universal church as a kind if ideal reality that only really existed to the extent that it was "concretized" in a local church.

Relationship between the Local Church and the Universal Church

Some have speculated that it was in large part in response to the kind of "ecclesiology from below" reflected in Boff's consideration of basic Christian communities that led the Congregation for the Doctrine of the Faith (CDF) to issue an instruction on the church as communion, *Communionis Notio*.[47] That document condemned any ecclesiology of communion that tried to give priority to the local church over the universal church or that viewed the universal church as a federation of autonomous local churches. Hence, the condemnation would hold not only for the approach of those like Boff who explicitly wished to develop an ecclesiology from below, but also for certain eucharistic ecclesiologies that would overemphasize the self-sufficiency of any eucharistic community. The document referred to these various approaches as instances of an unacceptable "ecclesiological unilateralism" (*CN*, 8). Rather, the CDF asserted, each local or particular church, constituted by both the Eucharist and the bishop, exists in a situation of "mutual interiority" with the universal church. Moreover, an authentic communion ecclesiology must insist on both the chronological and ontological priority of the universal church over the local church. According to the CDF, the story of Pentecost affirms the priority of the universal church, and the CDF goes on to cite early church sources that write of the church existing before creation itself (*CN*, 9).

This document, issued in 1992, soon occasioned a remarkable public debate between two esteemed curial figures, Cardinal Walter Kasper, who began the debate as bishop of Rottenburg-Stuttgart and continued it as a highly visible curial official, and Cardinal Joseph Ratzinger (later Pope Benedict XVI), then the prefect for the CDF and a likely participant in the drafting of *Communionis Notio*.[48] Kasper expressed concerns regarding the document's assertion of the ontological and chronological priority of the universal church over the local church. In particular, he called into question the CDF's reading of the Pentecost event. Kasper insisted that what Acts 2 asserted was that the universal church was no mere abstraction but was realized concretely in the local church of Jerusalem. At Pentecost, the universal and the local appeared as a single reality. Kasper feared that insistence on the priority of the universal over the local represented a veiled attempt to justify an excessive centralization of church authority in the papacy and Roman curia.

Ratzinger soon responded to Kasper in a German newspaper. He situated *Communionis Notio* in the context of a worrisome ecclesiological horizontalism or relativism that relied too exclusively on a sociological analysis of the church and failed to do justice to the sacramental dimensions of communion ecclesiology. A sociological analysis, it is true, might lead one to begin with where people actually experience the church, that is, the local church, but a properly theological starting point must begin with the unity of the church as the body of Christ. Ratzinger admitted the dangers of an over-centralization of church authority but insisted that this was a problem of jurisdiction and competency that had to be kept separate from the theological assertion of the priority of the universal church.

The debate ended in a kind of grudging *rapprochement* in which Kasper acknowledged the pre-existent mystery of the church but still insisted that this did not justify granting a priority to the universal church since the pre-existent mystery of the church must in some sense include both the universal and local dimensions of the church's eventual historical reality. For Ratzinger's part, he still held to the priority of the universal church but did not see this as contradicting the simultaneity of the universal and local church in history. Although the debate might appear rather technical and remote from concrete pastoral concerns, it is a debate with quite practical consequences, as we shall see later.

The Eastern Catholic Churches

By all accounts, the council's Decree on the Catholic Churches of the
Eastern Rite, *Orientalium Ecclesiarum*, must be viewed as one of the
secondary documents of the council. It is relatively brief and did not
receive the same attention as did the four constitutions and other declarations and decrees. Nevertheless, it was an important document
because it affirmed the extent to which a unity-in-diversity has, in
principle, always been present in the church in the Eastern Catholic
churches. We must consider now the extent and manner of this
decree's reception in the post-conciliar church.

A benchmark in the process of ecclesial reception is the 1990 promulgation of the Code of Canons of the Eastern Churches (CCEO).
This Eastern code was the culmination of a process that had actually
begun decades earlier. At the directive of Pope Pius XI, a commission
was created in 1929 to develop a canon law for the Eastern churches.
Sections of these newly revised canons were promulgated, not as a
unified code but in a series of four papal documents issued by Pope
Pius XII. After the council, Pope Paul VI created the Pontifical Commission for the Code of Eastern Canon Law in 1972 and charged it
with the task of producing a code of law for the Eastern churches.
This Eastern code was finally promulgated by Pope John Paul II in
1990. The code attempted to implement several of the key directives
of the council's decree, *Orientalium Ecclesiarum*.[49] A central directive of
that decree concerned the recovery and preservation of the ancient
tradition of the Eastern churches. Concern for this directive is reflected
in the code's attempt to preserve the tradition of synodality, that is, the
ancient practice of a standing body of bishops surrounding a patriarch
or metropolitan and exercising deliberative (rather than merely consultative) authority. Care to preserve the distinct Eastern traditions is
also evident in the 1990 code's treatment of the sacramental life of the
Eastern churches. The code affirms the Eastern practice of celebrating
as a unity the three sacraments of initiation, baptism, chrismation with
holy myron and Eucharist (cc. 695–97). It further codifies the practice
of celebrating these sacraments at infancy. Unlike in the West, where
the deacon is also an ordinary minister of baptism, in the Eastern code
it is the pastor who is the ordinary minister (c. 677). The code affirms
the tradition of priestly celibacy but also grants the possibility of

accepting married candidates to the diaconate and presbyterate (c. 373). It reflects ancient Eastern views of the sacrament of marriage when it requires not only that a marriage be contracted in the presence of an ordained minister, but that the "sacred rite" be celebrated in a context that includes a blessing from the priest (c. 828).

A second directive of the council's decree concerned the limited right to self-governance for the Eastern churches *sui iuris*. Here too the council recognized the distinctive role of synods and the synodal election of patriarchs, metropolitans, and bishops. In this regard, some critics would argue that the Eastern code's attempts at implementation were less successful. For example, although the election of a patriarch does not require papal confirmation, the election of an archbishop does and the election procedures for bishops allow only for the submission of a list of candidates to the Holy See (c. 149). In like manner, although the synod of a patriarchal church is competent to enact laws on its own authority in metropolitan and other autonomous churches, such laws are valid only after the church *sui iuris* has been notified by Rome (c. 167).[50] The code also does not allow for patriarchs to erect a parish, eparchy (the Eastern equivalent of a diocese), or exarchy (a portion of the people of God that does not have diocesan status, similar to an apostolic vicariate in the West), outside of their patriarchal territory. This can be done only by Rome. The Eastern code, in other words, falls well short of the goal of self-governance expressed in *Orientalium Ecclesiarum*.

We must also note the problematic manner in which the Code of Canons for Eastern Catholic Churches was promulgated. The code was issued by Pope John Paul II after extensive consultation with Eastern leaders but without any shared deliberative act of the patriarchal synods as Eastern ecclesiology would have dictated. This act of papal promulgation blurred a distinction vital to the Eastern churches, namely the distinction between the pope's role as universal pastor over the whole church, East and West, and his ministry as "Patriarch of the West." Many Eastern theologians contended that the pope's promulgation of the Code of Canon Law for the Western church was properly an exercise of his patriarchal rather than papal authority, since the code was directed to the Western church alone; the corresponding patriarchal synods of the Eastern churches should have played a similar role in the promulgation of the Eastern code. The papal promulgation of the

Eastern code thus appears as a canonical "concession" granted to the Eastern churches rather than a juridical acknowledgment of their status as co-equal "sister churches" to the church of the West.[51] As distinguished expert in Eastern canon law Victor Pospishil has observed, "the mode of promulgation is the reason why the CCEO—however well prepared—is not an Eastern Christian code, but a creation of the Western Church, imposed upon the Eastern Churches."[52] In the eyes of the Orthodox, this excessive assertion of papal authority over the Eastern Catholic churches raises questions regarding the extent to which Rome is really willing to return to an exercise of primacy more in keeping with the practice of the first millennium, as John Paul II suggested in his encyclical on ecumenism, *Ut Unum Sint* 55. Again, in Pospishil's view, the Eastern code "is an ecumenically embarrassing failure, because the CCEO is a documentary witness to the rigid centralization of the Papal Church, which seemingly disavows all the beautiful phrases of Vatican II in favor of Eastern Christianity."[53] Eastern Catholic theologians have stressed the difference between recognition of legitimate primacy of the church of Rome, something to which the Eastern Catholic churches have assented, often at great cost, and Roman centralization as an ecclesiastical pattern of engagement with the Eastern churches that has no theological justification.[54]

One particular difficulty regarding the reception of the Decree on the Catholic Churches of the Eastern Rite concerns the "diaspora" situation of many Eastern Catholics. Here in the United States there is a particularly sad history of at best neglect and at worst outright suppression of the Eastern churches. One problem that remains sensitive to this day is the continued unwillingness of Rome to grant the right of Eastern bishops to ordain married men for churches outside the Eastern churches' historic territories. But the larger issue, again, has to do with the question of self-governance. *Orientalium Ecclesiarum* 4 referred to the need to have regard for the spiritual welfare of the Eastern faithful and *Orientalium Ecclesiarum* 7 specified that bishops appointed outside their patriarchal territory remained attached to the hierarchy of their own Eastern church. Yet Rome has greatly circumscribed the ability of Eastern church leaders to provide for the spiritual needs of their faithful in Western lands.[55]

On a more positive note, we must call attention to the issuance in 1995 of Pope John Paul II's apostolic letter, *Orientale Lumen*. This remarkable document has been insufficiently appreciated, perhaps because it was soon eclipsed by his much longer encyclical on ecumenism, *Ut Unum Sint*, which was released a mere three weeks later. This apostolic letter is a veritable celebration of Eastern Christianity. The pope recognized that the East possesses a venerable theological, spiritual, and liturgical heritage from which Western Christians have much to learn. He offered a brief description of the Eastern concept of *theosis* or deification, the trinitarian theology of the Cappadocians, and the emphasis on the Holy Spirit in the East. He also included an extended reflection on monasticism as a shared patrimony of both East and West. Although this letter was written explicitly with the Eastern Orthodox churches in mind, the pope did make mention of the situation of the Eastern Catholic churches. He offered to the Orthodox the example of the Eastern Catholic churches, some of which, at various points in history, entered into full communion with Rome. They did this, he insisted, without in any way having had to sacrifice their unique Eastern heritage. This comment reflects an approach to the Eastern Catholic churches that has been consistent since the council's own decree. The Eastern Catholic churches are offered as a model for what ecumenical reunion without absorption might look like. The pope also observed that these Eastern Catholics carry with them the special wound of being deprived of full communion with their Orthodox brothers and sisters "... despite sharing in the heritage of their fathers" (*OL*, 21).

In conclusion, the situation facing the Eastern Catholic churches is still fraught with difficulties. They are despised "Uniates" in the eyes of the Eastern Orthodox churches not in communion with Rome, and their very small numbers dictate that within the Roman Catholic communion their venerable traditions will often be viewed as little more than exotic ornamentation superimposed upon a church that still sees itself in predominantly Western categories.

Unity with Other Christian Churches and Ecclesial Communities

In this section we have been considering the post-conciliar reception of the council's teaching on the catholicity of the church. We have done so with respect to the relationship between the local and the universal church and as regards the Eastern Catholic churches. Now I would like to consider catholicity with respect to other Christian traditions. Since another volume in this series is devoted exclusively to the question of ecumenism and interreligious dialogue, particularly as they are treated in *Unitatis Redintegratio* (the Decree on Ecumenism) and *Nostra Aetate* (the Declaration on the Relation of the Church to Non-Christian Religions), I will limit myself to reflection on one central theological debate. I will not be able to consider the many international and national dialogues that have so effectively advanced the cause of Christian ecumenism.

In both Parts One and Two we discussed the significance of the textual history of *Lumen Gentium* 8 and its assertion that the Church of Christ *subsists* in the Roman Catholic Church. Virtually all commentators recognize that this was not a question of semantics but of a substantive shift in church teaching that, at the least, affirmed some attenuated degree of ecclesiality for other Christian traditions. However, in the decades since the council, protracted debates have ensued regarding the extent of the shift in church teaching and its implications for how Catholics are to understand the status of other Christian communities.[56]

Leonardo Boff, in his *Church: Charism and Power,* interpreted *Lumen Gentium* 8 to mean that "the Church may also be present in other Christian churches."[57] Soon after, in 1985, The CDF issued a special *notificatio* that rejected Boff's interpretation. The CDF asserted that the council's teaching was that there was but one subsistence of Christ's church, namely the Roman Catholic Church; outside of the Roman Catholic Church there could be "only elements of the church."[58] One should note that the council never used the qualifier "only" but rather spoke of "many" elements of the church that were present outside the boundaries of Roman Catholicism. The CDF's interpretation might be defensible if one were to consider *Lumen Gentium* 8 alone. However, as Francis Sullivan has noted, if one also considers both *Lumen Gentium* 15 and *Unitatis Redintegratio* 3, both of which make reference to non-Catholic "churches and ecclesial communities," such a reading seems more difficult to sustain.[59]

In 2000, the CDF issued its controversial document, *Dominus Iesus,* stating that "the Church of Christ, despite the divisions which exist among Christians, continues to *exist fully* only in the Catholic Church."

It then asserts that "outside of her structure, many elements can be found of sanctification and truth." A few comments are in order.

First, the CDF is rendering the term *subsistit* as "continues to exist fully." As Sullivan has pointed out, it is the word "fully" that is crucial.[60] This addition allows the CDF to assert against Boff and others that there is only one subsistence of the body of Christ, the Roman Catholic Church, since only the Roman Catholic Church possesses the *fullness* of the means of salvation. If that is the meaning of *subsistit*, then by definition there can be only one subsistence of the church of Christ. This restrictive definition of *subsistit* would still require, however, that one recognize that Christ's church, while not technically *subsisting* in other Christian communities (since they would lack the "fullness" of means) would nevertheless be present in them in some other manner.

Second, the CDF's formulation that the church of Christ "exists fully only in the Catholic Church" is problematic insofar as it fails to preserve a distinction implicit in the council's formulation, namely the distinction between the institutional integrity which only the Roman Catholic Church can claim ("the fullness of the *means* of salvation"), and a more subjective or existential ecclesial vitality. Cardinal Walter Kasper has admitted that the CDF's formulation went beyond the teaching of the council in this regard.[61] The council *did* assert that the church of Christ continued to exist in the Catholic Church. It also taught that "it is through Christ's Catholic church alone, which is the universal help toward salvation, that *the fullness of the means of salvation* can be obtained" (*UR*, 3). However, the emphasis in the council's teaching is on the objective "means" of salvation present or absent within a Christian tradition. In other words, it was saying that, at a strictly formal level, the Catholic Church lacks nothing vital to manifesting God's grace and God's saving truth in the world. The Catholic Church possesses the scriptures, the sacraments, the apostolic office of bishops (entrusted with the responsibility for authenticating the apostolic faith proclaimed in the churches), the Petrine office (entrusted with securing the unity of the churches), and so on. The council readily acknowledged that many other Christian churches and ecclesial communities possess at least some of these "elements of sanctification and truth" and, consequently, these other Christian churches and communities are also means of salvation. The bishops could not ignore, however, that other Christian churches had, from the Catholic point of view, abandoned certain means of salvation (e.g., some of the sacraments or the apostolic office of the bishop) or celebrated them in a fashion that was, from the Catholic perspective, "defective."

Moreover, *Dominus Iesus* seemed to harden a distinction found in the conciliar documents between "churches" and "ecclesial communities." The CDF document claimed that only those Christian traditions with a valid episcopate and valid Eucharist were properly to be called churches. The late John Hotchkin, at the time the executive director of the U.S. Catholic Bishops' Committee on Ecumenical and Interreligious Affairs, claimed in an address to the Canon Law Society of America that this interpretation could not be supported by a careful reading of the council *acta*.[62] Such a study reveals that it was the intention of the council to affirm in a positive way the genuine ecclesiality of non-Catholic Christian communities rather than to insist on a restrictive use of the term "church." In part, the conjoining of the two terms, "churches" and "ecclesial communities," was proposed in sensitivity to the fact that most Protestant traditions in the West did not refer to their various worldwide memberships as if they were single "churches," preferring terms like "communion," "federation" or "alliance."[63] Although the council certainly assumed the importance of valid orders and eucharistic communion for church life, Hotchkin contended that the council wished to leave open the particular question of the status of orders and the Eucharist in individual non-Catholic Christian communions.

In short, there does not seem to be much justification for appealing to the teaching of the council in support of the view that other Christian traditions ought not properly be called churches.

CHURCH OFFICE AND THE EXERCISE OF LEADERSHIP

Perhaps no other area of church life was more in need of renewal than the structures and exercise of ecclesiastical leadership. Prior to the council, the responsibility for all church leadership was assigned exclusively to the clergy and the exercise of that leadership was understood in largely juridical language. Most issues concerning ecclesiastical leadership boiled down to questions of power: who had it and when and how could it be exercised. The council's new ecclesiological foundations effected a shift from a juridical to a properly theological conception of the church and ministerial leadership. The sacramental, relational, and pastoral dimensions of ordained ministry were brought to the foreground and key theological foundations were established which would later open the door to the possibility that the laity might also engage in ministry. However, the lion's share of the council's consideration of questions of church leadership was dedicated to the office of the bishop, with much less attention given to the presbyterate and hardly any consideration given to the diaconate or lay ministry.

When in Part Two we considered the council's teaching on ecclesiastical leadership, it seemed appropriate to limit that reflection to ordained ministry. The council had some important things to say about the laity and offered some provocative openings for the possibility of lay ministry, but it did not directly anticipate the flourishing of lay ministry that has occurred in the last four decades. Today, as we consider the post-conciliar reception of the council's teaching, it is no longer possible to consider ecclesiastical leadership without also considering the emergence of lay ministries in the church.

The Office of the Bishop

Since the council, numerous attempts have been made to develop the pastoral character of the bishop's office in relation to a theology of the local church. The 1983 Code of Canon Law draws from *Christus Dominus* 11 when it states:

> A diocese is a portion of the people of God, which is entrusted to a Bishop to be nurtured by him, with the cooperation of the presbyterium, in such a way that, remaining close to its pastor and gathered by him through the Gospel and the Eucharist in the Holy Spirit, it constitutes a particular Church. In this Church, the one, holy, catholic and apostolic Church of Christ truly exists and functions (c. 369).

This canon is significant in two regards. First, it defines the bishop in terms of his pastoral responsibilities to a local church and second, it eschews the language of power in favor of the language of pastoral care. As canonist Myriam Wijlens observes, "the bishop appears...not as a monarch but as a leader of a sacramental community."[64] The relative autonomy of the local bishop—an autonomy asserted at the council when it said that the bishop was a vicar and ambassador of Christ and not a vicar of the pope (*LG*, 27)—also finds expression in the 1983 code (c. 375).

In 2001 the synod of bishops met to reflect on the pastoral office of the bishop. As has become the custom, Pope John Paul II subsequently wrote a post-synodal apostolic exhortation, *Pastores Gregis*, on the synod theme. This exhortation has been largely overlooked. Yet it constitutes the most significant magisterial document on the ministry of the bishop in the post-conciliar period and therefore merits attention as the most extensive instance of the reception of both *Lumen Gentium* chapter 3 and *Christus Dominus*.

Pastores Gregis continued in the tradition of other post-conciliar documents to give pride of place to a theology of the bishop as shepherd, as is reflected in the very title of the exhortation, "The Shepherds of the Lord's Flock." The first chapter is titled, "The Mystery and Ministry of the Bishop." The chapter considers the bishop's membership in the college of bishops. Here we see a perpetuation of that theology of the bishop, found in certain conciliar texts and also present in both the 1983 Code of Canon Law and the 1990 Rite of Episcopal Ordination, which sees the bishop's membership in the episcopal college as *preceding* the bishop's relationship to a local church (*PG*, 8). It reflects a conception of the college of bishops succeeding to the authority of the college of apostles. The significance of this connection lies in the fact that the college of apostles was not comprised of individual pastors but of servants of the universal church.

The difficulty with this theology, however, is that the college of apostles and the college of bishops are distinct realities. The origins of the episcopate in the early centuries of the church clearly assumed that a bishop was ordained for ministry to a local church even as this ordination initiated him into communion with all other bishops. There is little sense in the early church that membership in the college of bishops was anterior to a bishop's pastoral charge to a local community. This is evident in the prohibition of absolute ordinations, that is, the ordination of a bishop without a call to serve a local community. In early Christianity, the only reason for an episcopal ordination was a local church's need for a pastor.

What we see in the perpetuation of this theology of the episcopate is the direct consequence of the debate on the relationship between the local and the universal church. If the universal church precedes the local, then membership in the college of bishops must precede a bishop's pastoral charge to a local church. If, on the other hand, the relationship between the local and universal church is seen as simultaneous and reciprocal, then one would expect that a bishop becomes a member of the college simultaneous with his being ordained to service of a local church. One's understanding of this debate also has a bearing on how one views the ecclesiological advisability of ordaining titular bishops, that is, bishops who are to be assigned to a diplomatic or bureaucratic (e.g., a curial office) post, rather than to pastor a local church. Such bishops are granted "title" to a church that no longer exists. We will evaluate this practice more fully in Part Four.

The second chapter of *Pastores Gregis* considers the spirituality of the bishop and addresses the danger of a bishop's ministry being reduced to that of an administrator (*PG*, 11). The chapter calls the bishop to a spirituality characterized by *kenosis*, the self-emptying that Christ himself embodied, and a life of simple service. The pope suggested that ultimately, as with all Christians, the spiritual journey of the bishop is grounded in the grace of baptism and confirmation. In this regard he cited the famous passage by St. Augustine:

> When I am frightened by what I am for you, then I am consoled by what I am with you. For you I am the bishop, with you I am a Christian. The first is an office, the second a grace; the first a danger, the second salvation.[65]

This episcopal spirituality, the pope insisted, could be further nourished through reliance on the maternity of Mary, the study of scripture, the celebration of the Eucharist, the prayer of the liturgy of the hours, and the practice of the evangelical counsels and beatitudes.

Chapter 3 turned to the ministry of the bishop as teacher. In this chapter we find a noteworthy meditation on the rite of episcopal ordination in which the Book of the Gospels is held above the head of the bishop-elect; it is a ritual that suggests that the bishop as teacher must always submit himself to the Word of God (*PG*, 28). This introduced a theme far too seldom reflected upon in any theology of the bishop's teaching office, namely the recognition that the bishop must first be a learner before he can be a teacher. The pope quoted St. Augustine: "with respect to the place which we occupy, we are your teachers; with respect to the one Master, we are fellow disciples with you in the same school." The pope developed this further, reminding bishops that "that which every Bishop has heard and received from the heart of the Church he must then give back to his brothers and sisters, whom he must care for like the Good Shepherd. In him the *sensus fidei* attains completeness" (*PG*, 28). Here we find an acknowledgment of the reciprocal relationship between the bishop as teacher and the sense of the faithful. The pope also recognizes the importance of the bishops' consultation with theologians:

> In carrying out this duty Bishops will derive particular benefit from open dialogue and cooperation with theologians, whose task it is to employ an appropriate methodology in the quest for deeper knowledge of the unfathomable richness of the mystery of Christ. Bishops will not fail to encourage and support them and the schools or academic institutions where they work, so that they can carry out their service to the People of God in fidelity to Tradition and with attentiveness to changing historical circumstances. (*PG*, 29)

In turn, of course, the bishop must exercise his own apostolic ministry to ensure that the unity and integrity of the faith is safeguarded.

The teaching ministry of the bishop, the pope contended, must serve the "new evangelization," that is, the evangelization of cultures and re-evangelization of countries that were historically Christian but in which the practice of the faith has waned. Bishops must make the authentic "inculturation of the Gospel" integral to their teaching ministry (*PG*, 30). They must see that their priests are trained to be good communicators of the faith.

Chapter 4 considers the sanctifying ministry of the bishop. Here the pope reflected on the conciliar teaching that the bishop's ministry was realized in its fullness when he presided at the Eucharist surrounded by the faithful of his church (*PG*, 33–37). Chapter 5 turns to the third of the three offices of the bishop, that of governance. The pope evoked Jesus' washing of feet as a gesture that captured the essence of the bishop's ministry of governance (*PG*, 42). The emphasis throughout this chapter is on the priority of pastoral service, which serves as the interpretive framework for any consideration of episcopal power. Here again the model of Christ the Good Shepherd was invoked. The pope also recommended that this ministry of governance be exercised in a consultative manner. He returned yet again to the language of St. Augustine, who insisted that *being for* the faithful does not preclude *being with* them (*PG*, 44). This openness to consultation, the pope warned, must not obscure the genuine responsibility for governance that is uniquely exercised by the bishop. The chapter then addresses the various groupings within the local church with whom a healthy and collaborative relationship must be cultivated.

The sixth chapter of *Pastores Gregis*, "In the Communion of the Churches," turns from the bishop's relationship to his local church to the bishop's ministry to the universal church. The pope mentioned the interventions of some of the bishops at the synod who raised questions regarding the possible application of the principle of subsidiarity to the relationship between the local bishop and the Holy See. He goes on to report, however, that "all the same, the Synod Fathers considered that, as far as the exercise of episcopal authority is concerned, the concept of subsidiarity has proved ambiguous, and they called for a deeper theological investigation of the nature of episcopal authority in the light of the principle of communion (*PG*, 56)." Finally, the apostolic exhortation also offers some developments regarding the bishop's relationship to the college of bishops and the ministry of the bishop of Rome, a topic we will explore further below. Although this papal document perpetuates some of the ambiguities of the conciliar teaching on the episcopate, it represents a genuine and positive development of the church's theology of the episcopate.

Episcopal Collegiality

No topic was more hotly debated at Vatican II than the notion of episcopal collegiality, and those debates have continued in the ensuing decades.

Papal Primacy and Episcopal Collegiality

In the council documents we find a number of passages in both the third chapter of *Lumen Gentium* as well as the *Nota Explicativa Praevia* that juxtapose two different ecclesiological frameworks. The first, evident in the *Nota*, is more juridical and accentuates the autonomous authority of the bishop of Rome in the exercise of his primacy. The second framework starts with the notion of communion and, without denying the supreme authority exercised by the bishop of Rome, emphasizes his role as head of the college. As head of the college, even when the pope acts on "his own authority," he is still to be in communion with his brother bishops. This latter view presumes a much higher degree of consultation and collaboration between pope and bishops than does the former.

In 1968 Cardinal Léon Josef Suenens, primate of Belgium and arguably the single most influential bishop at Vatican II, published a book, *Coresponsibility in the Church*, that laid out what he believed to be the full implications of the council's teaching.[66] The book explored the notion of shared responsibility in the church at multiple levels, but of particular interest was the cardinal's treatment of episcopal collegiality. Where the council had to be content with the juxtaposition of different conceptions, Suenens deliberately pursued the communion model of collegiality as that which best characterized the intentions of the council majority. In his memoirs, Cardinal Suenens reported a meeting with Pope Paul VI in which the pope expressed certain misgivings regarding what he saw as Suenens efforts to "democratize" the church.[67] In an interview held subsequent to his meeting with the pope, Suenens defended his views. His focus was on the pope's proper relationship to the college of bishops:

> For ecumenical reasons, as well as for theological reasons, we must avoid presenting the role of the Pope in a way that would isolate him from the college of bishops, whose head he is. When it is pointed out that the Pope has the right to act and to speak "alone," this word "alone" never means "separately" or "in isolation." Even when the Pope acts without the formal collaboration of the episcopal body—as he is indeed legally entitled to do—he always acts as its head.[68]

In 1969 an extraordinary synod of bishops was held to address the question of collegiality and the views of Suenens were much discussed. Indeed, the *instrumentum laboris* (a document drafted in advance of a synod which was used as the basis for synodal discussion) appeared to have been written largely as a rebuttal of Suenens. Suenens, however, felt himself vindicated by the many proposals that emerged from the language groups supporting his basic viewpoint. Yet other commentators viewed the synod as a repudiation of Suenens's conception of the relationship between papal primacy and episcopal collegiality.[69]

John Paul II adopted a more centralized view of papal primacy and appeared to hold a rather modest understanding of episcopal collegiality. In matters ranging from the appointment of bishops to the approval of vernacular translations of liturgical texts, the pontificate of John Paul II was marked by a pattern of expansive Vatican interventionism. This was further reflected, as we shall see below, in Vatican reservations regarding the authority of episcopal conferences and curial control over the conduct of the synod of bishops. This stock portrait of the pontificate of John Paul II has to be balanced, however, by a number of papal documents that offered insightful reflections on the papacy's relationship to the college of bishops.

His 1995 encyclical on ecumenism, *Ut Unum Sint*, was directed primarily toward Eastern Orthodoxy, a tradition that shares a historical episcopate but that has seen Vatican I's teaching on papal primacy as an obstacle to Christian reunion. In the view of the Orthodox, Catholic teaching on primacy presents the papacy as if it were an order of ministry superior to the episcopate, a fourth ministry within the sacrament of holy orders. The encyclical was an attempt to respond to this criticism. In *Ut Unum Sint* the pope presented a compelling vision of papal primacy with a striking similarity to the views of Suenens expressed decades before. It was a vision of primacy and collegiality understood as inseparable dimensions of the exercise of authority over the church universal. John Paul II portrayed the ministry of the bishop of Rome as one of service to the unity of the church. As such, the pope was not above the college but within it:

> This service of unity, rooted in the action of divine mercy, is entrusted within the College of Bishops to one among those who have received from the Spirit the task, not of exercising

power over the people—as the rulers of the Gentiles and their great men do—but of leading them towards peaceful pastures.... The mission of the Bishop of Rome within the College of all the Pastors consists precisely in "keeping watch" (*episkopein*), like a sentinel, so that, through the efforts of the Pastors, the true voice of Christ the Shepherd may be heard in all the particular Churches.... With the power and the authority without which such an office would be illusory, the Bishop of Rome must ensure the communion of all the Churches. For this reason, he is the first servant of unity.... All this however must always be done in communion. When the Catholic Church affirms that the office of the Bishop of Rome corresponds to the will of Christ, she does not separate this office from the mission entrusted to the whole body of Bishops, who are also "vicars and ambassadors of Christ." The Bishop of Rome is a member of the "College," and the Bishops are his brothers in the ministry. (*UUS*, 94–95)

In an unprecedented gesture, the pope also invited leaders of other Christian churches to explore with him ways in which the Petrine ministry might become less an obstacle and more a means to church unity.

One rather surprising response to *Ut Unum Sint* came in the celebrated 1996 Oxford lecture delivered by then retired Archbishop John Quinn. Quinn took up the pope's invitation to dialogue regarding the future of papal primacy.[70] This lecture, coming from a distinguished American archbishop, captured the imaginations of many and gave an unprecedented prominence to ecclesiological reflection on the exercise of papal primacy. Quinn noted the papal recognition in the encyclical that new forms of the exercise of primacy might be necessary as the church faces a "new situation." Quinn explored the principal features of this "new situation" and then proposed substantive institutional reforms necessary to redress certain dysfunctional aspects of present collegial structures.

John Paul II himself returned to the vision of primacy and collegiality first broached in *Ut Unum Sint*. In the final chapter of *Pastores Gregis* we find some provocative nods toward what might be called the

"Suenens position," that is, the view that the pope never acts alone in the sense of being separate from the college:

> [J]ust as the Bishop is never alone but always related to the College and its Head and sustained by them, so also the Roman Pontiff is never alone but is always related to the Bishops and sustained by them. This is yet another reason why the exercise of the supreme power of the Roman Pontiff does not destroy, but affirms, strengthens and vindicates the ordinary, proper and immediate power of each Bishop in his particular Church. (*PG*, 56)

In the teaching of both *Ut Unum Sint* and *Pastores Gregis* we are faced with an anomaly in the pontificate of John Paul II. The actual exercise of his papal authority, primarily through Roman dicasteries, often appeared authoritarian and thoroughly uncollegial, a point made delicately by Archbishop Quinn. To a large extent the curial activity of his pontificate was far more reflective of the juridical view of collegiality found in the *Nota Explicativa Praevia*. Yet this pattern of curial activity stood at odds with the pope's theology of primacy and collegiality, a theology far more reflective of the communion model that predominates in *Lumen Gentium*.

Institutional Expressions of Collegiality

So protracted were the conciliar debates over episcopal collegiality that relatively little attention was given to the various ways in which that collegiality could find institutional expression. Apart from numerous references in the council documents to ecumenical councils, there were also brief references to the synod of bishops and episcopal conferences, but without any real development. Since these two institutions have grown in significance in the decades since the council, it will be worth tracing their development and considering the debates regarding their status as expressions of collegiality.

Episcopal conferences as we know them today first emerged in the early nineteenth century, though one can find similar episcopal structures dating back to the particular synods of the early church. Since the council, the creation of episcopal conferences as a way to facilitate addressing common concerns by regional groups of bishops became much more common. Some conferences, such as the U.S. bishops' conference or CELAM in Latin America, became quite influential. The controversial promulgation of Pope Paul VI's encyclical on birth control, *Humanae Vitae*, led many episcopal conferences to issue formal interpretations of that document. In the 1980s the U.S. bishops' conference began to issue several well publicized pastoral letters. The high profile of these documents revived questions about the doctrinal teaching authority of these conferences.

At the 1985 extraordinary synod called by Pope John Paul II to assess the reception of the Second Vatican Council, the bishops requested a study of the status and authority of episcopal conferences. The result was a working paper introduced in 1988 by the Congregation of Bishops on the juridical and theological status of episcopal conferences.[71] The draft reflected a debate that had been brewing in certain ecclesiastical circles regarding episcopal conferences.

If in the 1960s Joseph Ratzinger and Jérôme Hamer were two proponents of the collegiality of episcopal conferences, by the mid-1970s their views had changed. After having become prefects for the Congregation for the Doctrine of the Faith and the Congregation for Religious, Cardinals Ratzinger and Hamer later revised their positions. This rethinking was instigated by a number of new considerations, not the least of which was the post-conciliar writing of an influential *peritus* at the council, the French Jesuit Henri de Lubac. In an important monograph written in the wake of the council, de Lubac considered the theological status of episcopal conferences from the perspective of a eucharistic ecclesiology.[72] According to him, in every celebration of the Eucharist two ecclesial modalities can be identified: first there is the communion of all believers gathered at the local celebration of the Eucharist, and second, there is the communion that exists among all local eucharistic communities. This communion of eucharistic communities is the universal church of Christ. The church is at the same time one and many, universal and local, but it is never something in between, at least not in the theological sense. Since episcopal collegiality flows out of the more fundamental principle of ecclesial communion, what holds for the communion of churches holds for the college of bishops. The individual bishop expresses collegiality precisely as bishop of a local church, and the whole episcopate expresses collegiality as a college. De Lubac concluded that a bishop could realize the collegial character of his ministry in only two ways: through the exercise of his ministry within the local church, and through his participation in the activity of the *whole college*. He admitted that episcopal conferences and world synods were *collective* acts of bishops that might be useful, but he resisted attributing to them a properly theological significance, since they were not manifestations of the whole college. Furthermore, de Lubac noted that episcopal conferences did not belong to divine law but rather were the product of ecclesiastical law.

While following de Lubac's line of argument, Ratzinger and Hamer also expressed concerns that the enhanced role of episcopal conferences could bring about a return to the kind of church nationalism that had appeared in times past under the guise of Gallicanism and Febronianism.[73] They further noted the danger of the bureaucratization of the ministry of the bishop in which individual bishops might become little more than functionaries who hide behind episcopal committees and vague declarations that inevitably lose their prophetic bite in the process of achieving episcopal consensus.

Of course, substantial arguments have also been marshaled in favor of episcopal conferences as legitimate if partial expressions of episcopal collegiality. The most important argument in favor of granting a doctrinal teaching authority to these conferences looks to the parallel situation of particular synods or councils in the early church. These regional gatherings of bishops, although clearly not representing the whole college, were considered authoritative, and often addressed properly doctrinal concerns.[74] Those who support this view follow the position taken by the early Ratzinger and Hamer in arguing for a more fluid understanding of collegiality, one grounded in the principle of ecclesial communion. This approach would recognize a gradation in the various ways of exercising collegiality, some of which may fall short of a full and formal collegiality (that possessed by the whole college) but which nevertheless possess a true theological character.

In 1998 Pope John Paul II promulgated the long awaited apostolic letter *Apostolos Suos*, addressing the question of the authority of episcopal conferences. In that document the pope offered a historical survey of the development of episcopal conferences and summarized the teaching of Vatican II and the Code of Canon Law. He confirmed the limited doctrinal authority of episcopal conferences and praised their contributions to the life of the church. *Apostolos Suos*, in its clear admission that these conferences were partial expressions of collegiality, went beyond the *instrumentum laboris* written a decade earlier. However, the pope stipulated that episcopal conferences could issue binding doctrinal statements only when: (1) they issued the document in a plenary session (not by way of a committee) and (2) the document was either approved unanimously or, having been approved by a two-thirds majority, it received a *recognitio* (formal approval) from Rome.

Apostolos Suos has not been without its critics. According to Joseph Komonchak, the document goes out of its way to avoid the comparison made at the council between episcopal conferences and regional synods of bishops.[75] Francis Sullivan has complained that the letter ultimately grants to episcopal conferences nothing more than either the aggregate authority of the individual bishops (when the bishops unanimously approve a document) or the authority of papal teaching (when the Holy See gives a document its *recognitio*).[76] It becomes difficult, from this perspective, to see any genuine collegial authority in such documents. With regard to Sullivan's position, much depends on how one understands the role of the canonical *recognitio*. Technically, in canon law, when the Vatican grants a *recognitio* to a document, it is not giving that document some new papal authority beyond that which it already possesses but is merely confirming that the contents of the document are in accord with the teaching and law of the universal church. Unfortunately, the actual process for obtaining a *recognitio*, at least in recent times, suggests that the Vatican sees its *recognitio* as more than merely confirming that the document is in accord with the present teaching and law of the church.[77]

Let us turn now to a second institutional expression of episcopal collegiality, the synod of bishops. Discussion of the draft schema on bishops during the second session of the council elicited numerous proposals for the reform of present ecclesiastical structures and the possible creation of new structures to better facilitate episcopal collegiality. The Eastern Catholic bishops, in particular, recommended their own experience with a standing synod of bishops that shares deliberative authority with a patriarch or metropolitan. Pope Paul VI's response to these requests came in the form of *Apostolica Sollicitudo*, a document hastily drafted by Cardinal Marella, creating the synod of bishops. The document was received with less than enthusiasm by many at the council. First, by issuing the document *motu proprio*, that is, by the pope's own authority, Paul VI was in some ways violating the spirit of the council in which decisions were being made collegially. Second, what was envisioned in the document was a far cry from what many bishops had called for. The synod of bishops, as proposed in *Apostolica Sollicitudo*, was not to be a standing synod with deliberative authority, but an occasional gathering of representative bishops for a limited period of time with strictly consultative power. As the synod of bishops has developed over the intervening four decades, three different synodal forms have emerged: ordinary synods that meet every three or four years; extraordinary synods that are convened to address special topics, often at the behest of the pope; and special synods that address issues of concern to particular regional churches.

The debate over the theological status and authority of the synod of bishops involves issues similar to the debate regarding the authority of episcopal conferences. Some argue that although synods, like episcopal conferences, represent less than a full expression of episcopal collegiality, collegiality can be realized in degrees and synods ought to be seen as real if partial collegial expressions.[78] Those who would grant collegiality only to an exercise of the whole college generally would not attribute any collegial authority to the world synod.[79] Representatives of the latter view have emphasized the synod's strictly consultative capacity and the prominence of the Holy See in determining the timing of the synod's convocation, its agenda, and the confirmation of its membership as indications that it should more appropriately be considered as a participation in papal primacy. This view is reflected in the treatment of the synod of bishops in the Code of Canon Law. In canons 342–48, there is no reference to the relationship between the synod of bishops and the whole college of bishops nor is there any consideration of the extent to which synods might be expressions of collegiality. Rather, the synod is related to the primacy of the bishop of Rome (c. 344).[80]

James Coriden has summarized a number of criticisms that have been raised regarding synods as presently configured: (1) the synodal process has been subject to excessive curial control; (2) there has been frustration regarding inaction on synodal proposals; (3) post-synodal exhortations have been written by popes, not the synods, and often have little relationship to synodal debates; (4) the synodal process itself involves participants having to listen to endless unrelated episcopal speeches; (5) real discussion of participants is limited; (6) the drafting committee often eliminates many proposals that emerge from the language groups; (7) only propositions garnering 95 percent approval of voting members are passed on to the pope.[81] Some of these concerns have been addressed by Pope Benedict XVI, who revised synodal procedures for the recent Synod on the Eucharist, shortening the length of the speeches and scheduling a daily session for open debate among the participants.

Subsidiarity

As we noted in Part Two, although the term *subsidiarity* is nowhere explicitly applied to the life of the church in the council documents, in the years since the council there has been a lively debate regarding the ecclesiological validity of this principle, particularly as regards attempts to determine the appropriate exercise and limits of papal primacy.[82]

In 1967 the synod of bishops recommended that the principle of subsidiarity guide the process of revising the code of canon law. Indeed, the preface to the new code explicitly affirms the applicability of the principle of subsidiarity to the life of the church even though the principle is largely avoided in the code itself. A decisive change in the evaluation of the principle of subsidiarity came at the 1985 extraordinary synod of bishops. At a gathering of cardinals assembled for the synod, Cardinal Hamer rejected the applicability of the principle, insisting that the council went to great lengths to avoid any ecclesial application of subsidiarity.[83] At a press conference after the conclusion of the 1985 synod, Cardinal Jan Schotte also rejected the legitimacy of subsidiarity as an ecclesiological principle. Both prelates insisted that the principle was inapplicable because the church was no mere sociological reality but rather a spiritual communion and therefore not subject to the sociological rules that apply to secular institutions.[84] This position was in keeping with the concerns expressed by Cardinal Ratzinger earlier regarding the dangers of a sociological reductionism and an ecclesio-logical relativism. The final report of the synod formally requested a study of the ecclesiological significance of the principle.

Since the 1985 synod the principle of subsidiarity has continued to be defended against its detractors. The distinguished social ethicist Oswald von Nell-Breuning, soon after the 1985 synod, insisted that subsidiarity remained applicable because the church was comprised of two dimensions, one social and the other pertaining to its supernatural mission. These two dimensions were inseparable.[85] Walter Kasper, then still a diocesan bishop, also spoke out against what he saw as an inappropriate spiritualization of the church. The council's elucidation of the theological concept of communion did not negate the claim that the church was still, at the same time, a *societas*, a human society.[86] Kasper's insistence on the continued relevance of seeing the church as a society did not constitute a return to a more juridical *societas perfecta* ecclesiology. Rather it presumed the incarnational character of the church as a human reality whose supernatural mission could not negate its humanity.[87] In a similar vein, Joseph Komonchak has pointed out the danger of responding to a sociological reductionism "with a *theological reductionism* which considers the Church so unique and transcendent that it can only be described in theological language."[88]

A concrete example of the pastoral implications of this debate was evident in an encounter between the Vatican and the German church leadership in the 1990s. According to German law at the time, a woman could obtain an abortion only after she had provided a certificate indicating that she had sought abortion counseling. The German bishops sponsored certain pastoral counseling centers with the specific purpose of dissuading women from obtaining abortions. Nevertheless, a woman could use the certificate obtained from a Catholic-sponsored consultation center to obtain an abortion even if she was advised against such action at the center. The German bishops argued that their continued pastoral support of these centers constituted a legitimate exercise of their pastoral authority within their local churches. Yet the Vatican intervened and demanded that the German bishops withdraw their sponsorship of these consultation centers. In the minds of many, the Vatican intervention amounted to a rejection of the applicability of the principle of subsidiarity to church life.

Reform of the Curia

The bishops at the council were eager to see a substantive reform of the Roman curia. In their mind, the curia was to serve not only the papacy but the whole college of bishops. The council limited its call for curial reform in *Christus Dominus* 9 and 10 because the pope had promised that a more specific reform would be undertaken after the council.[89] He began this process with the 1967 promulgation of *Regimini Ecclesiae Universae*, which expanded the number of curial departments, changed some of the names of the dicasteries, limited curial appointments to a five-year term, required the retirement of all curial prelates at the age of seventy-five, and added more diocesan bishops as members of various dicasteries. Paul VI also set about internationalizing curial appointments in order to lessen, somewhat, the influence of Italian prelates. In spite of the pope's efforts, complaints regarding the curia persisted and were heard at the 1969 extraordinary synod. Paul VI created a study commission on the reform of the curia in 1974, but he died before it could make its final report. Pope John Paul II reconstituted a commission to continue that work, resulting in the 1988 apostolic constitution, *Pastor Bonus*.

Pastor Bonus undertook a reform of the curia from the perspective of an ecclesiology of communion and a determination to orient treatments of papal and episcopal power in terms of *diakonia* (*PB*, 1). Such a framework, the pope insisted, demands that a collegial spirit undergird all the curia seeks to accomplish. The pope affirmed the legitimate authority of the individual bishops and the desire to preserve a genuine diversity in the life of the church. Nevertheless, the papacy must preserve the unity of the church and this requires, on occasion, a papal intervention that will often be exercised through the work of the curia and is justified in order to preserve a unity of faith and discipline (*PB*, 11).

In the norms promulgated by the constitution one must note a subtle but crucial shift in the description of the function of the curia. *Christus Dominus* had asserted that the departments of the Roma curia "perform their duties in his [the pope's] name and with his authority for the good of the churches and in the service of the sacred pastors" (*CD*, 9). *Pastor Bonus*, however, followed canon 360 of the 1983 Code of Canon Law in holding that the curia serves the pontiff directly and the local churches indirectly, making no mention of the pastors (bishops).

The new norms reduced the number of Vatican dicasteries and changed the title of several of the dicasteries that remained. Article 26 of the general norms called for greater consultation of episcopal conferences of the Latin church and synods of the Eastern Catholic churches. Roman congregations were expected to "assist" the bishops in the fulfillment of their role as "teachers and doctors of the faith" (*PB*, 50). The constitution highlighted the importance of *ad limina* visits (the traditional pilgrimage bishops are to make every five years "to the threshold" of the tombs of the apostles in Rome) which are to include a private meeting with the pope and other curial officials as an expression of communion between the pope and bishops.

The reforms called for by the pope's apostolic constitution fell short, in the minds of many, of the expectations of the council. It had called for a clearer distinction regarding the competencies of various dicasteries, but *Pastor Bonus* further muddied the waters, spreading competencies regarding certain matters (e.g., marriage law) across multiple dicasteries.[90]

Since the promulgation of that important document, Pope John Paul II continued in his efforts to internationalize the curia, and it is important to highlight the efforts that were made in his pontificate to appoint more laypersons to curial positions that do not involve the exercise of the power of governance. Still, criticisms have continued to haunt the curia regarding what many perceive as a consistent pattern of curial interventionism in the affairs of regional and local churches beyond that demanded by the legitimate concerns for the unity of the church.

A number of the proposals made by Archbishop Quinn in his Oxford lecture concerned "major structural reform of the curia." According to Quinn, in its present form the curia

> runs the real risk of seeing itself as a *tertium quid*. When this happens, in place of the dogmatic structure comprised of the pope and the rest of the episcopate, there emerges a new and threefold structure: the pope, the curia and the episcopate. This makes it possible for the curia to see itself as subordinate to the pope but superior to the College of Bishops. To the degree that this is so, and is reflected in the policies and actions

of the curia, it obscures and diminishes both the doctrine and the reality of episcopal collegiality.[91]

Quinn suggested that a special commission be created for the task of reforming the curia. There has, as yet, been no formal Vatican response to his proposal.

The Office of the Priest-Presbyter

As much of the council's teaching on the priesthood found in *Lumen Gentium* was elaborated in *Presbyterorum Ordinis*, a document whose reception will be explored in another volume in this series, I can only very briefly touch on post-conciliar reception of this element in conciliar teaching.

In Catholic theological studies on the priesthood since the council, one of the most important developments occurred as the result of the application of modern biblical and patristic scholarship to the study of the historical origins of the ministerial priesthood. Theologians such as Bernard Cooke, Edward Schillebeeckx, Kenan Osborne, and Thomas O'Meara would take advantage of these developments in their exploration of theologies of ministry.[92] They would highlight the relatively late emergence of the lay-clergy distinction in the early church, and point out that ordained ministry developed within a vision of the church that celebrated a diversity of gifts and charisms. All would agree that the term *ministry* needed to be expanded beyond the pre-conciliar identification with the priesthood.

Since the council, and particularly in the pontificate of Pope John Paul II, most magisterial documents have continued to give priority to the christological strand of the council's teaching on the priesthood, a strand that continues to stress the priority of the priest acting *in persona Christi capitis*, in the person of Christ the head of the church. This christological trajectory is reflected in Pope John Paul II's apostolic exhortation, *Pastores Dabo Vobis*. The pope describes the priest's ministry in the person of Christ as head and shepherd of the church. The pope emphasizes the servant dimension of the priest's role as shepherd:

Jesus Christ is head of the Church his body. He is the "head" in the new and unique sense of being a "servant," according to his own words: "The Son of Man came not to be served but to serve, and to give his life as a ransom for many" (Mk. 10:45). Jesus' service attains its fullest expression in his death on the cross, that is, in his total gift of self in humility and love....The spiritual existence of every priest receives its life and inspiration from exactly this type of authority, from service to the Church, precisely inasmuch as it is required by the priest's configuration to Jesus Christ Head and Servant of the Church. (*PDV*, 21)

Jean Galot and Avery Dulles have also offered fruitful explorations of this christological approach.[93] Galot grounded his theology of the presbyterate in scripture as well, focusing on the description of the priesthood of Christ in the Letter to the Hebrews. Galot contended that Christ inaugurated a new form of the priesthood, one that went well beyond the Levitical priesthood insofar as the Christian priesthood was to build up the church as a community of faith and love. Both the faithful and the ordained priest participate in Christ's priesthood, but each in distinctive ways. The ordained priest participates in the priesthood of Christ at the very level of his being. Galot rejected what he viewed as an overly functional theology of priesthood that stressed pneumatology over Christology and failed to attend to the ontological dimensions of the Christian priesthood.

Other theologians, like Edward Kilmartin, David Power, and Susan Wood, worry that an exclusive reliance on the claims that the priest acts *in persona Christi capitis* risks placing the priest outside the church. In order to avoid this, it is crucial, they contend, to place the priest's christological representation within the context of his representation of the church when he acts *in persona ecclesiae*.[94] This approach, guided by the ancient dictum *lex orandi, lex credendi*, follows the structure of the eucharistic prayers, which always place "the words of institution" (e.g., "do this in memory of me...") within the framework of the ecclesial "we" spoken by the priest-presider (e.g., "and so, Father, *we* bring you these gifts..."). The priest acting *in persona Christi capitis* can do so only in the power of the Spirit which is effected through the mediation of the church.

Three key issues have dominated the post-conciliar reception of the council's teaching on the priesthood: mandatory celibacy, the ordination of women, and the relationship between ordained and non-ordained ministry. The last of these will be considered below when we discuss the re-emergence of lay ministry in the church.

It is fairly well known that, during the council, Pope Paul VI asked the bishops not to address two pressing questions of the time, mandatory celibacy for clergy and the morality of artificial contraception. He promised to attend to both topics after the close of the council. This he accomplished with his 1967 encyclical, *Sacerdotalis Caelibatus*, and his 1968 encyclical, *Humanae Vitae*. Only the first concerns us here. In the wake of many pleas for a loosening of the restrictions on mandatory celibacy for diocesan priests, many were surprised when Paul VI offered a strong defense of the ancient tradition. He acknowledged the tradition of married clergy in the Eastern churches but insisted nevertheless upon a necessary link between celibacy and the priesthood. He did, however, open the door for the admission of married Protestant clergy into the Roman Catholic priesthood.[95] The issue has hardly gone away, with various individual bishops and bishops' conferences throughout the world continuing to send to Rome petitions for permission to ordain mature married men (often referred to by the Latin term, *viri probati*) in response to pressing pastoral needs. A number of bishops raised the question most recently in the 2005 Synod on the Eucharist.

A final issue that has dominated post-conciliar discussion of the priesthood concerns the possibility of the ordination of women. In 1976, the Congregation for the Doctrine of the Faith issued its statement, *Inter Insigniores*.[96] This statement concluded that both scripture and tradition supported the traditional prohibition of the ordination of women. It also produced a third argument made from "the analogy of faith" that was based on the priest's iconic representation of Christ as head of the church, a form of representation that demanded that the priest be male. This statement, far from quelling debate on the topic, only served to spur on numerous studies that addressed the historical and biblical arguments.[97] Some theologians rallied to support magisterial teaching, with a particular emphasis on developing the third, so-called iconic argument.[98] In the face of growing challenges to the church's official position, Pope John Paul II in 1994 issued his apostolic letter *Ordinatio sacerdotalis*, in which he stated that the church did not have the authority to ordain women since it was counter to the will of Christ. In spite of the elevated authoritative status that the pope's letter granted to this teaching, controversy has continued as many theologians have struggled to accept the arguments that have been offered in support of this teaching.

Many of the controversial issues regarding the ministerial priesthood that have emerged in the four decades since the council reflect the fact that, for all the council's many contributions, most of its energy on ordained ministry was spent on the episcopate, leaving little direction for a developed theology of the presbyterate and, as we shall see below, even less for a theology of the diaconate.

The Office of the Deacon

The Second Vatican Council wrote very little about the diaconate. Yet, by calling for a recovery of the diaconate as a stable ministry, one in which mature married men could apply, the council opened the door for one of the most dramatic new developments in the ministerial life of the church over the last four decades.[99]

The permanent diaconate was officially restored by Pope Paul VI in 1967 and has since become one of the fastest growing ministries in the North American church. Not only has the number of deacons mushroomed (there are more than thirteen thousand permanent deacons in the United States alone), so has their outreach. Some work as chaplains in jails and hospitals, others engage in catechetical ministry. Many preach and preside at baptisms, weddings, and funerals. Most assist liturgically at the celebration of the Sunday Eucharist. A growing number are serving as administrators for parishes without a resident priest-pastor. Yet, the permanent diaconate has not been fully received by the whole church. There are many regional churches that have made little use of this ancient ministry.

The status of the diaconate today is remarkably like that of lay ecclesial ministry: both are largely post-conciliar realities with ancient church roots. Both, in their contemporary forms, have grown at a rate that has outpaced theological reflection. I am not sure that we can adequately understand one without the other. In a recent review of literature on the diaconate, William Ditewig described the current pastoral theological context for the diaconate as a "confluence of three realities": (1) the growth of lay ecclesial ministry in the decades since the council, (2) the restoration of the diaconate as a permanent and stable ministry, and (3) the decline in the numbers of presbyters.[100]

The early decades of the development of the diaconate in the United States were difficult. Dioceses embarked on diaconal formation programs without much in the way of guidance regarding the content and structure of such programs. Oftentimes the theology of the diaconate was muddled. In the 1970s a particular emphasis was given to the liturgical functions of the deacon. In the 1980s emphasis on liturgical ministry tended to give way to a focus on the ministry of service and outreach, the exercise of *diakonia*. Since the permanent diaconate emerged at approximately the same time as the rapid growth of lay ecclesial ministry, there were some tensions that developed regarding the proper boundaries between these two sets of ministries, particularly since both deacons and lay ecclesial ministers often engaged in similar ministries (e.g., catechesis, visiting the sick).

Not all theologians welcomed the restoration of the diaconate. In 1983 George Tavard concluded that the restoration of the permanent diaconate was an ill-advised attempt to recover an ancient ministry that no longer had any real rationale. He thought it best to abandon the diaconate altogether.[101] More recently, some have complained of the sacerdotalization of the diaconate, with many deacons taking on elements of presidential ministry that are actually more appropriate to the priesthood.[102] Finally, an Australian biblical scholar, John N. Collins, has challenged the dominant theological understanding of the diaconate as a ministry grounded in humble service.[103] Collins holds that, in the New Testament, *diakonia* never referred to humble service, to what we might call acts of Christian charity. According to Collins, the tendency to think of *diakonia* as a kind of Christian "social work" crept into Christianity by way of early twentieth-century German biblical scholarship. His careful philological analyses suggest that the root meaning of *diakonia* lies, not in humble service, but rather in one's having been sent or commissioned to fulfill the work or mandate of another. In this sense, *diakonia* must be distinguished from ordinary Christian service to which all are called as followers of Christ. Collins insists that in the New Testament, and particularly in the writings of St.

Paul, *diakonia* describes a formal public ministry characterized by one's having been "sent" or "commissioned" on behalf of another. It is not yet clear to what extent Collins's work will have an impact on future theological reflection on the diaconate.

In spite of the difficulties that have emerged, in many churches in the United States the permanent diaconate has been very well received. Priests have found that deacons offer indispensable assistance in the exercise of their sacramental ministry. Early problems regarding inadequate diaconal formation have begun to be addressed both at the level of the universal church and here in the United States. An important turning point was the 1993 pastoral letter of Cardinal Bernardin on the permanent diaconate.[104] This document offered a developed and balanced exposition of the diaconate in terms of the threefold *munera:* the deacon was to exercise a ministry of service in the proclamation of the Word (teaching), in assistance at the liturgy and fulfillment of other liturgical functions (sanctification), and in the work of charity (governance). In 1998 the Congregation for Catholic Education and the Congregation for the Clergy issued two documents, *Basic Norms for the Formation of Permanent Deacons* and *Directory for the Ministry and Life of Permanent Deacons* that were intended to expand and standardize diaconal formation.[105] In 2004 the USCCB approved its own national directory for diaconal ministry and formation.[106]

Although most Catholics in the American church see the permanent diaconate as a positive gift to the life of the church, important issues remain. The theology of the diaconate is still at an early stage of development.[107] Tensions between lay ecclesial ministers and permanent deacons continue. Recently the ordination of women to the diaconate has received renewed attention. A report of the International Theological Commission offered a negative judgment on the question of whether ordaining women to the diaconate could be justified in the light of the existence of deaconesses in the early church. In their view, these deaconesses did not perform the same ministries as male deacons and therefore may not have shared in holy orders.[108] However, the report does not represent a formal judgment of the magisterium and significant studies have argued in favor of the restoration of women deacons.[109] Although the diaconate has, in the main, made significant and positive contributions to the life of the church, much work needs to be done in order to develop a theology of the diaconate that is faithful to both church tradition and the distinctive pastoral demands of the present moment.

Lay Ecclesial Ministries

The decades since the council have witnessed, particularly in the United States, a flourishing of numerous lay ministries. A 1999 study reported that in the United States alone there were over twenty-nine thousand lay ecclesial ministers, twenty thousand of whom worked in full-time ministry.[110] In some instances the increase in lay ministries has been due to a growing shortage of ordained ministers. This has certainly been the case regarding the emergence of parish administrators called to coordinate parish ministry and life in the absence of a resident pastor (a possibility provided for in c. 517, §2). In most instances, however, the emergence of lay ministries has been a direct consequence of a heightened appreciation of the council's teaching regarding the charisms that all the faithful possess by virtue of their baptism. In the fields of Christian formation, youth and campus ministry, family ministry, hospital chaplaincy, peace and justice advocacy, and a host of other ministries, church leaders have recognized the many gifts of the faithful that can contribute to the building up of the church and assist in the fulfillment of the church's mission in the world.

An important post-conciliar development that few at the council could have imagined has been the growing professionalization of these lay ministries, particularly in North America. Many laypeople have chosen to make ministry in the church their profession, often pursuing advanced degrees in theology and ministry formation. At a practical level this has raised new questions regarding such issues as just wages, health care and retirement benefits, the rights of lay ministers to due process in the filing of grievances, and the right to organize. Unfortunately, this growth in lay ministries has, in a real sense, "run ahead" of theological reflection on this new ministerial reality.

One trajectory of development in post-conciliar theologies of ministry has been to resist the pre-conciliar identification of ministry with ordination. The late Yves Congar remarked in the years after the council that his early work on a theology of the laity had focused too much on the lay/clergy pairing when in fact it made more sense to think in terms of community and ministries that serve that community.[111] Many since the council have followed Congar's lead and have imagined church ministries in terms of concentric circles, with ordained ministries in the center and other circles occupied by lay ministries distinguished by the varying degrees of commitment and formation that they require.[112]

The flourishing of lay ministries in the church has not been without its problems. Some in the church have complained of a new "lay clericalism" that has created yet another elitist caste in the church. A pressing concern raised by certain bishops and Vatican officials, and not a few priests and deacons, concerns the proper relationship between ordained and non-ordained ministry. Some fear that with the emergence of so many new lay ministries, conjoined with a decreasing number of priests, there has been an unacceptable "blurring" of the distinction between the ordained and lay ministers. This has led to an ambivalence in certain ecclesiastical documents regarding the role of the laity in the ministerial life of the church. For example, the 1983 Code of Canon Law, while affirming the positive contributions of the laity in participating in the life and mission of the church, was rather cautious in attributing the term *ministry* to the them. Elissa Rinere writes:

> In the code, "ministry" is a fulfillment of the hierarchical *munera* only. Laity may be brought into it by hierarchical invitation, but there is no ministry which belongs to the laity through baptism. There is no ministry which is fulfilled in the secular sphere, and there is no ministry which laity carry out on their own initiative.[113]

The 1997 Vatican interdicasterial document mentioned earlier prohibited using titles like "chaplain" in reference to lay ministers and seemed to suggest that the term *ministry* more properly referred to the ordained than to the laity. Some saw in this document a return to a pre-conciliar view of the lay minister as a kind of "priest's helper" rather than a true Christian minister. More recently we have seen Vatican documents like the revised *General Instruction on the Roman Missal* and *Redemptionis Sacramentum* that have tried to curtail liturgical abuses that were thought to blur the priests' unique role in the celebration of the Eucharist.

The American bishops have tried to respond to some of these concerns through the work of a special sub-committee on lay ecclesial ministry. As this volume goes to press, the U.S. bishops' conference is deliberating on a new statement, "Co-Workers in the Vineyard of the Lord: A Resource for Guiding the Development of Lay Ecclesial Ministry," that offers one of the most developed theologies of lay ministry to appear in an ecclesiastical document. One hopes that such a document will begin the hard work of building a consensus among theologians and church leadership on the rightful place of lay ecclesial ministry in the life of the church.

The length of Part Three is itself a testament to the impact of *Lumen Gentium, Christus Dominus,* and *Orientalium Ecclesiarum* on the church in the decades since the council. Virtually no area of church life has been untouched by the council's teaching. Yet arguments continue regarding the extent to which post-conciliar developments have been faithful to the vision of these council documents. The theological orientations introduced by the council have become broadly accepted, for the most part, in church life. Yet the institutionalization of these theological trajectories in church law and practice has been much more uneven. In Part Four we will consider what more work must be done both regarding the implementation of conciliar teaching and the formation of an agenda for some future council.

PART IV

The State of the Questions

Whenever I am invited to speak on the Second Vatican Council, one of the questions I inevitably receive concerns whether the time is ripe for a new council, a Vatican III or, as I sometimes suggest, Manila I! It is a difficult question to answer. On the one hand, as should be clear from our extended discussion in Part Three, one can hardly hold that the teaching of Vatican II has been fully implemented in the life of the church. There is much more to be done. On the other hand, history has shown that frequently the reception of a council's teaching came only with the teaching of a subsequent council. The Council of Nicea required the Council of Constantinople for its full reception. Surely a new council, at least in principle, would have the merit of being able to consider some of the questions that Vatican II left unanswered and to explore in greater depth topics the council touched on only briefly or omitted considering entirely.

In keeping with the format for this series, the title of this concluding section is "The State of the Questions." It could easily have been titled, "Where Do We Go From Here?" I see it as an opportunity for one theologian to consider where the church should go in continuing the process of ongoing reform and renewal encouraged by the council. I make no apologies for going beyond conciliar considerations. There are some in the church who would import into Vatican II studies the theory of "strict constructionism" that is often employed in American constitutional law. It is in this vein that William Dinges and James Hitchcock write:

> For many years a recurring issue in American politics has been the interpretation of the Constitution. There is a split between those who believe it should be understood narrowly and as far

as possible as the framers intended, and those who see it as embodying broad principles to be boldly applied in each age. The conservative-liberal split in Catholicism is of a similar nature, between those who read the texts of Vatican II carefully and cautiously—as "strict constructionists"—and those who see the Council not as the definitive word on the modern church but merely as the beginning of a continuing process by which the Church seeks to update itself.[1]

The late Cardinal Henri de Lubac pressed this distinction even further when he wrote of "the real Second Vatican Council" versus an alternative "para-Council" invoked by those liberals more preoccupied by what the council "ought to have said" or "meant to say."[2] Similarly, then Cardinal Joseph Ratzinger insisted that the ills of the post-Vatican II church were due not to the documents of the council but to a failure to attend adequately to the texts themselves.[3] As one who gives frequent presentations on the teaching of Vatican II, I certainly agree with these eminent church figures in their concerns that many who appeal to the council are in fact attributing to the council their own ideological agenda. Moreover, references to "the post-Vatican II church" often imagine a radical discontinuity between the council and the church before the council. However, I think it is a mistake to suggest, as Hitchcock does, that conservatives are the ones faithful to the intentions of the council (and hence, following the analogy from constitutional law, are "strict constructionists") while liberals have supplanted the council with their own reformist agendas. Hitchcock's analogy from constitutional law is simply inadequate.[4]

One of the reasons why the analogy of constitutional law does not hold is that, by definition, the American constitution is the foundational document in the American legal and political system. This constitution can be amended (though not easily), and there is an organic tradition of interpretation and precedent, but there will always be only one binding constitution. Councils and conciliar decrees do not function in the same way. The only truly foundational document in the Christian tradition is the Bible, and even it is foundational only as inspired testimony to the one full and comprehensive revelation of God in Christ, the living Word of God who is "both the mediator and the fullness of all revelation" (*DV*, 2). Conciliar decrees do not, for Catholics, constitute "new revelation." They offer binding articulations of the one revelation of God in Christ testified to in scripture. These articulations vary in their authority and relationship to that one revelation.

As Karl Rahner has famously observed, every ecumenical council—and every dogmatic formulation—is both an end and a beginning.[5] Conciliar documents, like all ecclesiastical documents, represent a normative expression of the church's response to the impulse of the Spirit as we seek to remain faithful to the gospel in each new historical epoch. And, as Yves Congar frequently reminded us, ecumenical councils are not primarily juridical events imposed upon the church from outside; they are formal manifestations of the church's own *conciliarity*, its ongoing life as an event of ecclesial communion.[6] Councils not only invoke and give normative status to past tradition, they impel the church into the future.

I have tried to honor the dynamic character of Vatican II and its teaching throughout this volume. I have outlined key moments in the genesis of the documents in Part One and sketched out the central themes from those documents in Part Two. In Part Three I surveyed the mixed reception and implementation of conciliar teaching, highlighting noteworthy theological debates. In this final section there will be fewer direct references to particular conciliar teachings. Instead, I will offer some modest analyses and proposals intended to help the church move forward on select issues raised by the texts and their postconciliar reception. In some cases, I will be considering the possibility of new syntheses where the council had to settle for juxtaposition. In other cases I will explore ways forward in the face of new pastoral and global contexts that the council members could not have anticipated.

THEOLOGICAL FOUNDATIONS OF THE CHURCH

As we stand four decades removed from the council, the time has come to get beyond the false polarization of a "people of God ecclesiology" and a "communion ecclesiology." The first is caricatured as a capitulation to secular democratic values while the second is derided for its a-historical, romantic, and overly spiritualized portrayal of the church. Attempts to make either of these trajectories a master ecclesiology are unwise. The council did not intend to impose one normative ecclesiology on the church but rather wished to highlight various dimensions of the church's nature and mission that must be given their due in any adequate theological understanding of the church. The church will continue to be enriched by a diversity of theologies that strive to render the church's nature and mission meaningful within new world horizons. Yet I am convinced that for those theologies to remain faithful to the council's nascent vision, they must continue to build on a theology of baptism.

The Priority of Baptism

When singing the praises of the council's most significant contributions, one invariably will mention the council's renewed theology of the laity. The standard narrative recounts the centuries-long preoccupation with the place of the clergy in Catholic ecclesiology and celebrates the council's placement of the laity in the foreground of its reflections on the church. It is true that the bishops made considerable advances in affirming the active participation of the laity in the life of the church and the church's mission in the world. The danger of this narrative, particularly when recounted by ordained church leadership, is that such a celebration of the laity can easily place the clergy behind a curtain where, like the wizard of Oz, they remain pulling church levers exempt from scrutiny.

It is all the more necessary then to privilege the council's rediscovery of a theology of baptism. By proposing a nascent baptismal ecclesiology, the council offered a line of reflection that could pull back the ecclesiastical curtain hiding the exclusive role of clerical leadership. This baptismal foundation encouraged a new mode of theological reflection on who we all are as church and, in particular, regarding how we might conceive the relationship between the ordained and the rest of the Christian faithful. It is a topic to which we will return.

We Are Baptized into Mission

We are baptized into mission. This mission is no mere extrinsic task imposed upon the church from without, it is the very *raison d'être* of the church. Because this volume was dedicated to an exposition of the teaching of *Lumen Gentium, Christus Dominus,* and *Orientalium Ecclesiarium,* I was not able to consider, as extensively as I would have liked, the essential missionary context for interpreting these three documents. This missionary context is more fully evident when we consider the contributions of *Gaudium et Spes* (the Pastoral Constitution on the Church in the Modern World) and *Ad Gentes* (the Decree on the Mission Activity of the Church). To read *Lumen Gentium* apart from *Gaudium et Spes,* in particular, risks a fundamental misapprehension of the council's vision of the church.

According to the council, the church's mission derives from its trinitarian origins. Salvation history reveals to us a God who sends forth Word and Spirit in mission as the very expression and fulfillment of God's love for the world. God's Word, spoken into human history from the beginning of creation and made effective by the power of the Spirit, in the fullness of time became incarnate in Jesus of Nazareth. The origins of the church, in turn, are inextricably linked to Jesus' gathering a community of followers who, after his death and resurrection, were empowered by his Spirit to continue his mission to serve, proclaim, and realize the coming reign of God. The council writes: "Proceeding from the love of the eternal Father, the church was founded by Christ in time and gathered into one by the holy Spirit" (*GS,* 40).

The affirmation of the missiological character of the whole church was one of the most important teachings of the Second Vatican Council. Although the council's desire to affirm a positive theology of the laity led it to attribute to the laity a particular apostolate for the transformation of the world, there are other instances where the council affirmed that it was in fact the mission of the whole church to transform the world in the service of the coming reign of God. Consequently, the attitudes and actions of all members of the church, including the clergy and consecrated religious, have social and political import and thus, in their own way, contribute to the furtherance of the church's mission to the world. Not all Christians will participate in the church's mission in the same manner, but none are exempt from the demands of the missionary character of the church. The Italian theologian Bruno Forte insists that

> the relationship with temporal realities is proper to all the baptized, though in a variety of forms, joined more to personal charisms than to static contrasts between laity, hierarchy and

religious state. . . . No one is neutral toward the historical circumstances in which he or she is living, and an alleged neutrality can easily become a voluntary or involuntary mask for ideologies and special interests. . . . It is the entire community that has to confront the secular world, being marked by that world in its being and in its action. The entire People of God must be characterized by a positive relationship with the secular dimension.[7]

When the council situated the whole church within the world and characterized the church as "sacrament of universal salvation" it insisted that all of the baptized, lay and clergy, have a responsibility toward the temporal order. This constitutes a thoroughgoing negation of any schema that posits two separate spheres of existence—the sacred and the profane. Rather, "there is the one sphere of existence with a complexity of definite relations that make up history."[8] It is this missionary perspective that most profoundly challenges certain enduring theologies of the laity that would present the laity as "foot soldiers" sent out by the clergy into the world in service of the world's transformation.

A Pneumatological Ecclesiology

In the many attempts at the institutionalization of the council's call for ecclesial reform and renewal far too little consideration has been given to the role of pneumatology, the council's theology of the Holy Spirit. John Beal, with an eye toward canon law's insufficiently trinitarian foundations, writes:

> The overemphasis on the christological perspective, which has even been described as a "christomonism," leads to the unspoken assumption that the Holy Spirit operates in the church primarily, if not exclusively, through the mediation of hierarchical authorities who act *in persona Christi* to mold and rule the priestly people in virtue of their sacred power.[9]

This failure is evident in the struggles many church leaders are having with the articulation of a theology of lay ministry and the cultivation of practices of communal discernment.

Power, Charism, and Office

Many bishops are well aware that the continued survival of their local churches depends on the exercise of the many charisms of the laity. Here in the United States bishops know that over 80 percent of those engaged in full time ministry are laywomen. Yet some balk at the articulation of any ecclesiology that would give a formal and constitutive role to the charisms of the baptized as anything more than a helpful augmentation to ordained ministry. One begins to suspect that what is actually at work here has to do with fear and power. Some church leaders would acknowledge the contributions of the lay faithful as long as church power remains exclusively in the hands of the ordained. The underlying framework motivating these fears is a "zero-sum" view of power that sees power as a finite commodity that must be divided up among church members. To give more power to some, in this view, means taking power away from others. This preoccupation with the distribution of ecclesiastical power is a stubborn remnant of a more juridical pre-conciliar ecclesiology. The future vitality of the church depends on the rejection of this exclusively juridical view of the church in the face of the council's budding pneumatology. The council consistently framed issues of power within the framework of service. This is reflected in its avoidance of "kingly" language in favor of the language of "shepherd/pastor" when treating the threefold office of priest, prophet, and king.

Power is not a dirty word. Canon lawyers will remind us that one of the appropriate and necessary tasks of canon law is to ensure the just apportionment and exercise of power.[10] Further, from a theological point of view, when exercised in the life of the church, power is not something that one possesses but a reality in which one participates, to the extent that one is open to the work of the Spirit. The council taught that the hierarchy does not compete with the rest of the faithful. The Spirit bequeaths to the church gifts both "hierarchic and charismatic" (LG, 4). Both those who hold church office and those who are called to exercise the gifts given to them at baptism do so empowered by the Spirit.

This pneumatological foundation for a contemporary ecclesiology has not yet been adequately explored in either church law or magisterial teaching. The council expressly affirmed the right of the faithful to use the charisms given them by the Spirit for service in the church and in the world. Yet, according to John Beal, this "is the only right asserted in the documents of Vatican II not incorporated into the revised code."[11] The contemporary concern of some church leaders that the presence of lay ecclesial ministers might threaten the role of the ordained reflects the continuing influence of the "zero-sum" view. When a theology of ministry shifts from power as control to a reflection on the charisms bequeathed to the church for its edification and mission, the primary question is no longer who has power and who does not. The main question now becomes: How can the various gifts exercised by all the Christian faithful be best employed in the fulfillment of the church's mission? In such a vision, lay ecclesial ministries will be seen not as a threat to the hegemony of the clergy but as a blessing to the church.

Communal Discernment

In the wake of the clerical sexual abuse scandals that racked the American Catholic Church at the beginning of the new millennium, one began to hear a renewed call for a greater accountability of church leaders.[12] But what could this language of accountability mean in a church that believes that its fundamental leadership structures are God-given and not subject to majoritarianism? Advocates for greater church accountability have hastened to point out that they are not calling for the church to become a liberal democracy. They recognize the unique ministry of apostolic leadership that is conferred by holy orders. However, they continue to assert that the exercise of this apostolic leadership cannot be undertaken in isolation from the life of the whole people of God.

Papal teaching has continued to support, in principle, the value of consulting the faithful. In his apostolic letter, *Novo Millennio Ineunte*, and in his apostolic exhortation on the office of the bishop, *Pastores Gregis*, Pope John Paul II affirmed the value of bishops exercising their ministry collaboratively.[13] In *Novo Millennio Ineunte* John Paul II quoted St. Paulinus of Nola: "Let us listen to what all the faithful say, because in every one of them the Spirit of God breathes" (*NMI*, 45).

Yet it must be said that, in spite of the lofty rhetoric in support of consulting the faithful, in the four decades since the close of the council there has been insufficient institutional implementation of the council's teaching regarding the supernatural instinct for the faith granted by the Spirit to all the baptized (*LG*, 12) nor of the constitutive role of the Christian faithful in the development of tradition (*DV*, 8). Many are convinced that the only Catholics being consulted by church leadership are those already disposed to agree with the present direction of church leaders. In the North American church there is a sense that what consultative structures exist are little heeded and that in the decisions that most affect the lives of Catholics, decisions in which the ancient church often turned to the whole faithful for Spirit-guided insight, there is little effort at real consultation. In short, contemporary Catholicism is in many ways still, in institutional terms, mired in the sixteenth-century distinction between a teaching church and a learning church. The task still lies before us to recover the ecclesiological vision of the early church that grasped that strong church leadership did not preclude consultation. There is no better witness to this conviction than that of St. Cyprian of Carthage, a third-century bishop committed to a strong episcopate but one who did not see strong leadership opposed to genuine consultation. He wrote the following in a letter to his clergy:

> [F]rom the beginning of my episcopate, I decided to do nothing of my own opinion privately without your advice and the consent of the people. When I come to you through the grace of God, then we shall discuss in common either what has been done or what must be done concerning these matters, as our mutual honor demands.[14]

Elsewhere he would reflect on the attitudes proper to a bishop:

> But it is unrepentant presumption and insolence that induces men to defend their own perverse errors instead of giving assent to what is right and true, but has come from another. The blessed apostle Paul foresaw this when he wrote to Timothy with the admonition that a bishop should be not wrangling or quarrelsome but gentle and teachable. Now a man is teachable if he is meek and gentle and patient in learning. It is thus a bishop's duty not only to teach but also to learn. For he becomes

a better teacher if he makes daily progress and advancement in learning what is better.[15]

It is safe to say that our present church polity is far removed from such a vision. When bishops are appointed from above with little input from the local church, when they are accountable to no one but the pope who appointed them, when widespread consultation is confused with polling or democratic balloting, when secrecy is maintained, not out of a concern for victims but to protect the guilty, then mutual accountability and a commitment to communal discernment so vital to the life of the early church is lost.

What we need are both new ecclesiastical structures capable of facilitating meaningful consultation of the faithful and the cultivation of habits and practices of communal discernment. I do not wish to ignore the significant advances that were made in the 1983 Code of Canon Law, but one of its most glaring weaknesses lies in its inability to institutionalize mechanisms for encouraging the church to become a genuine community of discernment. The church today requires a completely new code, one that begins with a pneumatological ecclesiology. Such an ecclesiology would acknowledge the constitutive role of the whole Christian faithful in the discernment of the Spirit and the creative reception of the one revelation of God in Christ. Such a code would have to establish structures that do not merely recommend consultation but require it as essential to the well-being of the church. As Pope John Paul II put it when addressing the U.S. bishops in September 2004:

> A commitment to creating better structures of participation, consultation, and shared responsibility, should not be misunderstood as a concession to a secular democratic model of governance, but as an intrinsic requirement of the exercise of episcopal authority and a necessary means of strengthening that authority.[16]

It is difficult to ignore the unusually strong language: consultation is an "intrinsic requirement" of the exercise of church authority.

As important as the reform of ecclesiastical structures for consultation is, perhaps more important is the cultivation of habits of consultation appropriate to church leaders. This is the kind of thing that cannot be institutionalized. By a habit of consultation I have in mind consultation not as a pragmatic exercise but as a genuine spiritual and ecclesial discipline. As a pragmatic exercise, consultation usually entails discussing one's views with those who are disposed to agree. It is no difficult matter to seek out close friends and ideological kindred spirits known to share one's convictions. Such consultation serves merely to confirm the rightness of one's views. The habit of ecclesial consultation, however, means consulting others out of a confidence that the Spirit might speak through others, even those who might present different and challenging viewpoints. Both the institution of formal structures of consultation and the cultivation of the habit of consultation will be necessary if church leadership is to respond courageously to the impulse of the Spirit in the church today.

A pneumatological ecclesiology situates the church in history seeking out, at every moment, the guidance of the Spirit. It sees the church as pilgrim, as a people who have not yet arrived at their final destination but who nevertheless are not aimless wanderers.

The Church as Pilgrim: Is Reform Constitutive for the Church?

The council's teaching on the eschatological dimension of the church made it easier to justify the need for substantive ecclesial reform. *Lumen Gentium* had taught that the church was always in need of "being purified" (*LG*, 8), and the Decree on Ecumenism insisted that insofar as the church was a human institution it would always be in need of "continual reformation" (*UR*, 6).[17] There are some in church leadership today, however, who challenge the continued focus on institutional or organizational reform, contending that the energy of the church today needs to be redirected from structural church reform to the church's mission to be an evangelizing presence in the world. Yet it would be a serious mistake to place in opposition the two imperatives of church reform and church mission. Structural church reform cannot be dismissed as a mere left-wing agenda, nor can it be placed in opposition to the church's mission in the world. Structural church reform is essential precisely in order that the church might better fulfill its mission in the world. The reason for this lies in the council's teaching that the church itself is a sacrament. The church does not merely administer seven sacraments; it is itself, in its visible reality, a sign and instrument of God's saving offer before the world.

But wherein lies the sacramentality of the church? If bread and wine are essential to the sacrament of the Eucharist because they serve as efficacious signs of a new sacramental reality, then what is it in the church that functions as an efficacious sign? The answer can only be, everything that comprises the church in its visible reality. The church certainly serves as a sacrament before the world not only in its members' ordinary life witness to the values of the gospel but also in its church law, offices, and ecclesial practices—all of these visible manifestations of the church participate in the church's sacramental reality.

This leads to a second question: if the whole of the church's visible reality participates in the church's sacramentality, what does this visible reality actually signify, that is, what does the church as sacrament "make present" to the world? In the language of scholastic sacramental theology, what is the *res* of the church as sacrament? The answer, I suggest, is the reign of God. The reign of God is a rich biblical metaphor that signifies God's active presence in history. This is why one of the most important teachings of the council was its recognition that the church was not itself the reign of God. God's active presence in history could be discerned beyond the boundaries of the church. Rather the church was the initial "budding forth" of God's reign. As sacrament of God's saving love, the church serves the liberative presence of God in history.

Now, since the church's sacramentality is grounded in its total visible reality, it is only as a visible, historical reality that the church can be sacrament of salvation and seed of the kingdom. What does this mean? It means that all things that participate in the visibility of the church participate as well in its sacramentality. Since not only Christian persons but also church laws, policies, and structures are part of the church's visibility, they too participate in the church's sacramental reality as a sign and instrument of God's reign. In other words, to assert the sacramentality of the church is to assert that church structures and policies matter. Church structures and policies can never be merely functional, "in-house" realities for a church that claims to be a sacrament of the kingdom. To the extent that these visible ecclesial realities are in keeping with the values of the kingdom of God, they share in the church's sacramentality. To the extent that any church structure, teaching, or policy is counter to the kingdom, it diminishes the church's sacramentality.

It is the commitment to the sacramentality of the church that renders questions of institutional/structural church reform more than a matter of church housekeeping or the rearrangement of ecclesiastical furniture. For the church to be an effective sacrament of the kingdom of God, one must be able to see in the whole visible reality of the church a "seed and sign" of that kingdom. When the visage of the church before the world reflects instead values and practices counter to the kingdom of God, the church's sacramentality is thereby compromised, and its mission undermined.

In the minds of many, church reform is associated with periods of church history, e.g., the Gregorian reforms or the Counter-Reformation. This historical view of reform movements can mistakenly suggest that reform is an only occasional church undertaking. The pilgrim status of the church suggests otherwise. Church reform is a permanent and constitutive dimension of ecclesial life. The only question to be asked is, what constitutes authentic church reform? The answer was provided by the council: "Every renewal of the Church is essentially grounded in an increase of fidelity to her own calling" (*UR*, 6). Authentic reform and renewal will always be motivated by a desire to make the church more fully what she is, the people of God, the body of Christ, the temple of the Holy Spirit, the sign and instrument of the reign of God.

THE UNITY AND CATHOLICITY OF THE CHURCH
IN A POSTMODERN WORLD

In a postmodern world, the questions surrounding the relationship between unity and diversity in the church have particular relevance. The term "postmodern" means many things to many people. It is often used to describe a certain critique of modernity. The postmodern mentality is suspicious of the modern tendency to subsume particular experiences into some overarching account of "how the world works." Modernity's penchant for grand theories (think of both capitalism and Marxism) that provide totalizing explanations of history or human nature is called into question by postmodern critics. They point out that these theories tend to take one perspective on the world at large or human experience and universalize that perspective. What inevitably ensues is the imposition of one perspective or interpretive scheme on all human experiences, often at the expense of those features of a set of experiences that may not fit into the interpretive scheme.

Globalization constitutes yet another salient characteristic of our postmodern situation. By globalization I am referring to a tension experienced between conflicting impulses.[18] In the wake of the Second World War, the birth of the United Nations, and the demise of the Soviet Union in 1989, there has been a pronounced impulse toward a more unified view of the world. This sense of global unification has been effected by advances in modern communications and transportation technologies that have compressed our sense of space and time. Global unification has also, in a sense, been furthered by the unfettered expansion of neoliberal capitalism which has brought the ethos of the free market and certain icons of Western culture to the world (consider the ubiquity of MacDonald's).

At the same time, the phenomenon of globalization has also brought with it a sense of social fragmentation. We have become more aware than ever of persistent cultural and religious differences that resist homogenization and force us to come to terms with a deep pluralism that often seems unbridgeable. This tendency, in its most extreme form, has been expressed in a violent tribalism and the growing appeal of various religious fundamentalisms. The tension between the unifying tendencies of neoliberal capitalism and a sense of social fragmentation brought on by new tribalisms is expressed in the title of Benjamin Barber's still helpful analysis of globalization, *Jihad vs. McWorld*. In that volume Barber writes:

> The forces of Jihad and the forces of McWorld operate with equal strength in opposite directions, the one driven by parochial hatreds, the other by universalizing markets, the one recreating ancient subnational and ethnic borders from within, the other making national borders porous from without."[19]

What impact has this new postmodern consciousness had on the church?

The postmodern critique of modernity's penchant for grand, universalizing narratives has its analogue in the church. In moral theology one might think of certain deductive approaches to natural law that naively assume that human nature itself is a universal and unchanging reality that can be easily understood. In ecclesiology, modernity manifested itself in abstract accounts of the church. During the 1950s, the French ecclesiologist Charles Journet would develop an ecclesiology that was built on an application of the four Aristotelian causes to the nature and mission of the church.[20]

A postmodern Catholic ecclesiology must challenge the adequacy of an abstract, formal treatment of the church.[21] We have already discussed Vatican II's reaffirmation of a theology of the local church. The postmodern emphasis on attending to the particular suggests the importance of the council's approach. Even more than the bishops could have known at the council, it appears today that the church can best be understood by careful reflection on the local church as an event, in its continuous, graced engagement with the world in geographically, temporally, and culturally specific contexts. This suggests the need for a renewed reflection on the catholicity of the church.

A New Catholicity

Robert Schreiter has called for a renewed and expanded understanding of the catholicity of the church.[22] Catholicity has for too long, at least in Roman Catholicism, been interpreted with an eye toward the geographic extension of the global reach of the church (often described as the church's universality) and in view of the orthodoxy of the church's faith. Yet these two aspects do not exhaust the meaning of the church's catholicity. It is true that catholicity is already an attribute of the church by virtue of the gift of revelation that was given in its fullness in Christ. The "whole" of the faith is already encountered in the gift of Christ. At the same time, catholicity denotes an eschatological value insofar as the fullness of divine revelation will never be in the full possession of this pilgrim church prior to the consummation of history. As *Dei Verbum* reminded us, the church is always moving toward the "plenitude of truth" (*DV*, 8).

How can we assert both the fullness of God's revelation in Christ and the church's movement toward "the plenitude of truth"? One answer lies in the theological category of reception. For much of the Catholic Church's modern history, at least since the Reformation, there has been a near-exclusive focus on a theology of tradition that attended to the ways in which the apostolic faith has been handed on. Contemporary hermeneutics and communications theory, however, have insisted on the importance of attending to not only the process of handing on the faith but also the process of its reception in concrete Christian communities. The faith of the church develops from generation to generation and place to place as concrete Christian communities receive the gospel and make it their own. This means that the apostolic faith must be conceived not as something static and unchanging but as a dynamic and living reality that is always embodied not simply in propositional statements and theological treatises but also in the lived faith of the people. Karl Rahner's famous observation that with Vatican II the Catholic Church was now on the brink of becoming a genuine "world church" itself suggests the direction that further reflection on the church's catholicity must take. Catholicity can no longer refer to a church already in possession of some *a priori* universal faith that is then shared in its missionary endeavors. As Rahner put it, the church is not to be "an export firm." Catholicity must refer to the dynamism by which the apostolic faith is growing in fullness through its various receptions in concrete space and time. One is reminded of Venerable Bede's observation that "every day the church gives birth to the church."[23] The catholicity of the church is manifested in this global, ecclesial birthing process. Commenting on this process, Joseph Komonchak writes:

> The apostolic Gospel comes with the power of the Spirit and is received by faith, and where this event of communication takes place, the Church is born again. Where this event does not take place, where the Gospel is preached in vain, no Church arises. Where the Gospel ceases to be believed, the Church ceases to exist. The whole ontology of the Church—the real "objective" existence of the Church—consists in the reception by faith of the Gospel. Reception is constitutive of the Church.[24]

Catholicity is realized dialogically. At one level this dialogue occurs by way of each local church's engagement with the world in its own social, cultural, economic, and political context. At a second level and simultaneously, this dialogue occurs as a series of ecclesial gift exchanges within the communion of churches. The catholicity of the church is built up wherever these exchanges are cultivated. The communion of churches is enriched when the diverse churches of Mexico City and Bangkok find ways to share their unique receptions of the gospel within the larger communion of churches.

This renewed emphasis on the church's catholicity can shed new light on the debate between Cardinals Kasper and Ratzinger regarding the relationship between the local and universal church. The question becomes less one of priority, the local or the universal, and more one of seeing the relationship between the local and universal as a relationship that preserves and enriches the church's catholicity. The "fullness" of the faith is realized in the numerous local receptions of the gospel within their distinctive social contexts as well as in the exchange of these local receptions of the gospel among the communion of churches. It is always within the communion of local churches that the "church gives birth to the church."

The catholicity of the church is not just realized globally. The challenges of postmodernity demand that the church develop a heightened sense of the catholicity of each local church, where, within local communities, we find ourselves enriched by the encounter with those whom we experience as "other" in some defined way. A paradox of global communications technologies and the emerging "information age" is that with the democratization of knowledge has come not more independent and open-minded dialogue about issues of import but a heightened partisanship and parochialism. *New York Times* columnist David Brooks writes:

> Once you've joined a side, the information age makes it easier for you to surround yourself with people like yourself. ...We don't only want radio programs and Web sites from members of our side—we want to live near people like ourselves....So every place becomes more like itself, and the cultural divides between places become stark. The information age was supposed to make distance dead, but because of clustering, geography becomes more important....[M]any of us find ourselves living in places that are overwhelmingly

liberal or overwhelmingly conservative. When we find ourselves in such communities, our views shift even further in the dominant direction. You get this self-reinforcement cycle going, which social scientists call "group polarization." People lose touch with others in opposing, now distant, camps. And millions of kids are raised in what amount to political ghettoes.[25]

This cultural phenomenon has its parallel in the church. Among the religious elites in the church (i.e., clergy, lay ecclesial ministers, theologians) a similar polarization is occurring. The politics of demonization are as much in evidence on the pages of the *Wanderer* or the *National Catholic Reporter* as they are on talk radio with Rush Limbaugh or Al Franken. It is easier than ever to associate oneself with other Catholics who share the same ideological predilections. Moreover, Catholic parishes are often as culturally and socio-economically segmented as the neighborhoods in which they are situated. This new situation presents new pastoral challenges to nourish the catholicity of the local church. Multicultural parishes are too often content to sustain quasi-independent African-American or Latino or East Asian subparishes alongside the Anglo parishioners in a way that does not encourage authentic interaction. The theological value of catholicity must not be reduced to mere tolerance. We must come to see our positive engagement with other cultures and ideological thought worlds as a means of enriching our own faith. To put the matter more strongly, we cannot be content with diverse cultures and ideologies simply co-existing at a respectful distance. The catholicity of the church demands that these diverse cultures and thought worlds engage one another in conversation and extended social and liturgical interaction. As many of our dioceses and parishes are becoming more multicultural in their make-up, and our ideologies more polarized, sustaining the catholicity of the local church may in fact be one of the North American church's greatest pastoral challenges.

A renewed appreciation for the catholicity of the church must also inform our sense of the place and contributions of the Eastern Catholic churches and those of Christian churches not in full communion with Rome.

Eastern Catholic Churches

Both during the council itself and in the intervening decades, the Eastern Catholic churches have been offered as a viable model for ecumenical reunion. It is a flawed strategy. Such an approach invites accusations of a renewed uniatism, that is, a strategy of using the Eastern Catholic churches as a kind of "bait" to encourage Orthodox reunion with Rome. The severely circumscribed autonomy granted to the Eastern churches in the CCEO makes it almost impossible to imagine any other Eastern Orthodox church willing to enter into visible communion with Rome on similar terms. In fact, both the Decree on the Catholic Churches of the Eastern Rite and the Eastern code acknowledge a certain provisionality to the situation of the Eastern churches and recognize that, in any imagined future with Eastern Orthodoxy, the status of the Eastern churches would have to change.

One knotty question that has emerged in the decades since the council concerns the diaspora status of many of the Eastern Catholic churches. Although the CCEO grants limited autonomy to the Eastern churches *within* their historical territories, beyond those territories that autonomy has been rigidly circumscribed, as is evident in the prohibition of the ordination of married men for the Eastern churches in eparchies beyond their traditional territorial boundaries. As Victor Pospishil has ruefully observed,

> It is truly a strange phenomenon . . . when a Christian community is prevented by law from preserving full ties with its own spiritual children, scattered in various parts of the globe.[26]

One can sympathize with the frustrations expressed by many Eastern Catholics. At the same time, in light of what was said above regarding the catholicity of local churches, we must consider other ecclesiological issues at play here beyond the perceived threat of Roman centralization.

One of the ancient principles that guided early Christian church polity was the axiom, "one bishop for one city," first articulated in canon 8 of the Council of Nicea. This axiom certainly had a pragmatic element as the early church adapted itself to pre-existing civic structures, but it also enshrined a central ecclesiological principle, namely the catholicity of the local church.[27] The rejection of multiple episcopal jurisdictions in one city was based in large part on a conviction that the unity of the exercise of *episkope* in one locality best preserved the catholicity of the church. It was important to maintain a local church in which Christians of various social-economic ranks and ethnicities could still gather at the one eucharistic synaxis presided over by the one bishop. Each eucharistic synaxis was a renewal of the Pentecost event in which ethnic and cultural differences were not repudiated but rather drawn into the larger communion of faith. This principle was largely preserved in early Christianity, both East and West. Yet in our contemporary situation it is now compromised on both sides.

Eastern Orthodoxy is having to grapple, particularly here in the United States, with multiple and overlapping episcopal jurisdictions, often based on historical ethnic identities. In the Roman Catholic Church we see some challenges to the principle in the establishment of a military ordinariate (a bishop assigned jurisdiction over military chaplaincies) and the existence of the personal prelature Opus Dei. However, it is the situation of the multiple Eastern Catholic churches that has challenged the ecclesiological rationale of this ancient axiom most dramatically. Hervé Legrand explains how multiple, overlapping jurisdictions among the Eastern Catholic churches first came about:

> It is in the setting of the Ottoman Empire that the different churches united to Rome found themselves with bishops juxtaposed one toward another, especially in the two refugee countries which became Lebanon and Egypt.[28]

This situation of multiple, territorially overlapping jurisdictions has developed anew in the diaspora situation in which many Eastern Catholics who have emigrated to the West find themselves. It has created a substantial pastoral dilemma. On the one hand, Eastern Catholics are more than justified in asking about their right to provide for their "spiritual children," as Pospishil put it, wherever they may be. To the extent that these spiritual needs are met by way of territorially overlapping episcopal jurisdictions, however, the catholicity of the local church can be compromised. An alternative proposed by

Legrand would be that, where Eastern Catholics live in a diaspora situation, there be a return to the principle of one bishop, one city. This principle would be modified, however, to include the possibility of a collegial exercise of the catholic ministry of *episkope*, perhaps by the use of a local "college" of bishops, one ordinary and the others auxiliary, within one city. In this situation, we would abandon the fiction of giving to auxiliary bishops a non-existent see situated in some now unpopulated region of the African Sahara. Instead we would grant to auxiliaries a collegial share in the exercise of the catholic ministry of *episkope* in one territorial diocese, delegating to some among them special concern for those who belong to a distinct Eastern Catholic tradition. Here the collegial exercise of *episkope* would honor the particular needs of Eastern Catholics while drawing them into the life of the local church catholic. Such a practice would not preclude, moreover, a situation in which the local bishop himself belonged to an Eastern church.

Finally, a real and not merely ceremonial affirmation of the integral place of Eastern Catholic churches would suggest the possibility of an intra-ecclesial reception of certain Eastern traditions. There is no reason why the Western church could not prayerfully consider the value of receiving certain Eastern ecclesial practices, such as the ordination of married men, the deliberative standing of a synod of bishops, and the synodal election of bishops.[29] I will have more to say about such proposals later, but here it is sufficient to note that such practices must not be evaluated as if they were novelties; they are revered traditions in the East and the best way to affirm the significance of the East must involve going beyond a reluctant accession to their ornamental role to a genuine consideration of the ways in which their traditions might enrich the whole communion of churches, East and West.

Catholicity and Ecumenism

A further consequence of the church's living in a postmodern situation is the need for a new assessment of the differences that obtain among the various Christian churches. Our experience of the broad diversity of world religions cannot help but shape the way we experience Christianity. The profound differences we see in our encounters with the

great religions of the world certainly relativize the differences that
obtain among the Christian churches.[30] Put differently, when considered against the horizon of our experience of world religions, the
commonalities shared among Christians will inevitably be greater than
the differences. This raises a number of questions regarding the future
of ecumenism, most of which are treated in depth in Cardinal Cassidy's contribution to this series. However, we must consider here the
debate regarding the ecclesiological status of other Christian traditions that has emerged as a result of the teaching of *Lumen Gentium*.

The last four decades have seen a lively discussion regarding the
authentic interpretation of the council's teaching that the church of
Christ "subsists in" the Roman Catholic church. The specific controversy concerns the extent to which other Christian traditions participate in the church of Christ and whether and to what extent they can
properly be called "churches." I provided a brief summary of that
debate in Part Three. Here I would like to consider the issue from a
different perspective.[31]

The council taught that the fullness of the means of salvation can
be found only in the Roman Catholic Church. The "fullness" the
council had in mind appears to be both objective and quantitative. It is
objective insofar as it is concerned with the verifiable presence or
absence of various "means of salvation" (e.g., the sacraments or the
scriptures) within a particular tradition. It is quantitative because it
imagines that one could enumerate these various means, developing a
quasi-checklist that could then be used to evaluate other Christian traditions. It is this emphasis on an objective and quantitative fullness
that, in my view, must be re-evaluated.

First, let us consider the council's focus on the objective means of
salvation and ask about what is not being addressed in this teaching.
No conciliar document, nor any post-conciliar document that I am
aware of, attends to the possibility that the Catholic Church, in certain circumstances, might fail to appropriate or activate the objective
"means of salvation" in its possession. Francis Sullivan puts the matter
well:

Of course it must be kept in mind that this is a question of
institutional integrity: of fullness of the *means* of salvation.
There is no question of denying that a non-Catholic commu-

nity, perhaps lacking much in the order of means, can achieve a higher degree of communion in the life of Christ in faith, hope and love than many a Catholic community.[32]

Cardinal Walter Kasper, current president of the Pontifical Council for Christian Unity, himself admitted that this language of a "fullness" abiding in the Roman Catholic church

> does not refer to subjective holiness but to the sacramental and institutional means of salvation, the sacraments and the ministries. Only in this sacramental and institutional respect can the Council find a lack (*defectus*) in the churches and ecclesial communities of the Reformation. Both Catholic fullness and the *defectus* of the others are therefore sacramental and institutional, and not existential or even moral in nature; they are on the level of the signs and instruments of grace not on the level of the *res*, the grace of salvation itself.[33]

This insight has implications for the pastoral situation of the church today that has not been sufficiently considered.

Let me situate the shared insight of Sullivan and Kasper more concretely. Imagine a pastoral situation in which we have in the same neighborhood Grace Lutheran Church and St. Bernadette's Catholic parish. Now, from the perspective of the council's teaching, Grace Lutheran would be lacking some specific means of salvation available, in principle, to St. Bernadette's. Presumably, they do not have access to a universal ministry of unity (the papacy), the sacrament of reconciliation, or the full reality of eucharistic communion. Yet in its concrete pastoral life Grace Lutheran Church might be building a Christian community that emphasizes fellowship, hospitality, and the dignity and importance of one's baptismal vocation. They might stress the importance of being biblically literate and living with fidelity a biblical vision of discipleship. On the other hand, St. Bernadette's, though possessing the fullness of the objective means of salvation, might be a community where Christian hospitality is almost completely absent, a community in which baptism is simply a christening ritual done to infants, a community in which the scriptures are poorly proclaimed and the homilies are filled with arcane, pious references and silly jokes but say little about the concrete demands of discipleship in daily life. In this scenario we must grant the possibility that Grace Lutheran, though lacking an ecclesial fullness at the level of objective means of salvation, might in fact, at the level of pastoral life, be fostering a form of Christian community that more effectively brings its members into communion with God and Christ and more effectively lives out Christ's call to discipleship and mission than is possible at St. Bernadette's.

This hypothetical situation helps explain a vexing pastoral reality experienced by many in the North American church. Many Catholics leave the Catholic Church for other churches, not because of doctrinal difficulties—they are not, by and large, troubled by papal infallibility or the Catholic belief in the eucharistic real presence—but because they do not experience in Catholic parishes the sense of fellowship or hospitality that they find in other churches. These former Catholics will tell you that the life of discipleship and the offer of communion with God in Christ are being *more effectively realized* for their family within the local Protestant congregation they have joined.

I am not trying to defend the decisions of these Catholics to leave Catholicism for another church. I worry about a dangerous congregationalism implicit in their decision that overvalues the local community at the expense of the participation in the larger communion of churches. But, even from a Catholic perspective, it cannot be denied that every Christian's access to the "universal church" comes only through participation in a concrete, flesh and blood, local community.

Now let us turn to the quantitative aspect of the council's teaching. The conciliar teaching suggests that one can enumerate the various "means of salvation" present in various Christian traditions (all of which are present in the Roman Catholic Church) and score them accordingly. The result would be a checklist for assessing various Christian traditions. Does this quantitative view do justice to the mystery of how Christians encounter God's saving love concretely in the life of the church? I am not saying that the council's teaching was wrong in suggesting the possibility of a list of the means of salvation present in the church. However, a review of the history of Christianity suggests that the genuine flourishing of ecclesial life has seldom been as dependent on possession of the quantitative *fullness* of the means of salvation as on the extent to which a given community has appropriated certain of these means in its pastoral life. If one looks at the history of Christianity as a totality, then, undoubtedly, the institutional integrity (e.g., the possession of a historical episcopate and a Petrine office) of the Roman Catholic Church has played an important role in its continued existence. If, however, one looks at particular moments of revitalization and renewal, the vitality of church life was more often the consequence of a renewed commitment to one or other aspect of Christian life that had fallen into desuetude. For significant periods in church history, certain "means of salvation" played a relatively peripheral role in the life of the church. For example, many of the churches of the first three centuries flourished with only minimal if any contact with the church of Rome. Or consider the Reformation. When one compares the atrophied state of Catholic sacramental life and the shameful corruption of the Renaissance papacy on the eve of the Reformation with the early vitality of the churches of the Reformation, is an assessment of which communion possessed the greater number of "means of salvation" really helpful?

Future reflection on this important topic must consider the catholicity of the church, as it extends to Catholicism's relations with other Christian traditions, not only quantitatively and objectively but also existentially and pastorally. At the least, we must conclude that our postmodern context is likely to require a different grid for reflecting on the unity and catholicity of the church. Full, visible unity among the churches must remain an indispensable goal of every authentic Christian tradition. What, concretely, full visible unity actually requires, however, will have to be thought anew.

CHURCH OFFICE AND THE EXERCISE OF LEADERSHIP

The Catholic Church has always assumed the necessity of formal leadership structures for the full realization of the church's mission in the world. A healthy church leadership can only serve the cause of the church's mission. A dysfunctional leadership, or a leadership racked by scandal, will only distract from the church's mission. A good example of this was in full view during the U.S. presidential election campaign of 2004. In that election there were numerous issues that deserved the attention of the American bishops, yet the credibility of the bishops, compromised by the clerical sexual abuse scandal, rendered their witness largely ineffective. I would like to consider in some detail the aspects of church leadership today that will require either reform or further theological development if our leaders are to guide the church effectively in the fulfillment of its mission. Any theology of church office, leadership, and ministry adequate to our times will have to account for both the essential role of the ordained and the re-emergence of lay ecclesial ministries.[34]

Our most distinctive Christian relationship comes from baptism. Yet the history of the church gives witness to many other ways in which Christians were ordered within the community. Up through the Middle Ages one continues to find evidence of a plurality of "orders" in the church: readers, virgins, widows, catechumens, penitents, and so on. What these groups shared was "a distinctive place in the church's public gathering, especially its worship...."[35]

Ministry represents a particular form of ecclesial ordering. In public ministry one is ordered for public service in the church. It follows that not every Christian activity will be an instance of church ministry, properly speaking. Of course all Christians possesses charisms to be exercised in their daily lives. These charisms may appear quite ordinary (making them no less vital), such as the charism of parenting[36] or imbuing the atmosphere of one's workplace with the values of the gospel. At other times these charisms may take on a more dramatic and even public character, as in the evangelical witness of Dorothy Day. The exercise of these charisms, however dramatic, does not call for undertaking any new ecclesial relationship for the sake of the church and its mission beyond that constituted by baptismal initiation.

There are other charisms, the manifestation of which does suggest the suitability of entering into a new, public, ecclesial relationship within the church. For a Christian activity to qualify as an ordered ministry it must be correlated to some distinctive public relationship within the community. The public character of this ministry is evident in the way in which we tend to hold such ministers to a higher moral standard. We recognize the possibility that their moral failings, because of their public character, might be a cause of scandal.

In this theology, ordered church ministry would denote a reality broader than the ministry of the ordained (though inclusive of it) and narrower than Christian discipleship. Entrance into an ordered min-

istry would generally involve the following: (a) personal call, (b) ecclesial discernment and recognition of a genuine charism, (c) formation
appropriate to the demands of the ministry, (d) authorization by community leadership, and (e) ritualization of this ministry in the form of
a prayer for the assistance of the Holy Spirit and a sending forth on
behalf of the community.

In this final section I will consider several forms of public or
ordered ministry in the church today. They are distinguished by the
distinctive ways in which they are ordered in the life of the church.
That is, they are distinguished relationally, not in terms of their distinctive powers or functions. The ordained offices of bishop, presbyter, and deacon, and the re-emergence of lay ecclesial ministry in
the church, can all be fruitfully considered by exploring the characteristic features of their distinctive *ordines* or relations within the church.

The Office of the Bishop

In the decades since the council we have seen extensive development
in the theology of the local church. More than anything else, it is this
renewed theology of the local church that demands a reconsideration
of the ministry of the bishop.

The Relationship between the Bishop and the Local Church

An ecclesiological ambiguity that emerged from the council teaching,
one that has been perpetuated in post-conciliar magisterial documents, concerns the proper configuration of a bishop's relationship to
both his local church and the college of bishops. The council appeared
to give a priority to the bishop's relationship to the college of bishops,
and in doing so it perpetuated a universalist ecclesiology that would
have been foreign to the church of the first millennium.

Early councils were unambiguous in their condemnation of
absolute ordination, that is, the ordination of a bishop without that
bishop's having a pastoral charge to a local community. Bishops were
ordained not for abstract ministry but for ministry to flesh-and-blood
communities. In some places bishops were assisted by chorbishops,
that is, bishops who were ordained to assist the ministry of the local

bishop within his diocese. These bishops shared, in a limited way, the pastoral charge given to the local bishop.

In the second millennium a new episcopal reality emerged, that of bishops who, in fact, had no church to pastor. After the Turkish conquest of large sections of the Christianized Mediterranean and Europe, Rome continued to appoint bishops to sees under Turkish rule and then assigned these bishops to assist ordinaries of large dioceses elsewhere. In the sixteenth century this practice was expanded at the Fifth Lateran Council to extend the assignment of lapsed or suppressed sees to all bishops without a local church. In 1882 the Congregation of Propaganda replaced the traditional title of such bishops, *episcopus in partibus infidelium*, with the phrase *titular bishops*, in deference to the civil governments of the countries where the titular sees were located. Consequently, the Roman Catholic Church now has a situation in which a significant number of its bishops, those assigned to curial or diplomatic posts and all auxiliary bishops, are given title to what are, in fact, non-existent churches.

The practice of granting bishops titular sees reflects the seriously weakened relationship of the bishop to the local church in our contemporary theology of the episcopate. Granting titular sees to bishops who will not serve as pastoral leaders to local churches obscures an authentic theology of the episcopate in two ways. First, it trivializes the relationship between a bishop and his local community. How can one speak meaningfully of a bishop's "communion" with a non-existent community? Second, it transforms what is properly a sacramental ministry within the church into an honorary or administrative title. This reinforces the impression, widespread in many quarters, that such ecclesial structures are more concerned with rank and domination than with ecclesial service.

Perhaps another way to grasp the attenuated relationship between bishop and local church is to consider the following thought experiment involving three scenarios. First, imagine that you are attending an episcopal ordination. Church law has decreed, since at least the early fourth century, that there must be three bishops participating in the ordination of a new bishop. The presence of these bishops is ecclesiologically significant because it manifests the necessary communion that must exist between the new bishop and the college of bishops, and between the new bishop's church and the communion of churches. Were a serious traffic accident to prevent all but one bishop from attending, the ordination would have to be rescheduled.

Second, imagine that somehow during the ordination of the new bishop, the consecrating bishop were to forget to offer the prayer of consecration with its epiclesis, a prayer for the Spirit to come down upon the *ordinand* and empower him with all that was necessary for the fulfillment of his office. Most canonists and sacramental theologians would agree that such an ordination would be invalid. Ordination is not the act of the consecrating bishop, it is the act of the Holy Spirit, and without a prayer for the Spirit's work, there can be no ordination.

Finally, let us imagine a third scenario. According to the Rite of Ordination of a Bishop, after the assembly has heard the reading of the apostolic letter of nomination from the pope, they are to respond with the acclamation, "Thanks be to God." This is often accompanied by applause. This is listed in the rite under the heading, "Consent of the People." What would happen if no one uttered the acclamation and no one applauded? My sense is that the assembly would be held at best to be inattentive and at worst rude, but no one would think the ordination invalid. There is little consciousness in the church that the consent of the people has anything like the importance given to the presence of three bishops or a prayer of epiclesis in the rite of episcopal ordination.

By way of contrast, in the early church there was a widespread assumption that a bishop could not be ordained without the consent of the people.[37] One of the first documents containing an ordination ritual, Hippolytus' early third-century *Apostolic Tradition*, forthrightly states:

> Let the bishop be ordained after he has been chosen by all the people; when he has been named and shall please all, let him, with the presbytery and such bishops as may be present, assemble with the people on Sunday. While all give their consent, the bishops shall lay hands upon him.[38]

St. Cyprian, third-century bishop of Carthage, wrote: "Moreover, we can see that divine authority is also the source for the practice whereby bishops are chosen in the presence of the laity and before the eyes of all, and they are judged as being suitable and worthy after public scrutiny and testimony."[39] In the fifth century, Pope Celestine I would declare that bishops should not be sent to churches unwilling to receive them: "The consent and the wishes of the clergy, the people and the nobility are required."[40]

As we have seen in the contemporary rite of ordination, there is still a place for the consent of the people, but I think it fair to say that few Catholics have a sense of the ecclesial significance of their acclamation. Why? Because the procedures for appointing a bishop provide for little if any input from the local church. In today's canon law, the laity's role in the selection of a bishop is reduced to selective consultation left to the discretion of the papal legate (c. 377, §3); this barely acknowledges the longstanding ideal of participation by the clergy and laity in the choice of their bishop. The current procedure for appointing bishops places most of the responsibility not on the local church but on the papal nuncio and the Congregation for Bishops. The nuncio and the Congregation for Bishops, in turn, are often influenced more by the opinions of prominent church leaders, "bishop makers," than by the needs of the local community and its own sense of who would be most suitable to lead.

The difficulty with calling for a greater role of the local church in the selection of a bishop is that such proposals are often met with the tired ecclesiological bromide, "the church is not a democracy." The maxim is true enough—though it is seldom pointed out that neither is the church a monarchy or an oligarchy—but it is also irrelevant to the question of local participation in the selection of a bishop. In the ecclesiology of the early church, the people were consulted and their consent was solicited in the appointment of the bishop, not because anyone thought the local church members were democratically electing their representative, but because it was believed that the Holy Spirit might disclose the divine will through the faith consciousness of the local church. The people of God submit themselves to the guidance of the Spirit in a process of corporate discernment that is intent upon serving the will of God in the community's corporate choice of a candidate.

Proposals for greater local participation in the selection of a bishop have been offered by any number of canonists and theologians. As but one possibility, it would not be difficult to imagine a vastly expanded role for diocesan pastoral councils and/or diocesan presbyteral councils in the process of selecting a local bishop.

Another way of strengthening the relationship between the bishop and the local church would be to recall the ancient canonical prohibitions, articulated in canon 15 of the Council of Nicea and maintained into the ninth century, against the "translation" of a bishop, that is, the transfer of a bishop from one diocese to another. Occasional exceptions to this canon were made, but they were rare. There were both theological and pastoral reasons for this prohibition. At the theological level, the transfer of a bishop violated the nuptial symbolism of a bishop's "marriage" to his people, a symbolism reinforced in the modern ritual by the newly ordained bishop's investiture with an episcopal ring. At a practical level, it forestalled episcopal careerism. As Michael Buckley has observed:

[T]he early Church saw quite practically in this effort to move from one see to another an endless source of clerical ambition, rivalry, and self-promotion, as well as, more theologically, the violation of the union that should exist between the bishop and the people of his diocese.[41]

If a bishop of a relatively small diocese has aspirations for "promotion" to a larger and more significant church, he may be more inclined to act cautiously, concerned about how his actions might be interpreted by those with the authority to assign him to a more influential post.

The church today is quite different in size and demographics from the church of the early centuries. It is not uncommon today to have a few large archdioceses with anywhere from one to ten million Catholics, a size unheard of in the early church. Given this new situation, it is possible to imagine cases where an exception to the prohibition of episcopal transfers might have to be made. There are some large archdioceses for which one would prefer to appoint a bishop who already possessed significant pastoral experience as a bishop. But these exceptions would, I think, be relatively few.

A bishop committed to his local diocese for life is going to be more likely to give priority to the concerns and needs of his own people. In the church in the United States, because of the frequent transfer of bishops, relatively small dioceses have had to come to grips with a sad pastoral reality. When they receive a new bishop, they know that if their bishop has the proper ecclesiastical "pedigree" he will be little more than a "rent-a-bishop," soon to be reassigned to a more prestigious post. Without serious consideration of these kinds of reforms in the office of the bishop, it will be difficult to redress the widespread assumption of many Catholics that their bishop is essentially a papal delegate with an at best tenuous relationship to the local church he was ordained to serve.

Papal Primacy and the Authority of Local Bishops

For all of the important steps forward made by Vatican II regarding a theology of the episcopate, the council seemed content to rely on a juxtaposition of its teaching on the episcopate and Vatican I's teaching on papal primacy. Thus the council gave only vague indications of how these two themes could be adequately integrated. That task has been left to the work of church leaders and theologians in the decades since the council. The difficulty boils down to this. Catholic teaching grants that a bishop has ordinary jurisdiction over his local church. As articulated at Vatican I, Catholic teaching also recognizes that the pope has ordinary, immediate, and universal jurisdiction over the whole church. These twin assertions suggest that both the local bishop and the bishop of Rome share jurisdiction of a bishop's local church. How is this jurisdictional overlap to be reconciled? Those favoring papal centralization say that it must always be reconciled in favor of the pope's universal jurisdiction. But this view seems to render the local bishop impotent and flies in the face of Vatican II's explicit declaration that a bishop is not to be viewed as a mere papal delegate. It turns out that the seeds of a resolution to this problem can actually be found in the immediate aftermath of Vatican I.

In Part One we mentioned the German bishops' response to the claim of Chancellor Bismarck that Vatican I had rendered the authority of the local bishop superfluous. They insisted against Bismarck that the council did not undermine the legitimate authority of the local bishop. The pope's ordinary, immediate, and universal jurisdiction implied only that proper to the bishop of Rome's office was the responsibility to ensure the welfare of the churches, intervening only because of the incapacity of the local bishop or because the good of the church required it. It is regrettable that this important clarification never found its way into the documents of Vatican II. Implicit in the statement of the German bishops is a recognition of the necessary autonomy of the local bishop with the clear implication that the intervention of the papacy in the affairs of the local church could be justified only by some incapacity of the local bishop or by an issue that threatened the unity of faith and communion.

The German bishops' clarification suggests that we consider two complementary modes of exercising papal primacy, *facilitative* and *interventionist*.[42] The most common exercise of primacy might be termed *facilitative*. This refers to the ordinary ministry of the bishop of Rome in which he "confirms his brothers" in the proper exercise of their ministry as pastors of local churches. This facilitative ministry might include the convocation of episcopal synods, papal visitations, and *ad limina* visits, along with other means of facilitating communion among the bishops. The facilitative exercise of papal primacy would not involve any direct intervention in the affairs of local churches.

Much less frequently there may also be a need for an *interventionist* exercise of papal primacy. This interventionist exercise of papal authority would be engaged only when the bishop of Rome, either directly or through curial offices, finds it necessary to intervene in the affairs of a local church or churches because the local structures of leadership have proven incapable of addressing a matter that threatens the unity of faith and communion. Unless the unity of faith and communion of the whole church is at risk, there seems to be little ecclesiological justification for Roman intervention. It is simply not sufficient for a Roman official, or even the pope, to disagree with the actions of a local bishop or bishops. Interventionist papal authority could be justified only when the action or inaction of local leaders is inadequate or imperils the unity of the church. Moreover, this interventionist authority functions best when the papal intervention comes at the request of the local church itself. I have in mind the celebrated "Feeney Affair" of the 1940s in which the archbishop of Boston, Cardinal Cushing, requested the intervention of the Holy Office in dealing with a renegade Jesuit priest who was preaching that salvation was absolutely excluded to all non-Catholics.

These two forms of papal primacy are not opposed to one another. The interventionist exercise of exceptional authority is simply a more direct and authoritative means of supporting and confirming the local bishops in the fulfillment of their pastoral responsibilities, namely, the building up of the body and the preservation of unity within the body.[43]

This distinction demands, I believe, a careful discernment on the part of the papacy regarding when and where the interventionist exercise of papal primacy is truly justified. Because of the widespread perception of excessive Vatican interventionism during the pontificate of Pope John Paul II, his eloquent vision of primacy in service of the college of bishops has had limited impact on ecumenical dialogue. For example, many of the Eastern Orthodox, in particular, are well aware of the current procedures for the appointment of bishops. These procedures systematically ignore the input of the local church and the Eastern principle of synodality. They have observed Vatican interventions rejecting vernacular translations of the lectionary and Roman missal approved by regional episcopal conferences. They have watched a Vatican congregation attempt to intervene in a bishop's remodeling of his cathedral and they have noted the recent universal church legislation regulating the kinds of materials suitable for chalices and patens. This pattern of Vatican intervention has, to many observers both outside and within the Catholic Church, shown little awareness of the distinction in the exercise of papal primacy developed above. Until that distinction becomes evident, not just in church rhetoric but also in church policy and practice, overtures toward other Christian traditions with the goal of restoring full visible unity under the primacy of the bishop of Rome are not likely to be effective.

The distinction I am proposing between the facilitative and interventionist exercise of papal primacy can be interpreted as an ecclesiological application of the principle of subsidiarity. But it also follows from what was said earlier regarding the mutual interiority of the local churches and the universal church. If one resists, as I believe one must, the temptation to give an ontological and/or chronological priority to either the local or the universal church, then the distinction between the two forms of primatial authority necessarily follow. Primacy must be seen as a ministry in service of the preservation of both the unity of the universal church as a communion of churches and the legitimate autonomy of each local church.

Episcopal Collegiality

One of the achievements of contemporary ecclesiology has been the effort made to overcome certain tensions found in the council documents regarding the relationship between papal primacy and episcopal collegiality. Papal primacy, while real and effective is, as Yves Congar once noted, "canonical and juridical, not sacramental."[44] Primacy must be understood with respect to the pope's episcopal ministry as bishop of Rome. The primacy of the bishop of Rome is, in turn, grounded in the primacy of the church of Rome, a primacy with origins that, in a limited sense, can be traced back to the second century. Once we recognize that papal primacy's sacramental basis is rooted not in papal election *per se*, but in the pope's episcopal ministry as bishop of Rome, then the relationship between primacy and episcopal collegiality becomes more apparent. Since the primacy of the pope is grounded in the pope's episcopal ministry, it is integrally connected to the pope's relationship to his brother bishops as both a member and head of the college of bishops. *Every* exercise of papal primacy is at the same time an exercise of the pope's episcopal office as member and head of the college. If this is the case, then every exercise of papal primacy must be at least implicitly collegial. Papal acts must be seen as, in some sense, genuine collegial acts as well.

Herein lie the difficulties many have with the present structure of the synod of bishops. The synod appears, in many ways, to be an instance of episcopal collaboration in an essentially papal initiative. This is only reinforced by the fact that such synods possess no deliberative authority and defer to the pope the task of issuing a post-synodal statement. If, as the council clearly taught, the bishops have a genuine share in the pope's universal pastoral ministry, then it is difficult to justify not granting episcopal synods (and episcopal conferences, for that matter) genuine deliberative authority.

The argument that authentic collegiality requires the participation of the whole college founders on a key conviction of our ancient tradition. Episcopal ordination required the participation of three bishops, not the entire college. Apparently, for the early church, the participation of the three bishops at an ordination represented a genuine collegial act. If the presence of three bishops is a genuine exercise of collegiality in an episcopal ordination, it is hard to understand why the participation of several hundred bishops at either an episcopal synod or in the deliberations of an episcopal conference would not possess a similarly genuine collegial status.

I would like to conclude this section on the office of the bishop by returning to a point made earlier. Our assessment of the role of the pope and bishops in the life of the church depends on our more fundamental understanding of the relationship between the local and universal church. If one develops an ecclesiology that gives priority to the universal church over the local churches, one will begin with the pope and bishops' supreme authority over the local church and locate episcopal authority in the bishop's membership in that college, overlooking entirely the significance of his relationship to his local church. From this perspective the authority of the pope and bishops is conceived as anterior to the communion of churches and will function as a kind of external governing board. That governing board, in turn, will have only two juridical modes of expression: (1) the pope exercising his supreme authority *solus* and (2) the pope and the whole college exercising their supreme authority in a solemn act of the whole college.

If, however, one denies a priority to either the local churches or the universal church but insists on their necessary simultaneity and mutual interiority, then a different configuration of church leadership emerges. This second ecclesiological stance requires that one see episcopal ordination as ecclesially reconfiguring the episcopal *ordinand* within a twofold relationship: (1) with the local church he is ordained to serve and (2) with the college of bishops (always in union with its head, the bishop of Rome), the sacramental embodiment of the communion of churches.

This second ecclesiological perspective has the merit of ensuring that the ministry of the local bishop functions to serve ecclesial communion by facilitating that communion in two directions: first, the bishop brings the received faith of the whole church to his local church, and second, he brings the unique faith witness of his local church to the consciousness of the whole communion of churches. This requires a reciprocal accountability. The bishop will honor an ascending accountability to the whole communion of churches through his membership in the college and submission to the primacy of the bishop of Rome. He will also attend to a descending accountability to the people of God as he submits himself, in humility and openness, to the Spirit-inspired insight and concerns of the community he was ordained to serve.

By correlating the college of bishops to the communion of churches, this second ecclesiological perspective also allows for a more fluid understanding of collegiality that would grant a *supreme* authority only to acts of the whole college but would acknowledge less complete modes of collegiality that would still give concrete expression to the communion of churches.

The Office of the Priest-Presbyter

In *Lumen Gentium's* chapter on the hierarchy, the bishops gave only passing attention to a theology of the ministerial priesthood. The topic received further consideration in *Presbyterorum Ordinis* and in *Optatam Totius*, documents that are treated in Maryanne Confoy's contribution to this series. It must suffice here to highlight some fruitful directions already being explored by theologians today regarding the ministerial priesthood.

Any authentic theology of the ministerial priesthood must take into account the post-conciliar shift from a theology of ministry based on power (e.g., ministries being distinguished by the powers they can exercise) to a theology of ministry based on relationship.[45] A relational theology of the ministerial priesthood sees ordination not as the conferral of power, nor as the conferral of some distinctive ontological state. A relational theology of ministry understands ordination as the ritual act that introduces a believer into a new ministerial relationship within the life of the church. This perspective presupposes, of course, that the most fundamental relationship of any Christian in the church is that constituted by baptism, namely discipleship. Ordination calls certain Christians into a new *ordo*, a new relationship within the church. At ordination, the priest is ministerially reconfigured within the church; he is called into a new ecclesial relationship. One can still speak of the conferral of ministerial power at ordination. But it is not the conferral of power that makes the ordained minister; rather, it is the reconfiguration of the person into a new ministerial relationship that requires the empowerment by the Holy Spirit necessary for the fulfillment of that ministry. The new "empowerment" is a function of the new ministerial relationship.

As was discussed in Part Three, there has been considerable hand wringing in the church today regarding the distinctive identity of the ordained priest. Here in the United States, recent studies have confirmed that this is a particular concern for the younger generation of priests, those who are currently under forty-five years of age.[46] This concern for a distinctive priestly identity may well be a symptom of a larger postmodern preoccupation with religious identity. A heightened emphasis on the distinctively cultic role of the priest—a role that would justify the preference of some of the newly ordained to return to cassocks and birettas—would represent a decisive move away from the vision of the council. It would also be another instance of treating the symptom rather than the problem. Many of the newly ordained are grasping for a distinctive priestly identity for the same reason that many young Catholics in general are preoccupied with cultivating a distinctive Catholic identity. The solution to a generation of young priests obsessing over what it means to be a priest is not to be found in yielding to a new iteration of Bing Crosby in *The Bells of St. Mary's*, but in a deeper communal reflection on the challenges of maintaining authentic religious identity in a postmodern world.

No authentic theology of the presbyterate can result by considering priestly identity in isolation. The ministerial priesthood must be correlated to the priesthood of all believers.[47] The council opened the door to such reflection in its assertion in *Lumen Gentium* 10 that "the common priesthood of the faithful and the ministerial or hierarchical priesthood" differ from one another "in essence and not only in degree." This passage has been frequently cited, but less frequently understood. There is a tendency to equate "the common priesthood of believers," with a priesthood of the laity. Such a reading assumes the council was positing two different types of priests, one lay and one clerical. This is a dangerously flawed reading of the council's teaching. In fact, the council was describing two interrelated realities. The priesthood of all the faithful was a synonym for Christian discipleship; all Christians, lay and clergy, participate in this common priesthood. All are called to make of their lives a sacrifice "holy and pleasing to

God." The ministerial priesthood was then placed in relation to the priesthood of the faithful. The ordained priest's ministry, in other words, could be understood only as a particular ministerial calling to be in service of the priesthood of all the baptized. This relationship is affirmed in the *Catechism of the Catholic Church*:

> While the common priesthood of the faithful is exercised by the unfolding of baptismal grace—a life of faith, hope, and charity, a life according to the Spirit—the ministerial priesthood is at the service of the common priesthood. It is directed at the unfolding of the baptismal grace of all Christians. (*CCC*, 1547)

There is little place in such a vision for the seventeenth-century theology of the priest as an *alter Christus*, another Christ, a man "set apart."

Priestly identity cannot be discovered by way of contrast and separation. It can be discovered only when we ask the more basic question: What does it mean to live out the common priesthood of the faithful? What are the demands of authentic Christian discipleship? Only when we have some sense of the answers to these questions can we then consider how the ministerial priesthood is to be understood. From this perspective the priest will emerge as a minister of the Word called to preach the gospel "in and out of season" to those he serves. The priest will serve the life of discipleship through the exercise of his sacramental ministry within and not above the Christian community. This sacramental ministry, however, will not develop along a provider/receiver model that sees the sacramental minister as a dispenser of grace and bestower of sacred mysteries. Rather, the sacramental ministry of the priest, always exercised within the community, will involve a distinctive and necessary presidency over the community's own celebration of its sacramental life. The priest will also serve the priesthood of all believers by cultivating the gift of discernment so that he can better recognize the charisms of believers. He will serve the common priesthood through pastoral leadership, through the empowerment of the people of God, and through the ordering of the many gifts of the baptized so that those gifts may build up the church in service of its mission in the world.

The Office of the Deacon

Although the permanent diaconate has grown dramatically in the United States, it is a ministry that has struggled to find an adequate theology.[48] Some have constructed a theology of the diaconate around those ministerial activities distinctive to deacons. The difficulty with this approach is that throughout church history deacons have exercised a broad range of ministries. We have early documentary testimony of the liturgical ministry of the deacon, of the ministry of preaching, the ministry to the sick, the administration of the temporal goods of the local church, and the ministry of catechesis. We have the historical witness of deacons who were accomplished theologians, like Ephrem of Nisibis or later, in the Middle Ages, of Alcuin of York. In the midst of this great diversity in pastoral ministry, the most consistent feature of diaconal ministry seems to have been the deacon's distinctive relationship to the bishop. This is evident in the ordination ritual for deacons found in Hippolytus's *Apostolic Tradition* in which the deacon is ordained not into the priesthood but into "service of the bishop" (*in ministerio episcopi*).[49] The testimony of our tradition indicates that what most distinguished the ancient diaconate was not what the deacon did or did not do, it was his commitment to be sent in service of the needs of the church as discerned by the one charged with apostolic oversight (the bishop).

If ordained ministry is best understood from the perspective of ministerial relationship, then a theology of the diaconate may be more fruitfully approached by considering the deacon's relationship to the bishop. Diaconal ministry is defined, in other words, by the deacon's service to the one charged with *episkope*, or apostolic oversight. The deacon is the one who is "sent forth" by the bishop (and, at times, indirectly by the local pastor) in service of the needs of the church as seen by the one charged with oversight of the local church. It is true that all ministries, lay and ordained, are subject to the ordering of the bishop or pastor, but the ministry of the deacon is not only *ordered by* the one responsible for apostolic oversight, his ministry is explicitly *placed at the service of* that ministry of oversight. The unique ministerial bond between deacon and bishop is expressed in the formal promise of obedience that a deacon makes to his bishop. It is also evident in the way in which the deacon's liturgical ministry is visibly aligned with the one who presides over the church's worship. Within the worshiping assembly the vested deacon stands at the side of the liturgical presider who exercises liturgical *episkope*. He is blessed by the presider prior to his proclamation of the gospel, and he explicitly serves the ministry of the presider in the petition for God's mercy during the penitential rite, in the preparation and distribution of the eucharistic gifts, and in the call for the gathered assembly to share the peace of Christ.

It will often be the case that the particular ministries engaged in by deacons and those of lay ecclesial ministers (such as the director of Christian formation) will overlap considerably. Deacons will often work side by side with lay ecclesial ministers in catechesis, youth ministry, peace and justice advocacy, or the administration of the business concerns of a parish or other Catholic institution. Their performance of these ministries will generally be, in substance, no different from that of lay ecclesial ministers.

Conversely, many of the ministries often thought of as distinctive to the deacon (e.g., preaching, presiding at baptisms, weddings, and funerals) can, in extraordinary circumstances, be engaged in by laypersons. What distinguishes the diaconate from lay ministry is not the substance of ministerial activity, but the way in which what the deacon does is explicitly a function of his service to the directives of the bishop and/or the pastor. The deacon is "sent" by the bishop into a particular pastoral field. By virtue of his promise of obedience to the bishop and his lifelong commitment to diaconal ministry, a commitment the church does not require of lay ministers, the deacon serves explicitly in response to the needs of the community as discerned by the bishop or his pastor.

One specific institutional reform that ought to be considered in the near future is the suppression of the practice of ordaining seminarians to the diaconate for a limited period of time prior to their presbyteral ordination. This practice is sometimes referred to as ordination into the "transitional diaconate."[50] The ancient tradition in no way presupposed that one must advance from one ordained ministry to the next. The most recent scholarship now suggests that a fixed sequence of ordination—deacon, presbyter, bishop—was not firmly in place before the Middle Ages.[51] The modern practice of a "transitional diaconate" risks denigrating diaconal ministry by reducing it to a kind of pastoral internship or field education assignment. Although seminarians clearly benefit from a pastoral internship that includes preaching and limited sacramental/liturgical ministry, there is no reason why these ministries could not be delegated to seminarians by their bishop without diaconal ordination.[52] As long as the transitional diaconate stands in institutional terms alongside the permanent diaconate it will be difficult for the diaconate to achieve the status, in the eyes of the faithful, of a stable ministry possessing its own ministerial integrity.

Lay Ecclesial Ministries

The most promising avenue for developing an integrated theology of ministry will extend to lay ministry the relational approach applied above to ordained ministries. Much of the debate about lay ministry is concerned with terminology. This is not an instance of theological nitpicking. Terminology often reveals an operative theology. In this volume, I have used the nomenclature of "lay ecclesial ministry" because it has become fairly widely accepted, at least here in the United States. This terminology, however, is not without its problems.

First, the term *lay* is only with difficulty shorn of its past historical associations with a kind of ecclesial passivity. To define a ministry as "lay" is almost reflexively to define it by what it is not, a ministry proper to the ordained. While the bishops at Vatican II worked mightily to develop a positive theology of the laity, the fruit of their work can better be read, I believe, as a positive theology of *all the baptized*, the *christifideles*, as followers of Jesus and members of the people of God.[53] Qualifying ministry as "lay" tends to vitiate the construction of such a theology.

Second, it is difficult to understand the point of the qualifier *ecclesial* in the term, *lay ecclesial ministry*. Does not all Christian ministry have an essentially ecclesial referent?

Third, as the term is used in the United States, lay ecclesial ministry refers only to those ministers who engage in long-term ministry on a full- or part-time basis, a ministry that generally will require extensive ministerial formation and, often, financial remuneration. This certainly describes, for example, a parish coordinator of Christian formation, but it doesn't describe the ministry of the liturgical lector.

Is it possible to develop a nomenclature for the exercise of ministry by those who are not ordained that is more theologically coherent and accounts for the diverse ministerial situations in the church today? Within the broader framework of ordered ministries outlined above, there are, I believe, a number of ways to do this. Thomas O'Meara has proposed that "[p]erhaps one should speak of three kinds of activities by which an individual is commissioned in the church: ordination, installation, and presentation." While acknowledging the three ordinations of deacon, presbyter, and bishop, O'Meara adds that "installation is for ministers who have an extensive education and whose ministry is full-time in the parish and diocese, while presentation is for readers, acolytes, visitors of the sick, assistants to other ministries."[54]

I agree with O'Meara in substance, but propose an alternative set of designations that would follow from the liturgical ritual that authorizes the person for ministry: ordination, installation, and commissioning. Ordained ministers are those ministers ordered for public service in the church by sacramental ordination. We have already discussed these essential forms of ministry. Installed ministry would refer to those ministries authorized not by sacramental ordination but by a ritual of installation and marked by a high degree of stability (one would be expected to hold a ministerial position for a number of years) and significant ministerial formation (e.g., a graduate degree or advanced ministerial certification). In the United States, many of these installed ministers would be professional, that is, ministers who would be paid a just wage and provided with basic benefits in keeping with Catholic social teaching. Beyond these ordained and installed ministries, we might speak of a third category, commissioned ministries, that is, ministries authorized by a commissioning ritual that would require a more limited stability (e.g., a commitment that might need to be renewed annually) and with more limited ministerial formation (e.g., a parish-based training program). By commissioned ministers I have in mind, for example, parish lectors, special ministers of communion, cantors, and catechists.

This proposal has the merit of understanding ministry not oppositionally, that is, ordained vs. non-ordained, but in terms of the positive ways in which these ministries are ritually ordered in service of the church's mission. Such a ministerial framework is in keeping with the council's tentative moves to incorporate pneumatology into its ecclesial reflections. It would insist on the essential place of sacramental orders while also affirming the rich diversity of gifts and charisms that the Spirit has bestowed upon the church.

This volume has been dedicated to the exposition of the teaching of Vatican II as reflected in three conciliar documents. I have also explored the mixed reception and implementation of that teaching over the last four decades. In this final section I have proposed ways in which several lines of thought found in the conciliar texts might be pressed further. Presupposed throughout is the conviction that councils are best read as dynamic ecclesial events. In turn, conciliar documents are best interpreted not on the analogy of the American constitution, but as a formal snapshot of a living church following the guidance of the Spirit into an unknown future. It is difficult to know in the present moment where attempts to fulfill the vision of Vatican II end and proposals anticipating Vatican III begin. We can affirm, however, with Venerable Bede, that "each day the church gives birth to the church." By baptism we are all active participants in this birthing process. Our baptismal vocation demands that we cooperate with the Spirit in the making of the church and the realization of the church's mission in the world.

NOTES

PREFACE

1. Pope Benedict XVI articulated this view most recently in a pre-Christmas address given on December 22, 2005. The text is found online at http://www.asianews.it/view.php?l=en&art=4944. The substance of his argument is similar to earlier critiques of the reception of Vatican II which he offered as prefect for the Congregation for the Doctrine of the Faith. See, for example, Joseph Ratzinger and Vittorio Messori, *The Ratzinger Report: An Exclusive Interview on the State of the Church* (San Francisco: Ignatius Press, 1985), 35.

2. See Giuseppe Alberigo and Joseph Komonchak, eds., *History of Vatican II*, 5 vols. (Maryknoll, NY: Orbis; Leuven: Peeters, 1995–).

3. Agostino Marchetto, *Il Concilio Ecumenico Vaticano II. Contrappunto per la sua storia* (Vatican City: Libreria Editrice Vaticana, 2005).

4. Ormond Rush, *Still Interpreting Vatican II: Some Hermeneutical Principles* (New York: Paulist Press, 2004), 7. See also John Thiel, *Senses of Tradition: Continuity and Development in Catholic Faith* (New York: Oxford University Press, 2000).

5. Hermann Pottmeyer, "A New Phase in the Reception of Vatican II: Twenty Years of Interpretation of the Council," in *The Reception of Vatican II*, ed. Giuseppe Alberigo, Jean-Pierre Jossua, and Joseph A. Komonchak (Washington, DC: Catholic University of America Press, 1987), 27–43.

6. Angel Antón, "Postconciliar Ecclesiology: Expectations, Results, and Prospects for the Future," in Latourelle, *Vatican II*, 1:423–24.

7. Antonio Acerbi, *Due Ecclesiologie: Ecclesiologia giuridica ed ecclesiologia di comunione nella "Lumen Gentium"* (Bologna: Dehoniane, 1975).

8. Rush, *Still Interpreting Vatican II*.

9. Rush refers to this as a "hermeneutics of the authors." See *Still Interpreting Vatican II*, 1–34.

10. Rush refers to this synchronic reading as a "hermeneutics of the texts." See *Still Interpreting Vatican II*, 35–51.

11. Rush refers to this third mode of interpretation as a "hermeneutics of the receivers." See *Still Interpreting Vatican II*, 52–68. For a much more fully developed theology of ecclesial reception, see Rush's dissertation, *The Reception of Doctrine: An Appropriation of Hans Robert Jauss' Reception Aesthetics and Literary Hermeneutics* (Rome: Gregorian, 1997).

PART I: THE DOCUMENTS

1. Robert Bellarmine, *De Controversiis: Christianae Fidei Adversus Haereticos* (Rome: Giunchi et Menicanti, 1836), II: Book III, Chapter 2, 90.

2. Part One of this volume is dedicated to a careful summary of the history of the three documents: the Dogmatic Constitution on the Church, the Decree on the Pastoral Office of Bishops in the Church, and the Decree on the Catholic Churches of the Eastern Rite. This kind of summary requires a great deal of distillation and subjective judgment over what to include and exclude. It is inevitable that such a summary treatment will have to rely on much more in-depth and foundational historical studies. Many fine historical works are available in French, German, and Italian. However, given the predominantly English-language readership for this present volume, the bulk of my citations will draw the attention of readers to the magisterial five-volume history of the council produced under the direction of Giuseppe Alberigo and Joseph Komonchak, *History of Vatican II*, 5 vols. (Maryknoll, NY: Orbis; Leuven: Peeters, 1995–).

3. Klaus Wittstadt, "On the Eve of the Second Vatican Council (July 1–October 10, 1962)," in Alberigo, *Vatican II*, 2:419ff.

4. Joseph Komonchak, "The Struggle for the Council during the Preparation of Vatican II," in Alberigo, *Vatican II*, 1:285.

5. For helpful discussions of this preparatory schema, see both Komonchak, "The Struggle for the Council," 287–301 and Giuseppe Ruggieri, "Beyond an Ecclesiology of Polemics: The Debate on the Church," in Alberigo, *Vatican II*, 2:285–98.

6. The Latin text of the schema can be found in *Acta Synodalia*, I/4, 12–91. Unless otherwise noted, the brief English translations of passages from the *De Ecclesia* text are drawn from the unpublished translation of the schema provided by Joseph Komonchak. I am grateful to him for making his translation available to me.

7. Komonchak, "The Struggle for the Council," 296.

8. Ibid., 303.

9. A summary discussion of the debate can be found in Gérard Philips, "Dogmatic Constitution on the Church: History of the Constitution," in

Vorgimler, *Commentary*, 1:107–10 and Ruggieri, "Beyond an Ecclesiology of Polemics," 328–40.

10. *Acta Synodalia* I/4, 138–41.

11. Ruggieri, "Beyond an Ecclesiology of Polemics," 328.

12. Jan Grootaers, "The Drama Continues Between the Acts: The 'Second Preparation' and Its Opponents," in Alberigo, *Vatican II*, 2:397.

13. Ibid., 413.

14. Philips, "Dogmatic Constitution on the Church," 112.

15. For an in-depth documentary history of the council's treatment of the diaconate in *Lumen Gentium* 29, see William T. Ditewig, "The Exercise of Governance by Deacons: A Theological and Canonical Study" (Ph.D. diss., Catholic University of America, 2002), 72–97.

16. Philips, "Dogmatic Constitution on the Church," 115–16.

17. Alberto Melloni, "The Beginning of the Second Period," in Alberigo, *Vatican II*, 3:105–8.

18. *Acta Synodalia*, II/1, 220.

19. *Acta Synodalia*, II/2, 60. See the discussion of this debate in Bonaventure Kloppenburg, *The Ecclesiology of Vatican II* (Chicago: Franciscan Herald Press, 1974), 128–29.

20. Evangelista Vilanova, "The Intersession (1963–64)," in Alberigo, *Vatican II*, 3:366–67.

21. *Acta Synodalia* II/3, 215. I depend here on Melvin Michalski, *The Relationship between the Universal Priesthood of the Baptized and the Ministerial Priesthood of the Ordained in Vatican II and in Subsequent Theology* (Lewiston, NY: Mellen University Press, 1996), 40–41.

22. For a consideration of the problems with insisting on an *essential* difference between the two priesthoods, see Heinz Schütte, *Amt, Ordination und Sukzession*, (Düsseldorf: Patmos Verlag, 1974), 353–56.

23. Aloys Grillmeier, "Dogmatic Constitution on the Church: Chapter II," in Vorgrimler, *Commentary*, 1:158.

24. For studies of the employment of this schema in the Vatican II documents, see Ormond Rush, "The Offices of Christ, *Lumen Gentium* and the People's Sense of the Faith," *Pacifica* 16 (June, 2003): 137–52; Peter Drilling, "The Priest, Prophet and King Trilogy: Elements of its Meaning in *Lumen Gentium* and for Today," *Eglise et théologie* 19 (1988): 179–206; Thomas Potvin, "Le baptême comme enracinement dans la participation à la triple fonction du Christ," in *Le laïcat: les limites d'un système*, ed. J.-C. Petit and C. Breton (Montreal: Fides, 1987), 141–90; Yves Congar, "Sur La Trilogie: Prophète-Roi-Prêtre," *Revue de sciences philosophiques et théologiques* 67 (1983): 97–115; Ludwig Schick, *Das Dreifache Amt Christi und der Kirche* (Frankfurt am Main-Bern: Lang, 1982).

25. Joseph A. Komonchak, "Toward an Ecclesiology of Communion, in Alberigo, *Vatican II*, 4:50–51.

26. Pope Paul VI would later grant Mary this title on his own authority.

27. Yves Congar, *L'Église de saint Augustin à l'époque moderne* (Paris: Cerf, 1970), 365–67.

28. Kloppenburg, *The Ecclesiology of Vatican II*, 222.

29. An English translation of this text can be found in Hans Küng, *The Council and Reunion* (London: Sheed and Ward, 1961), 283–95.

30. Cf. Denzinger-Schönmetzer, *Enchiridion symbolorum* [DS] 3112–17.

31. *Satis Cognitum* (June 29, 1896) *Acta Sanctae Sedis* 28, 732.

32. Komonchak, "The Struggle for the Council," 287.

33. Klaus Mörsdorf, "Decree on the Bishops' Pastoral Office in the Church," in Vorgrimler, *Commentary*, 2:167.

34. Grootaers, "The Drama Continues Between the Acts," 450.

35. A more in-depth treatment of the themes addressed in the fall 1963 debates can be found in Mörsdorf, "Decree on the Bishops' Pastoral Office," 170–83 and Joseph Famerée, "Bishops and Dioceses and the Communications Media," in Alberigo, *Vatican II*, 3:121–58.

36. The complete Latin text of these interventions can be found in *Acta Synodalia* II/4, 516–626.

37. René Laurentin, "Synod and Curia," *Concilium* 27 (1979): 93.

38. Quoted in Famerée, "Bishops and Dioceses," 127.

39. Ibid., 153.

40. The substance of Ratzinger's view at that time may be found in two essays, "Konkrete Formen bischöfliche Kollegialität," in *Ende der Gegenreformation?* ed. Johann Christophe Hampe (Stuttgart: Kreuz-Verlag, 1964), 155–63 and "The Pastoral Implications of Episcopal Collegiality," in *The Church and Mankind, Concilium* #1 (Glen Rock: Paulist Press, 1964), 39–67.

41. Jerôme Hamer, "Les conférences épiscopales exercice de la collégialité," *Nouvelle revue théologique* 85 (1963): 966–69.

42. Joseph Ratzinger, "The Pastoral Implications of Episcopal Collegiality," 64.

43. Vilanova, "The Intersession (1963–1964)," 384.

44. Komonchak, "Toward an Ecclesiology of Communion," 89.

45. Ricardo Burigana and Giovanni Turbanti, "The Intersession: Preparing the Conclusion of the Council, in Alberigo, *Vatican II*, 4: 597–98.

46. For a helpful survey of the Eastern Catholic churches, see Ronald Roberson, *The Eastern Christian Churches: A Brief Survey*, 6th ed. (Rome: Edizioni Orientalia Christiana, 1999).

47. Komonchak, "The Struggle for the Council," 200.

48. The precise number is between ten and fourteen—the numbering

varies in different accounts, depending on whether one counts only those schemata actually sent on to the Central Preparatory Commission and whether the schema on the sacraments is counted as one whole schema or its four chapters are each viewed as distinct schemata. See Komonchak, "The Struggle for the Council," 201.

PART II: MAJOR POINTS

1. Yves Congar *L'Église de saint Augustin à l'époque moderne* (Paris: Cerf, 1970), 102–12.

2. William Henn, *The Honor of My Brothers: A Brief History of the Relationship between the Pope and the Bishops* (New York: Crossroad, 2000), 107–8.

3. Walter Kasper, *Theology and Church* (New York: Crossroad, 1989), 151.

4. Robert Bellarmine, *De Controversiis: Christianae Fidei Adversus Haereticos*, (Rome: Giunchi et Menicanti, 1836), II: Book III, Chapter 2, 90.

5. Edward Schillebeeckx, *Christ the Sacrament of the Encounter with God* (Kansas City: Sheed & Ward, 1963); Otto Semmelroth, *Church and Sacrament* (Notre Dame: Fides, 1965); Karl Rahner, *The Church and the Sacraments* (New York: Crossroad, 1963).

6. Bonaventure Kloppenburg, *The Ecclesiology of Vatican II* (Chicago: Franciscan Herald Press, 1974), 17.

7. Jerome Murphy-O'Connor, "Eucharist and Community in I Corinthians," in *Living Bread, Saving Cup*, ed. Kevin Seasoltz (Collegeville: Liturgical Press, 1982), 4.

8. Yves de Montcheuil, *Aspects de l'Eglise* (Paris: Cerf, 1949), 51.

9. St. Augustine, *Sermon 272*.

10. St. John Chrysostom, *In Epistolam I ad Corinthios Homiliae*, 24, 2.

11. The translation is my own.

12. Yves Congar, "Pneumatologie ou 'Christomonisme' dans la traditione latine," in *Ecclesia a Spiritu Sancto edocta* [Festschrift for Gérard Philips] (Louvain: Duculot, 1970), 41–63.

13. The translation is my own.

14. I am drawing this account of the exchange between Newman and Talbot from Michael J. Himes, "What Can We Learn from the Church in the Nineteenth Century?" in *The Catholic Church in the 21st Century*, ed. Michael J. Himes (Liguori, MO: Liguori Publications, 2004), 73–74.

15. Giovanni Magnani, "Does the So-Called Theology of the Laity Possess a Theological Status?" in Latourelle, *Vatican II*, 1:597ff.

16. Ibid., 611.

17. *Acta Synodalia* III/1, 282. This also appeared in the *relatio* introducing chapter 4; see *Acta Synodalia* III/3, 62.

18. Magnani, "Does the So-Called Theology of the Laity Possess a Theological Status?"609–12.

19. Translation is my own.

20. The translation is my own.

21. Heribert Mühlen, *Una Persona Mystica* (Rome, 1968), 572.

22. St. Ignatius of Antioch, *Letter to the Smyrnaeans*, in *The Apostolic Fathers*, trans. Francis X. Glimm, Joseph M.-F. Marique, and Gerald G. Walsh (New York: Christian Heritage, 1946), 121.

23. *The Martyrdom of Polycarp* in *The Apostolic Fathers*, 151.

24. For a helpful summary treatment of early theological understandings of catholicity, see Avery Dulles, *The Catholicity of the Church* (Oxford: Clarendon Press, 1985), 13–29.

25. See Werner Elert, *Eucharist and Church Fellowship in the First Four Centuries*, trans. N. E. Nagel (St. Louis: Concordia Publishing House, 1966); Kenneth Hein, *Eucharist and Excommunication: A Study in Early Christian Doctrine and Discipline* (Frankfurt: Lang, 1975).

26. For further consideration of the issues around the terms local vs. particular church, see Gianfranco Ghirlanda, "Universal Church, Particular Church, and Local Church at the Second Vatican Council and in the New Code of Canon Law," in Latourelle, *Vatican II*, 2:233–71; Hervé Legrand, "La realization de l'Eglise en un lieu," in *Initiation à la pratique de la théologie*, ed. Bernard Lauret and François Refoulé, 5 vols. (Paris: Cerf, 1993), 3:145–59.

27. Henri de Lubac identified the particular church with the diocese, the church gathered at the Eucharist under the ministry of the bishop. In his view, "local church" was a term that could be used in various ways to define a church, not theologically, but in terms of various socio-cultural factors. Henri de Lubac, *Les églises particulières dans l'Église universelle* (Paris: Aubier, 1971), 43–56. The Code of Canon Law tended to follow de Lubac in equating the particular church with the diocese. For a compelling theological argument for the use of the term "local church" over "particular church," see Gilles Routhier, "'Église locale' ou 'Église particulière': querelle sémantique ou option théologique?" *Studia Canonica* 25 (1991): 277–334.

28. Jean Jacques von Allmen, "L'Église locale parmi les autres églises locales," *Irénikon* 43 (1970): 512.

29. Joseph A. Komonchak, "Ministry and the Local Church," *CTSA Proceedings* 36 (1981): 58.

30. Xavier Rynne, *Letters from Vatican City: Vatican Council II (First Session): Background and Debates* (New York: Farrar, Straus & Co., 1963), 201–2.

31. Michael Plishka, "From Easternization to Inculturation: Re-interpreting the Mission of the Eastern Catholic Churches," *Worship* 71 (July 1997): 317–35, at 319.

32. See George D. Gallaro, "'Orientalium Ecclesiarum' Deserves More Attention," *Nicolaus* (1986): 293–302.

33. Robert F. Taft, "Eastern Catholic Churches (*Orientalium Ecclesiarum*)," in *Modern Catholicism: Vatican II and After*, ed. Adrian Hastings (New York: Oxford University Press, 1991), 135.

34. Latin text is found in DS 2885–88.

35. Translation is taken from Jacques Dupuis, ed., *The Christian Faith in the Doctrinal Documents of the Catholic Church* (New York: Alba House, 2001), 376.

36. *Mystici Corporis*, 103.

39. In 1949 the Holy Office loosened this prohibition.

38. Quoted in Giuseppe Alberigo, "The Announcement of the Council," in Alberigo, *Vatican II*, 1:15. Alberigo notes that the official Latin version sanitized this text in typical fashion, substituting the word "communities" for "churches," "follow" for "participate," and "search" for "feast."

39. *Acta Synodalia* I/4, 15.

40. Francis A. Sullivan, "The Significance of the Vatican II Declaration that the Church of Christ 'Subsists in' the Roman Catholic Church," in Latourelle, *Vatican II*, 2:272–87; idem, *The Church We Believe In: One, Holy, Catholic and Apostolic* (New York/Mahwah, NJ: Paulist Press, 1988), 23–33.

41. *Acta Synodalia* II/3, 202.

42. Quoted in Paul Lakeland, *The Liberation of the Laity* (New York: Continuum, 2003), 105.

43. The term appears in *LG*, 21, 22; *CD*, 4, 5; *PO*, 7. It appears a sixth time in #2 of the *Nota Explicativa Praevia*.

44. Kasper, *Theology and Church*, 156–61.

45. For an attempt to retrieve the notion of "hierarchy" by distinguishing between "command hierarchy" and "participatory hierarchy," see Terence L. Nichols, *That All May Be One: Hierarchy and Participation in the Church* (Collegeville: Liturgical Press, 1997).

46. This view of the church as an ordered communion parallels in some ways Ghislain Lafont's presentation of the post-conciliar church as a "structured communion." See his *Imagining the Catholic Church: Structured Communion in the Spirit* (Collegeville: Liturgical Press, 2000).

47. For a fuller consideration of the various modes in which bishops can exercise their teaching office, and the appropriate response of the faithful to their teaching, see Richard R. Gaillardetz, *By What Authority? A Primer on Scripture, the Magisterium and the Sense of the Faithful* (Collegeville: Liturgical Press, 2003).

48. Gérard Philips, "Dogmatic Constitution on the Church: History of the Constitution," in Vorgrimler, *Commentary*, 1:129.

49. For more discussion of the teaching office of the pope and bishops see, Richard R. Gaillardetz, *By What Authority? A Primer on Scripture, the Magisterium and the Sense of the Faithful*; idem, *Teaching with Authority: A Theology of the Magisterium in the Church* (Collegeville: Liturgical Press, 1997); Francis A. Sullivan, *Creative Fidelity: Weighing and Interpreting Documents of the Magisterium* (New York/Mahwah, NJ: Paulist Press, 1996); *Magisterium: Teaching Office in the Catholic Church* (New York: Paulist Press, 1983); Ladislas Örsy, *The Church: Learning and Teaching: Magisterium, Assent, Dissent, Academic Freedom* (Wilmington: Michael Glazier, 1987).

50. This point has been made quite cogently by Hervé Legrand in his important essay, "Collégialité des évêques et communion des églises dans la réception de Vatican II," *Revue des sciences philosophiques et théologiques* 75 (1991): 545–68. See also Joseph Ratzinger, "Die bischöfliche Kollegialität nach der Lehre des Zweiten Vatikanischen Konzils," in *Das neue Volk Gottes: Entwürfe zur Ekklesiologie* (Dusseldorf: Patmos-Verlag, 1969), 184–87.

51. Pope Pius XII made this statement in an address to newly created cardinals, *AAS* 38 (1946): 144–45. He reaffirmed the ecclesial implications of the principle of subsidiarity in an address to the Second World Congress of the Lay Apostolate in 1957, see *AAS* 49 (1957): 926–28. In the section that follows, I have been aided by a valuable survey of the literature on this topic by John Burkhard, "The Interpretation and Application of Subsidiarity in Ecclesiology: An Overview of the Theological and Canonical Literature," *The Jurist* 58 (1998): 279–342.

52. Wilhelm Bertrams, "De principio subsidiaritatis in iure canonico," *Periodica* 46 (1957): 3–65; "Das Subsidiaritätsprinzip in der Kirche," *Stimmen der Zeit* 160 (1957): 252–67.

53. The principle of subsidiarity does appear as a social principle in *Gravissimum Educationis* 3, 6 and *Gaudium et Spes* 86.

54. See Joseph Komonchak, "Subsidiarity in the Church: The State of the Question," *The Jurist* 48 (1988): 298–349, at 309–12.

55. This included, within defined limits, the regulation of the liturgy with particular regard to the approval of the use of the vernacular, the approval of liturgical translations, and the approval of cultural adaptations.

56. Maurice Vidal, "Presbyterat," *Dictionnaire de spiritualité*, (Paris: Beauchesne, 1985), 2093–94.

57. Abbot Columba Marmion, *Christ—The Ideal of the Priest* (St. Louis: Herder, 1952).

58. The diaconate is also briefly mentioned in *AG*, 16; *SC*, 35; and *DV*, 25.

59. This material is drawn from Richard R. Gaillardetz, "Are Deacons the Answer?" *Commonweal* 130 (August 15, 2003): 22–24.

PART III: POST-CONCILIAR RECEPTION AND IMPLEMENTATION

1. Quoted in Angel Antón, "Postconciliar Ecclesiology: Expectations, Results, and Prospects for the Future," in Latourelle, *Vatican II*, 1:409.

2. See Segundo Galilea, "Latin America in the Medellín and Puebla Conferences: An Example of Selective and Creative Reception of Vatican II," in *The Reception of Vatican II*, ed. Giuseppe Alberigo, Jean-Pierre Jossua, and Joseph A. Komonchak (Washington, DC: Catholic University of America Press, 1987), 59–73.

3. Eugenio Corecco, "Aspects of the Reception of Vatican II in the Code of Canon Law," in *The Reception of Vatican II*, 249–96, at 261.

4. Ibid., 264.

5. See Eugene Bianchi and Rosemary Radford Reuther, eds., *A Democratic Catholic Church: The Reconstruction of Roman Catholicism* (New York: Crossroad, 1992).

6. See the website of the Association for the Rights of Catholics in the Church: http://arcc-catholic-rights.net/.

7. As but two examples, see Yves Congar, *Sainte Eglise. Etudes et Approches ecclésiologiques* (Paris: Cerf, 1963); Henri de Lubac, *Catholicism* (French original, 1938; London: Burns and Oates, 1950).

8. Dennis M. Doyle, *Communion Ecclesiology: Vision and Versions* (Maryknoll, NY: Orbis, 2000), 13.

9. See Avery Dulles, "The Reception of Vatican II at the Extraordinary Synod of 1985," in *The Reception of Vatican II*, 349–63. For a more in-depth treatment of the synod, see Xavier Rynne, *John Paul's Extraordinary Synod* (Wilmington: Glazier, 1986).

10. "Final Report," *Origins* 15 (December 19, 1985): 444–50.

11. Leonardo Boff, *The Church: Charism and Power* (New York: Crossroad, 1985), 145.

12. Ibid., 152.

13. Doyle, *Communion Ecclesiology*, 124–26.

14. John Henry Newman, *On Consulting the Faithful in Matters of Doctrine* (1859; reprint, Kansas City: Sheed & Ward, 1961).

15. Sharon Euart, "Structures for Participation in the Church," *Origins* 35 (May 26, 2005): 18–25. The treatment of the canonical structures for the consultation of the faithful in this section is largely drawn from Sr. Sharon Euart's address.

16. Hans Küng, *The Church* (New York: Image Books, 1976); Edward Schillebeeckx, *The Church with a Human Face* (New York: Crossroad, 1985); Gotthold Hasenhüttl, *Charisma: Ordnungsprinzip der Kirche* (Freiburg: Herder, 1969); Roger Haight, *Christian Community in History*, 2 vols. (New York: Continuum, 2004–5).

17. An important exception is Paul Lakeland, *The Liberation of the Laity* (New York: Continuum, 2003).

18. For one book-length bibliography that only covers the first two decades since the council, see Leonard Doohan, *The Laity: A Bibliography* (Wilmington: Glazier, 1987).

19. Aurelie Hagstrom, "The Secular Character of the Vocation and Mission of the Laity: Toward a Theology of Ecclesial Lay Ministry," in *Ordering the Baptismal Priesthood*, ed. Susan K. Wood (Collegeville: Liturgical Press, 2003), 152–74.

20. "Some Questions Regarding Collaboration of Nonordained Faithful in Priests' Sacred Ministry," *Origins* 27 (November 27, 1997): 397–410.

21. Hagstrom, 167. See also Richard R. Gaillardetz, "Shifting Meanings in the Lay-Clergy Distinction, "*Irish Theological Quarterly* 64 (1999): 115–39.

22. Pope Paul VI, "Talk to the Members of the Secular Institutes," *AAS* 64 (1972): 208.

23. Luigi Accattoli, *When a Pope Asks Forgiveness: The Mea Culpa's of John Paul II* (Boston: Pauline Books, 1998).

24. International Theological Commission, *Memory and Reconciliation: The Church and the Faults of the Past* (Boston: Pauline Books, 2000).

25. Francis A. Sullivan, "The Papal Apology," *America* (April 8, 2000): 17–22. See also Christopher Bellitto, "Teaching the Church's Mistakes: Historical Hermeneutics," in *Memory and Reconciliation: The Church and the Faults of the Past,*" *Horizons* 32/1 (2005): 123–35; Bernard P. Prusak, "Theological Considerations—Hermeneutical, Ecclesiological, Eschatological Regarding *Memory and Reconciliation: The Church and the Faults of the Past,*" *Horizons* 32/1 (2005): 136–51.

26. In this section I am drawing on Stefano De Fiores's essay assessing post-conciliar Mariology, "Mary in Postconciliar Theology," in Latourelle, *Vatican II*, 1:469–539.

27. Yves Congar, "Sur la conjoncture présente de la publication de l'exhortation 'Marialis cultus,'" *La Maison-Dieu* 121 (1975): 118.

28. De Fiores, "Mary in Postconciliar Theology," 475.

29. Ivone Gebara and Maria Clara Bingemer, *Mary: Mother of God, Mother of the Poor* (Maryknoll, NY: Orbis, 1989).

30. Elizabeth Johnson, *Truly Our Sister: A Theology of Mary in the Communion of Saints* (New York: Continuum, 2004).

31. Ibid., xiv.

32. Elizabeth Johnson, *Friends of God and Prophets: A Feminist Theological Reading of the Communion of Saints* (New York: Continuum, 1998).

33. Andrew Greeley, "A Cloak of Many Colors," *Commonweal* (November 9, 2001): 10–13.

34. Charlene Spretnak, *Missing Mary: The Queen of Heaven and Her Reemergence in the Modern Church* (New York: Palgrave Macmillan, 2004).

35. See Jeanette Rodriguez, *Our Lady of Guadalupe, Faith and Empowerment among Mexican-American Women* (Austin: University of Texas Press, 1994).

36. Hans Urs von Balthasar, *Sponsa Verbi* (Einsiedeln: Johannes Verlag, 1961), 189–283. See also David Schindler, *Heart of the World, Center of the Church: Communio Ecclesiology, Liberalism and Liberation* (Grand Rapids: Eerdmans, 1996).

37. ARCIC, "Mary: Grace and Hope in Christ," *Origins* 35 (June 2, 2005): 33–50.

38. One can find attention paid to the unity and diversity issue in the following passages: *SC*, 37–40, 123; *OE*, 2, 5; *UR*, 14, 16–18; *LG*, 13, 23; *AG*, 8–11, 16, 22–23, 26; and *GS*, 53–55, 58, 61, 91.

39. Karl Rahner, "Basic Theological Interpretation of the Second Vatican Council," in *Theological Investigations*, vol. 20, *Concern for the Church* (New York: Crossroad, 1981), 78.

40. See Peter Phan, *Being Religious Interreligiously: Asian Perspectives on Interfaith Dialogue* (Maryknoll, NY: Orbis, 2004).

41. Marcello de Carvalho Azevedo, *Basic Ecclesial Communities in Brazil: The Challenge of a New Way of Being Church* (Washington, DC: Georgetown University Press, 1987).

42. Fr. Joseph Cardijn was a Belgian priest who in the early twentieth century played an important role in the Lay Apostolate movement and was later made cardinal.

43. Peter Lwaminda, "A Theological Analysis of the AMECEA Documents on the Local Church with Special Emphasis on the Pastoral Option for Small Christian Communities," in *The Local Church with a Human Face*, ed. Agatha Radoli (Eldoret, Kenya: AMECEA Gaba Publications, 1996), 96–99.

44. There is a huge literature on this movement. As but two examples, see Bernard J. Lee, et al., *The Catholic Experience of Small Christian Communities* (New York/Mahwah, NJ: Paulist, 2000); John Paul Vandenakker, *Small Christian Communities and the Parish: An Ecclesiological Analysis of the North American Experience* (Kansas City: Sheed & Ward, 1994).

45. Leonardo Boff, *Ecclesiogenesis: The Base Communities Reinvent the Church* (Maryknoll, NY: Orbis, 1977), 13.

46. Boff's argument for a revision of current church law in order to provide for these communities' right to the Eucharist may be found in *Ecclesiogenesis*, chapter 6.

47. Dennis Doyle, "Communion Ecclesiology and the Silencing of Boff," *America* 167 (September 12, 1992): 139–43.

48. This debate is summarized by Kilian McDonnell in "The Ratzinger/ Kasper Debate: The Universal Church and Local Churches," *Theological Studies* 63 (2002): 227–50.

49. For assessments of the Code of Canons of the Eastern Churches, see Frederick R. McManus, "The Code of Canons of the Eastern Catholic Churches," *The Jurist* 53 (1993): 22–61; David Motiuk, "The Code of Canons of the Eastern Churches: Some Ten Years Later," *Studia Canonica* 36 (2002): 189–224.

50. McManus, "The Code of Canons of the Eastern Catholic Churches," 50.

51. Robert Barringer, "'Orientalium ecclesiarum' Deserves More Attention," *Eastern Catholic Life* (December 8, 1985): 8.

52. Victor J. Pospishil, *Eastern Catholic Canon Law* (Brooklyn: Saint Maron Publications, 1993), 60.

53. Pospishil, 59; For a similar view, see George D. Gallaro, "'Orientalium Ecclesiarum' Deserves More Attention," *Nicolaus* (1986): 296.

54. Thomas E. Bird, "The Vatican II Decree on the Eastern Catholic Churches Thirty Years Later," *Sophia* 21 (1994): 23–29.

55. Gallaro, "'Orientalium Ecclesiarum' Deserves More Attention," 297.

56. Francis A. Sullivan, "The Significance of the Vatican II Declaration that the Church of Christ 'Subsists in' the Roman Catholic Church," in Latourelle, *Vatican II*, 2:272–87.

57. Boff, *Church: Charism and Power*, 75. The English translation renders "subsists" as "present in," thus softening Boff's claim of multiple subsistences of the one church of Christ.

58. "Doctrinal Congregation Criticizes Brazilian Theologian's Book," *Origins* 14 (April 4, 1985): 683–87.

59. Sullivan, "The Significance of the Vatican II Declaration that the Church of Christ 'Subsists in' the Roman Catholic Church," 280–81.

60. Francis A. Sullivan, "The Impact of *Dominus Iesus* on Ecumenism," *America* (October 20, 2000): 9–12.

61. He, however, gives the passage in *Dominus Iesus* a more irenic reading. The observation is made in his *prolusio* given to the Pontifical Council for Promoting Christian Unity during its plenary meeting, November 12–17, 2001. Cardinal Walter Kasper, "Present Situation and Future of the Ecumenical Movement," *Information Service* 109 (2002): I–II.

62. John Hotchkin, "Canon Law and Ecumenism: Giving Shape to the Future," *Origins* 30 (October 19, 2000): 289–98.

63. Ibid., 294.

64. Myriam Wijlens, "'For You I Am Bishop, with You I Am a Christian': The Bishop as Legislator," *The Jurist* 56 (1996): 68–87 at 75.

65. St. Augustine of Hippo, *Sermon* 340, 1.

66. Cardinal Léon Josef Suenens, *Coresponsibility in the Church* (New York: Herder and Herder, 1968).

67. Cardinal Léon Josef Suenens, *Memories and Hopes* (Dublin: Veritas, 1992), 189.

68. Quoted in Suenens, *Memories and Hopes*, 210.

69. See Avery Dulles, "The Pope and the Bishops: Who Leads and How?" *The Tablet* (June 28, 1997): 836.

70. Archbishop John R. Quinn, "The Exercise of the Primacy: Facing the Cost of Christian Unity," *Commonweal* 123 (July 12, 1996): 11–20. It was reprinted with a number of responses in *The Exercise of Primacy: Continuing the Dialogue*, ed. Phyllis Zagano and Terrence W. Tilley (New York: Crossroad, 1998). Quinn later developed the themes of his lecture in *The Reform of the Papacy: The Costly Call to Christian Unity* (New York: Crossroad, 1999).

71. "Draft Statement on Episcopal Conferences," *Origins* 17 (1987–88): 731–37. A good overview of the debate concerning the ecclesiological status of episcopal conferences is provided by Joseph Komonchak in his introduction to *Episcopal Conferences: Historical, Canonical and Theological Studies*, ed. Thomas Reese (Washington, DC: Georgetown University Press, 1989), 1–22. See also Hervé-M. Legrand, Julio Manzanares, and Antonio García y García, eds., *The Nature and Future of Episcopal Conferences* (Washington, DC: The Catholic University of America Press, 1988) and Hubert Müller and Hermann J. Pottmeyer, eds., *Die Bischofskonferenz: theologischer und juridischer Status*, (Düsseldorf: Patmos, 1989).

72. Henri de Lubac, *The Motherhood of the Church followed by Particular Churches in the Universal Church* (San Francisco: Ignatius Press, 1982, originally published in French, 1971).

73. Joseph Ratzinger with Vittorio Messori, *The Ratzinger Report* (San Francisco: Ignatius Press, 1985), 58–61; Jerôme Hamer, "La responsabilité collégiale de chaque évêque," *Nouvelle revue théologique* 105 (1983): 641–54.

74. Hermann J. Sieben, "Episcopal Conferences in Light of Particular Councils During the First Millennium," and Antonio García y García, "Episcopal Conferences in Light of Particular Councils During the Second Millennium," in *The Nature and Future of Episcopal Conferences*, 30–67.

75. Joseph Komonchak, "On the Authority of Bishops' Conferences," *America* (September 12, 1998): 7–10.

76. Francis A. Sullivan, "The Teaching Authority of Episcopal Conferences," *Theological Studies* 63 (September 2002): 472–93.

77. One might consider, for example, the American bishops' attempts at obtaining a *recognitio* for vernacular translations of liturgical texts or their efforts to arrive at juridical norms for implementing *Ex Corde Ecclesiae*.

78. Angel Antón, "Verso un collegialità più effettiva nel Sinodo dei vescovi," *La Revista Clero Italiano* 64 (1983): 482–98.

79. Joseph Ratzinger, "The Structure and Task of the Synod of Bishops," in *Church, Ecumenism and Politics: New Essays in Ecclesiology* (New York: Crossroad, 1988), 46–62.

80. James Coriden, "The Synod of Bishops: Episcopal Collegiality Still Seeks Adequate Expression," *The Jurist* 64 (2004): 116–36, at 120–21.

81. Ibid., 125.

82. As in Part Two, here as well I am depending on John Burkhard's survey of the literature, "The Interpretation and Application of Subsidiarity in Ecclesiology: An Overview of the Theological and Canonical Literature," *The Jurist* 58 (1998): 279–342, along with the essay by Joseph Komonchak, "Subsidiarity in the Church: The State of the Question," *The Jurist* 48 (1988): 298–349 and the monograph by Ad Leys, *Ecclesiological Impacts of the Principle of Subsidiarity* (Kampen: Kok, 1995).

83. The text of his address can be found in *Synode extraordinaire, Célébration de Vatican II* (Paris: Cerf, 1986), 598–604.

84. For a review of this argument see Leys, *Ecclesiological Impacts of the Principle of Subsidiarity*, 113–19; Komonchak, "Subsidiarity in the Church," 336–37.

85. Oswald von Nell-Breuning, "Subsidiarität in der Kirche," *Stimmen der Zeit* 111 (1986): 147–57.

86. Walter Kasper, "Der Geheimnischarakter hebt den Sozialcharakter nicht auf. Zur Geltung des Subsidiaritätsprinzips in der Kirche," *Herder-Korrespondenz* 41 (1987): 232–36.

87. Leys, *Ecclesiological Impacts of the Principle of Subsidiarity*, 140–42.

88. Komonchak, "Subsidiarity in the Church," 339; emphasis is mine.

89. Pope Paul VI, "Allocution to the Roman Curia, September 21, 1963," *AAS* 55 (1963): 798–99.

90. James Provost, "*Pastor Bonus:* Reflections on the Reorganization of the Roman Curia," *The Jurist* 48 (1988): 499–535, at 523.

91. Quinn, *The Exercise of Primacy*, 12–13.

92. Bernard Cooke, *Ministry to Word and Sacraments* (Philadelphia: Fortress, 1976); Edward Schillebeeckx, *The Church with a Human Face: A New and Expanded Theology of Ministry* (New York: Crossroad, 1985); Kenan

Osborne, *Priesthood: A History of Ordained Ministry in the Roman Catholic Church* (New York/Mahwah, NJ: Paulist, 1989); Thomas O'Meara, *Theology of Ministry*, rev. ed. (New York/Mahwah, NJ: Paulist, 1999).

93. Jean Galot, *Theology of the Priesthood* (San Francisco: Ignatius Press, 1984); Avery Dulles, *The Priestly Office: A Theological Reflection* (New York/ Mahwah, NJ: Paulist Press, 1997).

94. Edward Kilmartin, "The Active Role of Christ and the Holy Spirit in the Sanctification of the Eucharistic Elements," *Theological Studies* 45 (1984): 225–53; "Lay Participation in the Apostolate of the Hierarchy," *The Jurist* 41 (1981): 343–70; David N. Power, "Church Order: The Need for Redress," *Worship* 71 (July, 1997): 296–308; "Representing Christ in Community and Sacrament," in *Being a Priest Today*, ed. Donald J. Goergen (Collegeville: Liturgical Press, 1992), 97–123; Susan K. Wood, *Sacramental Orders* (Collegeville: Liturgical Press, 2000), 86–142.

95. Pope Pius XII had set the precedent for this in the 1950s by allowing a small number of German Lutheran clergy who were married to be accepted into the Roman Catholic communion and be ordained as priests.

96. *Inter insigniores, Origins* 6 (February 3, 1977): 517–24.

97. As but two examples of the many collected studies challenging the historical and biblical arguments of the CDF, see Ute E. Eisen, *Women Officeholders in Early Christianity: Epigraphical and Literary Studies* (Collegeville: Liturgical Press, 2000) and Carroll Stuhlmueller, ed., *Women and Priesthood: Future Directions*, (Collegeville: Liturgical Press, 1978). An important historical study defending the official church position but published prior to the CDF statement is Haye van der Meer, *Women Priests in the Catholic Church: A Theological Historical Investigation* (Philadelphia: Temple University Press, 1973).

98. See Donald J. Keefe, "Sacramental Sexuality and the Ordination of Women," *Communio* 5 (Fall 1978): 228–51.

99. Material in this section is drawn from Richard R. Gaillardetz, "Toward a Contemporary Theology of the Diaconate," *Worship* 79 (September 2005): 419–38.

100. William Ditewig, "The Once and Future Diaconate: Notes from the Past, Possibilities for the Future," *Church* 20 (Summer 2004): 51–54.

101. George H. Tavard, *A Theology of Ministry* (Wilmington: Michael Glazier, 1983), 91. See Owen F. Cummings's review and rebuttal of a number of theological critiques in "Theology of the Diaconate: The State of the Question," in Owen Cummings, William T. Ditewig, and Richard R. Gaillardetz, *Theology of the Diaconate: The State of the Question* (New York/Mahwah, NJ: Paulist Press, 2005), 1–29.

102. Sherri L. Vallee, "The Restoration of the Permanent Diaconate: A Blending of Roles," *Worship* 77 (November 2003): 530–42; Richard R. Gaillardetz, "Are Deacons the Answer?" *Commonweal* 130 (August 15, 2003): 22–24; Hervé Legrand, "Le diaconat dans sa relation à la théologie de l'Église et des ministères," in *Diaconat, XXIe siècle. Actes du Colloque de Louvain-la-Neuve 13–15 septembre 1994*, ed. André Haquin and Philippe Weber (Brussels: Lumen Vitae, 1997), 13–41.

103. John N. Collins, *Diakonia: Re-interpreting the Ancient Sources* (New York: Oxford University Press, 1990); *Are All Christians Ministers?* (Collegeville: Liturgical Press, 1992); *Deacons and the Church: Making Connections Between Old and New* (Harrisburg, PA: Morehouse Publishing, 2002), 21.

104. Cardinal Joseph Bernardin, *The Call to Service: Pastoral Statement on the Permanent Diaconate* (Chicago: Archdiocese of Chicago, 1993).

105. Congregation for Catholic Education and the Congregation for the Clergy, *Basic Norms for the Formation of Permanent Deacons and Directory for the Ministry and Life of Permanent Deacons* (Washington, DC: USCCB, 1998).

106. Bishops' Committee on the Diaconate, *National Directory for the Formation, Ministry, and Life of Permanent Deacons in the United States* (Washington, DC: USCCB, 2004).

107. Walter Kasper, *Leadership in the Church* (New York: Crossroad, 2003), 13.

108. International Theological Commission, *From the Diakonia of Christ to the Diakonia of the Apostles* (Mundelein: Hillenbrand Books, 2004).

109. Ad Hoc Committee of the Canon Law Society of America, *The Canonical Implications of Ordaining Women to the Permanent Diaconate* (Washington, DC: CLSA, 1995); Phyllis Zagano, *Holy Saturday* (New York: Crossroad, 2000).

110. Philip J. Murnion and David DeLambo, *Parishes and Parish Ministers* (New York: National Pastoral Life Center, 1999), 45–46. For an informative study of this new ministerial phenomenon, see Zeni Fox, *New Ecclesial Ministry: Lay Professionals Serving the Church*, revised and expanded ed. (Franklin, WI: Sheed & Ward, 2002).

111. Yves Congar, "Mon cheminement dans la théologie du laïcat et des ministères," in *Ministères et communion ecclésiale* (Paris: Cerf, 1971), 17.

112. See Thomas O'Meara, *Theology of Ministry* and Edward Hahnenberg, *Ministries: A Relational Approach* (New York: Crossroad, 2003).

113. Elissa Rinere, "Conciliar and Canonical Applications of 'Ministry' to the Laity," *The Jurist* 47 (1987): 219.

PART IV: THE STATE OF THE QUESTIONS

1. William D. Dinges and James Hitchcock, "Catholic Activist Conservatism in the United States," in *Fundamentalisms Observed*, ed. Martin E. Marty and Scott Appleby (Chicago: University of Chicago Press, 1991), 109.

2. Henri de Lubac, *A Brief Catechesis on Nature and Grace* (San Francisco: Ignatius Press, 1984), 235–60.

3. Joseph Cardinal Ratzinger, *The Ratzinger Report* (San Francisco: Ignatius Press, 1985), 29–42.

4. These terms are increasingly seen as inadequate even within the field of constitutional law. See Christopher Wolfe, "How to Read and Interpret the Constitution," in *Constitutionalism in Perspective: The United States Constitution in Twentieth Century Politics*, ed. Sarah Baumgartner Thurow (New York: University Press of America, 1988), 3–22.

5. Karl Rahner, "Current Problems in Christology," in *Theological Investigations*, vol. 1, *God, Christ, Mary, and Grace* (Baltimore: Helicon Press, 1961), 149–54.

6. Yves Congar, "The Conciliar Structure or Regime of the Church," in *The Ecumenical Council: Its Significance in the Constitution of the Church*, ed. Peter Huising and Knut Walf (New York: Seabury, 1983), 3–9.

7. Bruno Forte, *The Church: Icon of the Trinity* (Boston: St. Paul Books & Media, 1991), 54–55.

8. Ibid., 58–59.

9. John Beal, "It Shall Not Be So Among You! Crisis in the Church, Crisis in Church Law," in *Governance, Accountability and the Future of the Catholic Church*, ed. Francis Oakley and Bruce Russett (New York: Continuum, 2004), 96–97.

10. Ibid., 101.

11. Ibid., 97.

12. Paul Lakeland, *The Liberation of the Laity* (New York: Continuum, 2003); David Gibson, *The Coming Catholic Church: How the Faithful Are Shaping a New American Catholicism* (San Francisco: HarperSanFrancisco, 2004); Donald Cozzens, *Faith that Dares to Speak* (Collegeville: Liturgical Press, 2004); idem, *Sacred Silence: Denial and the Crisis in the Church* (Collegeville: Liturgical Press, 2002).

13. See *NMI*, 45 and *PG*, 44.

14. St. Cyprian of Carthage, *Epistle* 14, 4.

15. Ibid., 74, 10.

16. Quoted in Thomas J. Healey, "A Blueprint for Change," *America* (September 26, 2005): 15.

17. Richard R. Gaillardetz, "Ecclesiological Perspectives on Church Reform," forthcoming in *Church Ethics and Its Organizational Context: Learning from the Sex Abuse Scandal in the Catholic Church*, ed. Jean Bartunek, Mary Ann Hinsdale, and James F. Keenan (Kansas City: Rowman and Littlefield).

18. The literature on globalization is immense. For a good summary assessment, see Robert J. Schreiter, *The New Catholicity: Theology between the Global and Local* (Maryknoll, NY: Orbis, 1997), 1–27.

19. Benjamin Barber, *Jihad vs. McWorld* (New York: Times Books, 1995), 2.

20. Charles Journet, *L'Église du Verbe Incarné*, 3 vols. (Bruges: Desclée de Brouwer, 1941, 1951, 1969).

21. See Roger Haight's excellent exposition of the challenges that post-modernity presents for contemporary ecclesiology, in *Christian Community in History*, 2 vols. (New York: Continuum, 2004–5), 1:17–66.

22. Schreiter, *The New Catholicity*, 116–33.

23. *Patrologia Latina* 93:166d.

24. Joseph Komonchak, "The Epistemology of Reception," *The Jurist* 57 (1997): 193.

25. David Brooks, "Age of Political Segregation," *New York Times* (June 29, 2004).

26. Quoted in Thomas E. Bird, "The Vatican II Decree on the Eastern Catholic Churches Thirty Years Later," *Sophia* 21 (1994): 24.

27. Hervé Legrand, "'One Bishop per City': Tensions around the Expression of the Catholicity of the Local Church since Vatican II," *The Jurist* 52 (1992): 369–400.

28. Ibid., 379.

29. I am grateful to Ormond Rush for having pointed out the value of such an intra-ecclesial reception.

30. This viewpoint informs Haight's exploration of a postmodern ecclesiology in *Christian Community in History*.

31. Richard R. Gaillardetz, "Catholic Teaching on Membership in the Body of Christ," forthcoming in *Through Divine Love: The Church in Each Place and All Places*, ed. Jeffrey Gros and Walter Klaiber (Sherborne, England: Kingswood Books).

32. Francis Sullivan, *The Church We Believe In: One, Holy, Catholic and Apostolic* (New York/Mahwah, NJ: Paulist Press, 1988), 26. The chapter cited here is a reworking of the essay cited above from the Latourelle collection.

33. Cardinal Walter Kasper, "Present Situation and Future of the Ecumenical Movement," *Information Service* 109 (2002): I–II.

34. Richard R. Gaillardetz, "The Ecclesial Foundations of Ministry within an Ordered Communion," in *Ordering the Baptismal Priesthood*, ed. Susan K. Wood (Collegeville: Liturgical Press, 2003), 26–51.

35. David Power, "Church Order," in *The New Dictionary of Sacramental Worship* (Collegeville: Liturgical Press, 1990), 214.

36. Wendy Wright, "The Charism of Parenting," in *Retrieving Charisms for the Twenty-First Century*, ed. Doris Donnelly (Collegeville: Liturgical Press, 1999), 85–101.

37. Richard R. Gaillardetz and John Huels, "The Selection of Bishops: Recovering the Enduring Values of Our Tradition," *The Jurist* 59 (1999): 348–76.

38. *Apostolic Tradition* 1, 2, 3.

39. *Epistle* 67, 4. For the ecclesiological presuppositions that framed Cyprian's perspective, see Paul J. Fitzgerald, "A Model for Dialogue: Cyprian of Carthage on Ecclesial Discernment," *Theological Studies* 59 (June, 1998): 236–53.

40. Pope Celestine I, *Ep.* 4, c. 5.

41. Michael J. Buckley, "What Can We Learn from the Church in the First Millennium?" in *The Catholic Church in the Twenty-First Century*, ed. Michael J. Himes (Liguori, MO: Liguori, 2004), 20.

42. In an earlier essay I referred to these two modes as *confirmatory* and *exceptional*. See Richard R. Gaillardetz, "Reflections on the Future of Papal Primacy," *New Theology Review* 13 (November 2000): 52–66.

43. For a quite similar account of this distinction in papal primacy, see Michael J. Buckley, *Papal Primacy and the Episcopate: Toward a Relational Understanding* (New York: Crossroad, 1998), 62–74.

44. Yves Congar, *Fifty Years of Catholic Theology: Conversations with Yves Congar* (Philadelphia: Fortress, 1987), 55.

45. See Edward Hahnenberg, *Ministries: A Relational Approach* (New York: Crossroad, 2003), and Susan K. Wood, ed., *Ordering the Baptismal Priesthood.*

46. Katarina Schuth, "A View of the State of the Priesthood in the United States," *Louvain Studies* 30 (2005): 8–24 at 19.

47. Edward Hahnenberg, "One Priestly People: Ordained and Lay Ministries in the Church," forthcoming in *Priests for the Twenty-First Century*, ed. Donald Dietrich and Michael J. Himes (Kansas City: Sheed & Ward, 2006).

48. Richard R. Gaillardetz, "Toward a Contemporary Theology of the Diaconate," *Worship* 79 (September 2005): 419–38.

49. Bernard Botte, ed., *La Tradition Apostolique, Sources Chretiennes* 11 (Paris: Cerf, 1984), chapter 8. It is noteworthy that while *Lumen Gentium* 29 draws on this formula, *non ad sacerdotium, sed ad ministerium*, it does not make any explicit reference to the clause found in the *Apostolic Tradition* regarding service to the bishop. This point was made by the International Theological Commission in its document as well, *From the Diakonia of Christ to the Diakonia of the Apostles*, 85.

50. Susan K. Wood, *Sacramental Orders* (Collegeville: Liturgical Press, 2000), 166–71.

51. See Wood's discussion in *Sacramental Orders*, 167. For recent research on the topic, see John St. H. Gibaut, *The Cursus Honorum: A Study of the Origins and Evolution of Sequential Ordination* (New York: P. Lang, 2000); Louis Weil, "Aspects of the Issue of *Per Saltem* Ordination: An Anglican Perspective," in *Rule of Prayer, Rule of Faith: Essays in Honor of Aidan Kavanagh, O.S.B.*, ed. Nathan Mitchell and John F. Baldovin (Collegeville: Liturgical Press, 1996), 200–217; Balthasar Fischer, "Hat Ambrosius von Mailand in der Woche zwischen seiner Taufe und seiner Bischofskonsekration andere Weihe empfangen?" in *Kyriakon* [Festchrift for Johannes Quasten], vol. 2, ed. Patrick Granfield and Josef A. Jungmann (Münster/Westfalem: Aschendorff, 1970), 527–31; Ormonde Plater, "Direct Ordination: The Historical Evidence," *Open* 37 (1992): 1–3.

52. However, it should be noted that *Redemptionis Sacramentum*, recently published by the Congregation for Divine Worship and the Sacraments, has prohibited even seminarians from preaching in the context of the Eucharist. *Origins* 33 (May 6, 2004): 801–22, see #66.

53. Richard R. Gaillardetz, "Shifting Meanings in the Lay-Clergy Distinction," *Irish Theological Quarterly* 64 (1999): 115–39.

54. Thomas O'Meara, *Theology of Ministry*, rev. ed. (New York/Mahwah, NJ: Paulist, 1999), 224.

PART V
FURTHER READING

I. THE SECOND VATICAN COUNCIL

A. Historical Studies and Reminiscences

Alberigo, Giuseppe and Joseph A. Komonchak, eds. *History of Vatican II.* 5 vols. Maryknoll, NY: Orbis, 1995–.

Congar, Yves. *Mon Journal du Concile.* 2 vols. Paris: Cerf, 2002.

Hurley, Denis. *Vatican II: Keeping the Dream Alive.* Pietermaritzburg, South Africa: Cluster Publications, 2005.

Madges, William, and Michael J. Daley, eds. *Vatican II: Forty Personal Stories.* Mystic: Twenty-Third Publications, 2003.

O'Malley, John W. *Tradition and Transition: Historical Perspectives on Vatican II.* Wilmington: Glazier, 1989.

O'Meara, Thomas F. *A Theologian's Journey.* New York/Mahwah, NJ: Paulist Press, 2002.

Rynne, Xavier. *Vatican Council II.* Maryknoll, NY: Orbis, 1999; originally published in 1968.

Stacpoole, Alberic, ed. *Vatican II by Those Who Were There.* London: Chapman, 1985.

Suenens, Léon-Josef Cardinal. *Memories and Hopes.* Dublin, Veritas, 1992.

Wenger, Antoine. *Vatican II.* Westminster, MD: Newman Press, 1966.

Wiltgen, Ralph M. *The Rhine Flows into the Tiber: A History of Vatican II.* Devon [Eng]: Augustine Pub. Co., 1978.

B. Commentaries on Vatican II Documents

Congar, Yves, and Guilherme Baraúna, eds. *L'Église de Vatican II.* 3 vols. *Unam Sanctam* 51 a-c. Paris: Cerf, 1967.

Hastings, Adrian, ed. *Modern Catholicism: Vatican II and After.* New York: Oxford University Press, 1991.

Hünermann, Peter and Bernd Jochen Hilberath. 3 vols. *Herders Theologischer Kommentar zum Zweiten Vatikanischen Konzil.* Freiburg im Breisgau: Herder, 2004–.

McNamara, Kevin. *Vatican II: The Constitution on the Church: A Theological and Pastoral Commentary.* Chicago: Franciscan Herald Press, 1968.

Philips, Gérard. *L'Église et son mystére au IIe Concile du Vatican.* 2 vols. Paris: Desclée, 1967.

Vorgrimler, Herbert, ed. *Commentary on the Documents of Vatican II.* 5 vols. New York: Crossroad, 1989.

C. Post-Conciliar Syntheses and Assessments of Conciliar Teaching

Alberigo, Giuseppe, Jean-Pierre Jossua, and Joseph A. Komonchak, eds. *The Reception of Vatican II.* Washington, DC: Catholic University of America Press, 1987.

Burns, Robert A. *Roman Catholicism after Vatican II.* Washington: Georgetown University Press, 2001.

Butler, Christopher. *The Theology of Vatican II.* Rev. ed. Westminster, MD: Christian Classics, 1981.

Daly, Bernard, Mae Daly, and Bishop Remi J. De Roo. *Even Greater Things: Hope and Challenge after Vatican II.* Toronto: Novalis, 1999.

Fagin, Gerald M., ed. *Vatican II: Open Questions and New Horizons.* Wilmington: Glazier, 1984.

Kloppenburg, Bonaventure. *Ecclesiology of Vatican II.* Chicago: Franciscan Herald Press, 1974.

Latourelle, René, ed. *Vatican II: Assessment and Perspectives.* 3 vols. New York/Mahwah, NJ: Paulist Press, 1988.

Markey, John J. *Creating Communion: The Theology of the Constitutions of the Church.* Hyde Park: New City Press, 2003.

Miller, John H., ed. *Vatican II: An Inter-faith Appraisal.* Notre Dame: University of Notre Dame Press, 1966.

O'Connell, Timothy E., ed. *Vatican II and Its Documents: An American Appraisal.* Wilmington: Glazier, 1986.

Ratzinger, Joseph with Vittorio Messori. *The Ratzinger Report.* San Francisco: Ignatius Press, 1985.

Richard, Lucien, Daniel Harrington, and John W. O'Malley, eds. *Vatican II: The Unfinished Agenda.* New York/Mahwah, NJ: Paulist Press, 1987.

Tracy, David, ed. *Toward Vatican III: The Work That Needs to Be Done.* New York: Seabury Press, 1978.

D. Popular Treatments of the Council and Conciliar Themes

Doyle, Dennis M. *The Church Emerging from Vatican II: A Popular Approach to Contemporary Catholicism.* Mystic: Twenty-Third Publications, 2002.

O'Sullivan, Maureen. *101 Questions and Answers on Vatican II.* New York/Mahwah, NJ: Paulist Press, 2002.

Pennington, Basil. *Vatican II: We've Only Just Begun.* New York: Crossroad, 1994.

II. CONCILIAR THEMES AND POST-CONCILIAR DEVELOPMENTS

A. Theological Foundations of the Church

Azevedo, Marcello de Carvalho. *Basic Ecclesial Communities in Brazil: The Challenge of a New Way of Being Church.* Washington, DC: Georgetown University Press, 1987.

Boff, Leonardo. *Ecclesiogenesis: The Base Communities Reinvent the Church.* Maryknoll, NY: Orbis, 1977.

———. *The Church: Charism and Power.* New York: Crossroad, 1985.

Doyle, Dennis M. *Communion Ecclesiology: Vision and Versions.* Maryknoll, NY: Orbis, 2000.

Forte, Bruno. *The Church: Icon of the Trinity.* Boston: St. Paul Books & Media, 1991.

Kasper, Walter. *Theology and Church.* New York: Crossroad, 1989.

Küng, Hans. *The Church.* New York: Image Books, 1976.

Lafont, Ghislain. *Imagining the Catholic Church: Structured Communion in the Spirit.* Collegeville: Liturgical Press, 2000.

Lakeland, Paul. *The Liberation of the Laity.* New York: Continuum, 2003.

Lee, Bernard J. et al., *The Catholic Experience of Small Christian Communities.* New York/Mahwah, NJ: Paulist Press, 2000.

Phan, Peter C., ed. *The Gift of the Church: A Textbook on Ecclesiology.* Collegeville: Liturgical Press, 2000.

Ratzinger, Joseph. *Church, Ecumenism and Politics: New Essays in Ecclesiology.* New York: Crossroad, 1988.

Sullivan, Francis A. *The Church We Believe In: One, Holy, Catholic and Apostolic.* New York/Mahwah, NJ: Paulist Press, 1988.

Tillard, Jean-Marie R. *Church of Churches: The Ecclesiology of Communion.* Collegeville: Liturgical Press, 1992.

B. Unity and Catholicity in the Church

Borelli, John, and John Erickson, eds. *The Quest for Unity: Orthodox and Catholics in Dialogue.* Crestwood: St. Vladimir's Seminary Press, 1996.

Burgess, Joseph, and Jeffrey Gros, eds. *Building Unity: Ecumenical Dialogues with Roman Catholic Participation in the United States.* New York/Mahwah, NJ: Paulist Press, 1989.

———. *Growing Consensus: Church Dialogues in the United States, 1962–1991.* New York/Mahwah, NJ: Paulist Press, 1995.

de Lubac, Henri. *The Motherhood of the Church followed by Particular Churches in the Universal Church.* San Francisco: Ignatius Press, 1982.

Dulles, Avery. *The Catholicity of the Church.* Oxford: Clarendon Press, 1985.

Every, George. *Understanding Eastern Christianity.* Bangalore: Dharmaram Publications, 1978.

Kilmartin, Edward. *Toward Reunion: The Orthodox and Roman Catholic Churches.* New York/Mahwah, NJ: Paulist Press, 1979.

Meyer, Harding, and Lukas Vischer, eds. *Growth in Agreement: Reports and Agreed Statements of Ecumenical Conversations on a World Level.* New York/Mahwah, NJ: Paulist Press, 1984.

Nichols, Aidan. *Rome and the Eastern Churches.* Collegeville: Liturgical Press, 1992.

Pospishil, Victor J. *Eastern Catholic Canon Law.* Brooklyn: Saint Maron Publications, 1993.

Ramet, Pedro, ed. *Eastern Christianity and Politics in the Twentieth Century.* Durham: Duke University Press, 1988.

Roberson, Ronald. *The Eastern Christian Churches: A Brief Survey.* 6th ed. Rome: Edizioni "Orientalia Christiana," 1999.

Rusch, William G., and Jeffrey Gros, eds. *Deepening Communion: International Ecumenical Documents with Roman Catholic Participation.* Washington, DC: USCC, 1998.

Schreiter, Robert J. *The New Catholicity: Theology between the Global and Local.* Maryknoll, NY: Orbis, 1997.

Stormon, E.J., ed. *Towards the Healing of Schism: The Sees of Rome and Constantinople.* New York/Mahwah, NJ: Paulist Press, 1987.

Stransky, Thomas F. and John B. Sheerin, eds. *Doing the Truth in Charity: Statements of Pope Paul VI, Popes John Paul I, John Paul II, and the Secretariat for Promoting Christian Unity 1964–1980.* New York/Mahwah, NJ: Paulist Press, 1982.

C. Church Office and Ecclesiastical Leadership

Allen, John L., Jr. *All the Pope's Men: The Inside Story of How the Vatican Really Thinks.* New York: Doubleday, 2004.

Bianchi, Eugene, and Rosemary Radford Reuther, eds. *A Democratic Catholic Church: The Reconstruction of Roman Catholicism.* New York: Crossroad, 1992.

Collins, John N. *Deacons and the Church: Making Connections between Old and New.* Harrisburg, PA: Morehouse Publishing, 2002.

Cooke, Bernard. *Ministry to Word and Sacraments.* Philadelphia: Fortress, 1976.

Cummings, Owen F. *Deacons and the Church.* New York/Mahwah, NJ: Paulist Press, 2004.

Ditewig, William T. *101 Questions and Answers on Deacons.* New York/Mahwah, NJ: Paulist Press, 2004.

Dulles, Avery. *The Priestly Office: A Theological Reflection.* New York/Mahwah, NJ: Paulist Press, 1997.

Fox, Zeni. *New Ecclesial Ministry: Lay Professionals Serving the Church.* Revised and expanded ed. Franklin, WI: Sheed & Ward, 2002.

Gaillardetz, Richard R. *By What Authority? A Primer on Scripture, the Magisterium and the Sense of the Faithful.* Collegeville: Liturgical Press, 2003.

———. *Teaching with Authority: A Theology of the Magisterium in the Church.* Collegeville: Liturgical Press, 1997.

Galot, Jean. *Theology of the Priesthood.* San Francisco: Ignatius Press, 1984.

Hahnenberg, Edward. *Ministries: A Relational Approach.* New York: Crossroad, 2003.

Hasenhüttl, Gotthold. *Charisma: Ordnungsprinzip der Kirche.* Freiburg: Herder, 1969.

Kasper, Walter. *Leadership in the Church.* New York: Crossroad, 2003.

Legrand, Hervé-M., and Christoph Theobald, eds. *Le ministère des évêques au concile et depuis.* Paris: Cerf, 2001.

Legrand, Hervé-M., Julio Manzanares, and Antonio García y García, eds. *The Nature and Future of Episcopal Conferences.* Washington, DC: The Catholic University of America Press, 1988.

Leys, Ad. *Ecclesiological Impacts of the Principle of Subsidiarity.* Kampen: Kok, 1995.

Müller, Hubert, and Hermann J. Pottmeyer, eds. *Die Bischofskonferenz: theologischer und juridischer Status,* Düsseldorf: Patmos, 1989.

Nichols, Terence L. *That All May Be One: Hierarchy and Participation in the Church.* Collegeville: Liturgical Press, 1997.

O'Meara, Thomas F. *Theology of Ministry*. Revised ed. New York/Mahwah, NJ: Paulist Press, 1999.

Osborne, Kenan. *Priesthood: A History of Ordained Ministry in the Roman Catholic Church*. New York/Mahwah, NJ: Paulist Press, 1989.

Pottmeyer, Hermann J. *Towards a Papacy in Communion: Perspectives from Vatican Councils I & II*. New York: Crossroad, 1998.

Quinn, John R. *The Reform of the Papacy: The Costly Call to Christian Unity*. New York: Crossroad, 1999.

Reese, Thomas J., ed. *Episcopal Conferences: Historical, Canonical and Theological Studies*. Washington, DC: Georgetown University Press, 1989.

————. *Inside the Vatican: The Politics and Organization of the Catholic Church*. Cambridge: Harvard University Press, 1996.

Schillebeeckx, Edward. *The Church with a Human Face*. New York: Crossroad, 1985.

Suenens, Léon Josef. *Coresponsibility in the Church*. New York: Herder and Herder, 1968.

Sullivan, Francis A. *Magisterium: Teaching Office in the Catholic Church*. New York/Mahwah, NJ: Paulist Press, 1983.

————. *From Apostles to Bishops: The Development of the Episcopacy in the Early Church*. New York: Newman Press, 2001.

Wood, Susan K. *Sacramental Orders*. Collegeville: Liturgical Press, 2000.

————, ed. *Ordering the Baptismal Priesthood*. Collegeville: Liturgical Press, 2003.

INDEX